Utopian and Science Fiction by Women

Liverpool Science Fiction Texts and Studies
General Editor David Seed
Series Advisers
I. F. Clarke   Edward James   Patrick Parrinder
Brian Stableford

1. Robert Crossley, *Olaf Stapledon: Speaking for the Future*

2. David Seed, ed., *Anticipations:
Essays on Early Science Fiction and its Presursors*

3. Jane L. Donawerth and Carol A. Kolmerten, eds.,
Utopian and Science Fiction by Women: Worlds of Difference

From Sarah Robinson Scott, *A Description of Millenium Hall and
the Country Adjacent* . . . 2d ed. London: Printed for J. Newbery
at the Bible and Sun in St. Paul's Church-Yard, 1764. Illustra-
tor: A. Walker. Courtesy of the Library of Congress.

UTOPIAN AND SCIENCE FICTION BY WOMEN

WORLDS OF DIFFERENCE

EDITED BY

JANE L. DONAWERTH

AND

CAROL A. KOLMERTEN

Foreword by SUSAN GUBAR

LIVERPOOL UNIVERSITY PRESS

Published in Europe by
LIVERPOOL UNIVERSITY PRESS
PO Box 147
Liverpool
L69 3BX

Published in the rest of the world by
Syracuse University Press

Copyright © 1994 by Syracuse University Press

British Library Cataloguing-in-Publication Data
A British Library CIP Record is available
ISBN 0 85323 269 5 *cased*
ISBN 0 85323 279 2 *paper*

Printed and bound in the United States of America

Contents

Illustrations

Foreword

Susan Gubar

I t always seemed somehow, though mysteriously, appropriate to me that Sandra M. Gilbert's first book of poetry, *In the Fourth World*, began with "Getting Fired, or 'Not Being Retained' " and concluded with a visionary meditation that gave the volume its title. Of course, as a poet she must have chosen her opening and closing poems quite self-consciously. But, to fall into Gertrude Stein's idiom, I did not know at the time what I knew she knew. After Jane Donawerth and Carol Kolmerten asked me to compose a foreword for this collection of essays, not only their subtitle—*Worlds of Difference*—but also their subject seemed to echo in my mind with my collaborator's poetic debut and thus to hold out the promise of a solution to that mystery.

A sardonic, surrealistic fantasy about a hostile, invasive letter telling the poet she has been dismissed from her job, "Getting Fired" imagines the grinning, cigarette-smoking missive as "a secret agent who slips through a door when no one is looking," as an "uncle who had not seen me for twenty years," and as a "movie actor / who makes his fortune from his teeth and hair and lovable shoulders." Though the poet-speaker attempts to stay calm outside in her garden, the letter dislodges her completely, taking over the care of her kitchen, her children, and her husband, even replacing the books on her study's shelves with "its own collection, all / black paperbacks, all untitled." By the end of the poem, while the members of the household accept the epistle-usurper "as though it really were a badtempered old uncle," the daunted woman poet falls into Dickinsonian hesitations as she broods ineffectually beneath the rhododendrons:

> 'If first I—
> Then perhaps I—
> after which, of course,
> and so forth—'

Clearly the opening poem in the first book of Sandra Gilbert's poetic corpus recounts a tale of female alienation (the family following its social routines with poet stalking apart in joyless, pointless reverie), of self-division (the sinister letter appropriating her role inside the house and she herself cast out), and of a dispossession that becomes associated with her own diminishment, if not her death (she has, after all, been terminated). Yet, as if imaginatively as well as professionally "fired," the poet is launched on a book of verse and ultimately appears revitalized at the end of the volume. Indeed, in the collection's concluding text, "In the Fourth World," vitiated subjectivity is countered by physical spontaneity, self-fragmentation by creative clairvoyance, and dispossession or death by the poet's confident dream of an indefinite, infinite survival.

Within a magical realm beyond that of the three dimensional, the exuberant writer explains that she "grew wings and began to dance"; she "started to write poems and couldn't stop"; and she "always knew who the murderer was." Replacing Dickinsonian stutterings with one of Dickinson's most optimistic projects, namely her efforts to "dwell in Possibility—," the speaker of "In the Fourth World" envisions a publicly acknowledged self poised on the threshold of a succession of universes:

> in the fourth world
> someone I had never met before called me by my name
> 'come here a minute, Sandra'
> and gave me a map on which was clearly marked
> the way through suburbs airports deltas avenues
> letters windmills tulips galaxies
> to the fifth world
> and the sixth world
> and the seventh

Uninhibited by capital letters or punctuation, the verse here spins out a moment when a gratuitously benevolent stranger confers the gifts of a social identity harmonious with the author's sense of personal destiny and a map of mysteriously other places, promising future adventures in as yet unknown physical and metaphysical domains.

Sandra Gilbert's arithmetic of infinite progression may seem far removed from the utopian and science fiction narratives studied in the essays collected here by Jane Donawerth and Carol Kolmerten. However, *In the Fourth World* resembles these narratives in seeking to imagine changed, charged dimensions of social and linguistic freedom for its female creator. And it does so by eerily recounting the speaker's actualization in the past tense, as if it had already occurred (in dream? in youth? on another planet?) and thus could be recovered. Was the verse connected, then, to our critical efforts to excavate a literary past for women? Only after some twenty years of collaboration with Sandra have I realized that her solitary creative ventures often offered a clue to our common critical endeavors.

Published in 1979 (the same year as *The Madwoman in the Attic*), *In the Fourth World* proposes a dialectic between the outsider of "Getting Fired," banished by a male letter who might stand for other hostile men of letters or letters of the law, and the bold voyager of *In the Fourth World*, at home with and in all conceivable creations. The malevolent, avuncular letter nullifying the woman poet is replaced at the end of the book by a self-generating, healthy woman of letters, one who "slept well woke early / didn't smoke," one who looks at nature without the distorting lens of culture: "my eyes were butterflies / opening." Thus, the book of poems (most composed before we met) undoubtedly (if unconsciously) shaped our critical efforts to trace a utopian strain in even the most Gothic female traditions just as it reminds us that the feminist literary critical enterprise itself participates in utopian desires.

As Jane Donawerth and Carol Kolmerten explain in their Introduction, the essays in the volume they have edited establish a continuous literary history of female-authored utopias and science fiction novels. Distinctive as those evolving genres are, their represented "Worlds of Difference" resonate with the words of difference repeatedly uttered by nineteenth- and twentieth-century literary women working within apparently nonutopian and non–science fiction conventions, words that counter female alienation from male-dominated structures and strictures by dwelling in and on the possibilities of a better place before, beyond, or behind masculinist history. Thus, Sandra Gilbert and I have continually found that the flip side of the literary woman's critique of her status as a "nobody" exiled or marginalized in patriarchal culture (hiding out beneath the rhododendrons) is her dream of becoming "somebody" in the utopian no-where of (fourth, fifth, sixth, and seventh) worlds elsewhere.

In *The Madwoman in the Attic*, we proposed that the yearning of many nineteenth-century women of letters for motherly or sisterly aesthetic precursors was translated into a vision of a mother country and functioned as an antidote to the painful dis-ease we traced in Victorian women's novels and verse. When Sandra Gilbert and I decided to compose a sequel to *The Madwoman*, we entitled our three-volume series *No Man's Land: The Place of the Woman Writer in the Twentieth Century* in order to allude to the importance in modern times of the Great War and to the sex wars waged because of the continuing hostility of Western culture to female aesthetic ambition. But we were also hinting at the inherently utopian nature of that ambition. For in opposition to the "no man's land" of patriarchal history we set a vision that energized many modernist and contemporary literary women, a dream of Herland that inspired not only the feminist polemicist Charlotte Perkins Gilman, the author of the early twentieth-century utopian narrative *Herland*, and not only speculative or fantasy writers from Olive Schreiner to Joanna Russ and Ursula Le Guin, but also women of letters usually defined in terms of quite different aesthetic moods and modalities.

To some extent, of course, feminist criticism is itself inevitably a utopian project, born of the effort to counter women's more than probable estrangement from a male-dominated history of letters with the possibilities of an artistic matrilineage commensurate to our desires. As educators committed to finding or inventing gender assignments less debilitating to men and women than those we have inherited, we have much to learn from the speculations of earlier generations of writers seeking different worlds in which women could experience agency and actualization, community and consummation. The critics included in *Utopian and Science Fiction by Women*—appearing during a resurgence of language about "family values" and "right to life," euphemisms that make it seem as if the 1990s might degenerate into a kind of retro-1950s—explore a range of texts that resist platitudes about any essential or universal "female nature" and instead testify to many women's quite dissimilar efforts to multiply the ways in which we imagine ourselves, our families, and our values so we can engender fresh words for future lives in new worlds.

Acknowledgments

Because this is a book about utopias and science fiction as envisioned by women, we shall begin our acknowledgments with a parable. When Carol moved into her hundred-year-old house in Catonsville, Maryland, sixteen years ago, one of the first things she did was plant a cherry tree close to the sidewalk, so that passersby could, in good utopian fashion, enjoy the cherries that would be produced every June. For years, when the cherries ripened, Carol would put a sign on her tree inviting people to help themselves. No one ever did: this is not a utopian world where people trust freely offered gifts. For us, though, this book has been a utopian book and we have accepted many freely offered gifts of time and support from many people.

From its beginnings, this book has been a collaborative project that has given us enormous intellectual pleasure, without many of the pains of writing. The annoyances of writing and editing were diminished by having two of us working together, almost always at Jane's or Carol's dining-room table, while eating good food.

At a 1988 NEMLA (Northeast Modern Language Association) meeting where we first met, we formulated a need for a book that hypothesized a history neither of us had had, as yet, time to write. Carol had organized a panel at the meeting on "Women Seeing Utopia." That session led to a similar one at the 1989 National Women's Studies Association, and in 1990 to another panel at NEMLA that Jane organized. Most recently we joined again in a 1992 panel at the Society for Utopian Studies Conference. We thank all the panel members who have participated in these sessions and who helped us conceptualize our project at an early stage, in particular, Carol Farley Kessler, Lee

Cullen Khanna, and Naomi Jacobs. We further thank countless students at the University of Maryland and at Hood College, who discussed with us early formulations of some of these ideas on utopias and science fiction by women.

Since our conceptual phase, our debts are more specific. We both appreciate having had sabbaticals at crucial times from our respective institutions (University of Maryland at College Park and Hood College). We also appreciate immensely the efforts of the staffs at the University of Maryland and Hood College who converted disparate manuscripts into a uniform word-processing format, especially Grace Crussiah, Johnnie Klute, and Diana White at Maryland and Ruth Watson at Hood. We also thank our contributors to this collection, who became our collaborators, often advising us. We further thank the readers from Syracuse University Press, especially Lyman Tower Sargent, whose knowledge and good sense helped us shape the book. Jean Pfaelzer gave us extremely useful comments on the Introduction. We are also grateful to Stephen M. Ross, for editing the Introduction and for spending several weeks compiling a comprehensive bibliography from the separate contributors' lists—without his computer skills we might have given up the project. We also greatly value the support of Cynthia Maude-Gembler, executive editor of the press. Furthermore, we gratefully acknowledge the support of the General Research Board of the Office of Graduate Studies and Research of the University of Maryland at College Park.

Finally, we would like to thank our families: our spouses, Stephen M. Ross and Woody Scally, and our children, Laura Kolmerten McAfee, who introduced Carol to science fiction more than fifteen years ago, and Kate and Donnie Scally, who kept problems to a minimum and gave gifts of joy that kept work on this book a pleasure.

Contributors

RUTH CARVER CAPASSO received her doctorate in French literature from Harvard University in 1983. She is currently Assistant Professor of French at Kent State University in Ohio. Her research and publications focus on women writers, particularly seventeenth-century figures such as Mlle. de Scudéry, Mme. d'Aulnoy, and Mme. de Lafayette. She has also published on George Sand.

JANE L. DONAWERTH is an Associate Professor of English and an Affiliate Faculty in Women's Studies at the University of Maryland at College Park, teaching courses she has designed in science fiction by women, women writers of the English Renaissance, and the history of rhetorical theory. She has published articles and a book on Shakespeare, as well as articles on science fiction by women and rhetorical theory by women. With two small children, she is working slowly on her third book, *Feminist Approaches to Science Fiction by Women*.

LINDA DUNNE has been an administrator of nontraditional college programs for adults at Antioch University, The City University of New York, and, currently, the New School for Social Research. She is completing her doctorate in literature at CUNY and is writing about the figures of the monster, freak, and physically deformed in narrative fiction by American women writers of the late nineteenth and early twentieth centuries.

MICHELLE ERICA GREEN received her B.A. from the University of Pennsylvania and her M.A. from the University of Maryland. Currently working on her Ph.D. at the University of Chicago, she teaches part-time at DePaul University. Although she is a lifelong Trekkie, her academic interests lie primarily in Renaissance drama and *film noir*. She works with community theater groups, writes for local literary magazines, and collects movie memorabilia.

NAOMI JACOBS, Associate Professor of English at the University of Maine, is the author of *The Character of Truth: Historical Figures in Contemporary Fiction* (Southern Illinois Univ. Press, 1990). She has also published articles on utopian literature, on pedagogy, and on writers including Aphra Behn, Dickens, and the Brontës. Her current project is a book entitled *When Silence Speaks: Dialogue and the Brontës*.

CAROL FARLEY KESSLER, Professor of English, American Studies and Women's Studies, Penn State–Delaware County Campus, wrote *Elizabeth Stuart Phelps*, and edited *Daring to Dream: Utopian Stories by United States Women 1836–1919* and *The Story of Avis* by Elizabeth Stuart Phelps (1877). Forthcoming publications include *Charlotte Perkins Gilman: Progress Toward Utopia* and a revised, expanded edition of *Daring to Dream* covering 1836–1949. She has contributed to *The Heath Anthology of American Literature*, and her articles have appeared in *Extrapolation*, *Frontiers*, *Legacy*, and *Women's Studies*.

LEE CULLEN KHANNA is Professor of English at Montclair State University. She has published on Renaissance and modern utopias, including work on Thomas More and Edward Bellamy. Her essays on women's utopias have appeared in *Feminism, Utopia, and Narrative*, ed. Jones and Goodwin (Univ. of Tennessee Press, 1990); *Utopian Studies International Forum*, and *Alternative Futures*. Currently she is completing a book, *Utopia and Gender*.

CAROL A. KOLMERTEN is Professor of English and Director of the Honors Program at Hood College. Her book, *Women in Utopia; The Ideology of Gender in the American Owenite Communities* (Indiana Univ. Press, 1990), was cited by Phi Beta Kappa as "Recommended Reading" for 1990. She is the editor of the 1991 Syracuse University Press reprint of the 1893 *Unveiling a Parallel* by Alice Ilgenfritz Jones and Ella Merchant. Currently, she is working on a cultural biography of Ernestine L. Rose.

SARAH LEFANU is a free-lance writer and editor. She is the author of *In the Chinks of the World Machine: Feminism and Science Fiction* (joint winner of the 1990 Emily Toth Award). She is coeditor of three anthologies of original fiction, *Despatches from the Frontiers of the Female Mind* (1985), *Colours of a New Day: Writing for South Africa* (1990) and *God: An Anthology of Fiction*. She has three children and lives near Bristol.

JEAN PFAELZER is the author of *The Utopian Novel in America 1886–1896: The Politics of Form*. She has published on utopianism in *Science Fiction Studies*, *Extrapolation*, *ATQ*, and in the anthologies *America as Utopia* and *Feminism, Utopia, and Narrative*. Currently, she is working on a critical biography of Rebecca Harding Davis and an anthology of Davis's short stories. She is Associate Professor of English and American Studies at the University of Delaware.

RAE ROSENTHAL is an Associate Professor of English at Essex Community College, where she teaches courses in British fiction and women's literature. Her publications have appeared in *Studies in Contemporary Satire*, *The D. H. Lawrence Review*, and *Focuses*, where her article, "Male and Female Discourse: A Bilingual Approach to English 101," won the Edward P. J. Corbett Award for the most outstanding essay submitted in 1990. Currently, she is working on a project that will examine visions of feminist revolution in Victorian novels.

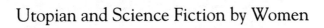

Utopian and Science Fiction by Women

1

Introduction

Jane L. Donawerth and Carol A. Kolmerten

This collection of essays postulates that utopias and science fiction by women—women's "literatures of estrangement"—constitute a continuous literary tradition in the West from the seventeenth century until the present day.[1] One of the most important tasks of recent feminist scholarship has been to recover texts by women and to reevaluate forgotten, neglected, and underrated women writers and their works. Through such scholarship, feminists are reconceptualizing their past and, consequently, their future.[2] Although a great deal of work has been done on women's utopian and science fiction, this volume is the first, to our knowledge, to argue that these fictions historically speak to one another and together amount to a literary tradition of women's writing about a better place. Thus our purpose in this volume is to recover these worlds imagined by women, from forgotten texts, from reevaluated texts, and from a lost tradition. Although these women writers may only have known one or two other texts by women in this tradition—and early writers may each have reinvented the form—from our vantage point we are able to piece together the squares to see the design of this history as a whole.

Part of the design becomes clear if we look at the descriptions by feminist critics of "literatures of estrangement." The past fifteen years has seen an explosion of writing about women's utopias, apologues, science fiction, speculative fiction, and feminist fabulation.[3] One of the reasons women's utopian and science fiction has become so popular in the last twenty years is that gender roles can be more easily revised when the reader is estranged from her ordinary world. In 1972, Joanna Russ reflected that science fiction, the "*What If* literature," should be "the perfect literary mode in which to explore (and explode) our assumptions about 'innate' values and 'natural' social arrangements, . . . about differences between men and women, about family structure, about sex, . . . about gender roles" ("Image" 79–80). Seventeen years later, Sarah Lefanu described contemporary science fiction as "subversive, satirical, iconoclastic," drawing on the "freedom that science fiction offers from the constraints of realism," and "mingling . . . the rational discourse of science with the pre-rational language of the unconscious . . . [as] a means of exploring the myriad ways in which we are constructed as women" (*Feminism* 4–5).

Most theorists admit that notions of utopia, science fiction, and fantasy overlap to some degree.[4] Thus arises the problem of what to call women's writing about a better place. Some critics have created new ways of naming this literature that consistently crosses generic boundaries. Refusing the term "science fiction," Natalie M. Rosinsky combines fantasy and science fiction under the title "speculative fiction," because "women's studies research and the new physics indicate that such conventional concepts of im/possibility [as that marking the boundary between fantasy and science fiction] are limited and value laden" (115n. 2). Marleen Barr has also argued for a new term, "feminist fabulation," which "modifies the tradition of speculative fiction with an awareness that patriarchy is a contrived system, a meaning-making machine which constructs and defines patriarchal fictions—myths of female inferiority—as integral aspects of human culture," and which accepts, "as fictional points of departure," "the insights of this century's waves of feminism" ("Food for Postmodern Thought" 22).

We have found particularly useful to our discussions Anne Cranny-Francis's description of "literature of estrangement" as "a literature concerned primarily with the alienation experienced by individual subjects, realized textually by a setting displaced in time and/or space" (26). This notion of displacement in form and content, borrowed originally from the Russian formalists, has been the subject of many scholars' approaches to utopian and science fiction. In the 1970s and 1980s, Darko Suvin, for example, defined utopia as "the verbal construction of a particular [more perfect] quasi-human community . . . based on estrangement arising out of an alternative historical hypothesis" ("Defining" 132), and called science fiction the "literature of cognitive estrangement" (*Metamorphoses* 4). For feminists, and for this project, "literature of estrangement" is an especially useful category, because it draws together the several genres that women have used to talk about a better place, and because it exposes the ways in which a text's workings embody its politics.

Indeed, recent feminist scholarship has expanded definitions of estrangement and has illustrated how women writing utopian and science fiction embody their politics in the structures of their works. In 1983, Daphne Patai argued that, because of the effect of "defamiliarization," there is great potential for feminist writers in "the way in which utopias estrange us from our present and thereby allow us to see it more clearly" ("Beyond Defensiveness" 150–151). In an extremely influential article, Rachel Blau DuPlessis described feminist apologues—including utopian and science fiction—as "teaching stories contain[ing] embedded elements from 'assertive discourse'—genres like sermon, manifesto, tract, fable— . . . in which elements like character and plot function mainly as the bearers of philosophical propositions or moral arguments" ("Feminist Apologues" 1). Discussing the common ground shared by utopian and science fiction as genres of estrangement, Jean Pfaelzer has cautioned that "the political defiance inherent in utopian novels needs to be understood as part of the aesthetic structures themselves" (*Utopian Novel* 14–15). And Deborah Rosenfelt has further suggested that the post-1960s feminist utopia embodies ideology in its structure: "Conscripting readers as participants in the same linear evolution, the narrative enacts the central feminist myth in its purest form—a woman's progress from passivity to action, from weakness to strength, from victimization to agency, from silence to expression, from oppression to liberation" (273). Carol Farley Kessler has, moreover, asserted the relation between utopian writing and political change: for women writers the utopia is "a refuge or shelter wherein we may safely envision a changed society," a form "unashamedly didactic" but not "a social blueprint"; instead it "offer[s] alternative *vicarious* experience, spur[ring] us as readers to reevaluate and act upon our own world" (*Daring to Dream* 3–5).

All these descriptions share an emphasis on the imaginative freedom of alternate worlds, the crossing of generic boundaries, the didactic politics of the writing, and the overturning of gendered stereotypes in women's use of the genres. It is significant that all of these terms have been applied to fictions as different as Charlotte Perkins Gilman's *Herland*, Joanna Russ's *The Female Man*, and Marge Piercy's *Woman on the Edge of Time*. Throughout the last four centuries, women writers have invented or appropriated techniques of the literature of estrangement to write about a better place, a place where gender will not be so limiting as in their own experience.

The design of this tradition becomes yet clearer as we consider women's literatures of estrangement in the historical context of the development of Western feminism. In the dedicatory poem to Margaret Cavendish's *The Description of a New World, Called the Blazing-World* (1668), her husband, the duke of Newcastle, compares her, not to Thomas More, but to Columbus: she is, he writes, better than Columbus, because Columbus merely found, but she created a world. Like Cavendish's husband, we see the tradition of women's utopias as distinct from men's. We see women's utopias arising from the nascent feminism of the movement to acquire education for women in seventeenth-century Europe, with some influence from the male utopian tradition. As a woman, Cavendish could not explore a new world, but in the seventeenth century, with the benefit of an education she wanted to see extended to all women, Cavendish could create a world in writing.[5] Margaret Cavendish's *Blazing-World* lies at the North Pole, where an Empress is given "an absolute power to rule and govern all the World as she pleased" (sig. C3^r). With this power the Empress first summons all the philosophers and scientists of her time to discuss and speculate on the nature of things—indeed, this speculation is what makes her book a prototype of our science fiction, as well as of our feminist utopias. Second, the Empress decides how best to teach other women: she institutes "a Congregation of Women" and since "Women . . . generally had quick wits, subtile conceptions, clear understandings, and solid judgments," they soon become expert theologians and "devout and zealous Sisters" (sig. I2^v). Third, the Empress chooses a scribe and adviser, Margaret Cavendish, who is "a plain and rational Writer"—a true achievement for a seventeenth-century Englishwoman—and who learns from the woman ruler of the Blazing-World how to make her own world (sigs. N1r–O2^v).

Cavendish's *Blazing-World* embodies the qualities that we saw emphasized in recent critics' descriptions of women's literatures of estrangement, offering the freedoms for women of an alternate world, crossing the generic boundary between romance and essay, and didactically confronting the sexual politics of seventeenth-century England, pronouncing women equal to men if the women are educated.[6] As Lee Cullen Khanna explains in chapter 2 in this volume, *Blazing-World* "foregrounds the issue of revision as a necessary precondition to expressions of feminist desire"; in that sense it is a precursor to a whole set of feminist utopias in England and France during the next century and a half that estrange the reader from her ordinary world, teach her that the good life consists of education for women along with seclusion from the world of men, and offer her a subject position in that separate world.[7]

The fantasies of the aristocratic seventeenth-century French writers Mme. d'Aulnoy and Mlle. de Scudéry, which Ruth Capasso discusses in chapter 3 of this volume, follow this pattern: set on islands, aristocratic women with fine educations enjoy a life of intellect and aesthetically appreciated sensual pleasure until that life is destroyed by a man. Capasso also discusses Mlle. de Montpensier's utopia, outlined in letters to a female friend, where "admittance would be denied to married couples, and falling in love would be cause for expulsion."

Because so few have as yet been recovered, it is difficult to trace the connections between these early seventeenth- and eighteenth-century utopias. We suppose that many more such utopias will be found. Nevertheless, we can suggest some connections. Cavendish was praised by Bathsua Makin in her 1673 treatise proposing an education for women, and surely Cavendish, as well as Makin, would have been read by Mary Astell before she constructed her own utopia in *A Serious Proposal* (Part 1:1694, Part 2:1697): a women's "seminary" or college, where women could escape from the world of men, could be educated as well as men, and could form a community with other women through which to make an effectual inroad against the evils in the world around them.

Sarah Scott seems to have gathered up all these previous works as influences for *A Description of Millenium Hall* (1762). Scott had a mother who was said to have been educated in Makin's academy, perhaps providing Scott with a model for her school, and Scott found another model in Astell's proposal for a women's college and community, perhaps taking the title of *Millenium Hall* from Astell's treatise on marriage.[8] As Linda Dunne writes, Sarah Scott, like Astell, presented "a bitter critique of eighteenth-century society, and . . . an alternative to the traditional marriage plot of the eighteenth- and nineteenth-century novel" (see chapter 4). Scott perhaps had an antecedent in the utopian tradition for her overturning of the marriage plot, as well as for her college of charitable women. One of the most popular French romances to precede Scott's novel was Françoise de Graffigny's *Lettres d'une Péruvienne*, published in English as *Letters Written by a Peruvian Princess* in 1748, and going through thirty editions in French, English, and Italian in the next thirty years. In this critical utopia, in the tradition of those romances discussed by Ruth Capasso, an Incan princess, stolen by Spaniards, is rescued by the French and taken to Europe, where her perspective as a citizen of a utopian civilization allows her to critique French society. She writes her letters to her former Incan lover, but instead of marrying him, and instead of rewarding with marriage the French chevalier who has rescued her, she chooses a country estate with a large library, a small circle of friends, and no husband as her ideal. This model of the utopia based on women's education and seclusion from the world, and often exclusion from marriage, is still active in the nineteenth century in England, as Rae Rosenthal's essay on Elizabeth Gaskell's *Cranford* (1851–53) argues (see chapter 5).

The models for these early women's fictions of estrangement are thus not those of Sir Thomas More, who is concerned with outward travel to a new world in his *Utopia*, but, instead, the feminist models of women's education: the cloister, the salon, the country house with a large library. Although the connections between them, in the current state of scholarship, are tenuous, we project that feminist scholars will recover in the next few decades enough additional texts to be able to establish significant links. Sarah Scott's novel, for example, was imported to the United States: Did Scott's English novel, or another in this early French and English tradition, serve as a model for Sarah Pierce's 1792 utopian poem in Connecticut? In this poem beginning "On rising ground we'll rear a little dome," Pierce recapitulates the emphases on the secluded country house, female community, women's education, and hostility to marriage that inform many of these works (see Von Frank).

In the nineteenth century, literatures of estrangement by women began incorporating scientific solutions of social problems, and creating greater participation for women in public offices and business, a change that reflects the nineteenth-century goals of feminism to secure property rights, divorce, suffrage, and careers for women. In the area of nineteenth-century feminist utopias, there has been a great deal of productive scholarship, and we can summarize these histories, rather than cite the individual works by writers such as Mary Griffith, Mary Bradley Lane, Florence Dixie, Elizabeth Stuart Phelps, Annie Denton Cridge, and Lois Waisbrooker.

In her introduction to *Daring to Dream*, a study of United States feminist utopias from 1836 to 1919, Carol Farley Kessler has pointed out that these works by women critique men's control of women's labor and sexuality, and offer as correctives "marriage reform" (7–8) and "paid work, education, suffrage, and co-operation" (11). In chapter 8 in this volume, Kessler analyzes in detail the more realistic cooperative scenarios that Charlotte Perkins Gilman offers in her early short stories for reform of women's domestic servitude and of women's participation in the work and economy of United States and British society. In a chapter on feminist utopias in *The Utopian Novel in America 1886–1896*, Jean Pfaelzer has argued that United States utopian writers in the late nineteenth century "believed [women] wanted political equality and fundamental rearrangements at home" (143), and that both are facilitated by idealizing science, and by positing "collective or mechanical alternatives" to the housework and childcare that constitute women's work (143, 150). In chapter 6 in this volume, Pfaelzer further argues that Rebecca Harding Davis and Louisa May Alcott offer critiques in their fiction of male utopias that "demystify the Western notion of self . . . as separate, bounded, and autonomous" and project, instead, a "feminist notion" of "a dialectical relationship between the individual and society."

In *Women's Utopias in British and American Fiction*, Nan Bowman Albinski similarly stresses, for utopias written by women from the 1830s through 1919, a radical revision in gender roles, but she finds this difference between countries: while both "endorse the industrial revolution" (16), British writers emphasize suffrage, socialist solutions to public problems, and women in public roles, while United States writers emphasize marital reform, private solutions to public problems, and a transformation of women's work through "technology and commercialization" (54). Thus the recurrent figure of British women's utopias is the female prime minister, who reforms public evils through her political position, while the recurrent figure of United States women's utopias is the artful female cook, who studies chemistry, uses the latest technology, and sits down to dinner as a respected guest of the family she serves (Albinski 30, 63). That the British and United States utopias yet remain part of the same tradition might be seen by looking at Alice Ilgenfritz Jones and Ella Merchant's *Unveiling a Parallel* (1893) in the light of these conclusions. This novel critiques men's control of women's labor and sexuality, offering, instead, economic reform that allows women meaningful work, and thereby a real possibility for women to choose to remain single. This novel further offers political equality: all women vote along with men, and women's roles are granted importance; the cook in the utopian country of Caskia is also an important scientist. Social problems are thus solved by a combination of advanced technology and women's employment in public roles. As Carol Kolmerten points out in chapter 7 in this volume, however, these nineteenth-century women, writing out of a tradition that identified the utopia with the sentimental romance, faced an almost unresolvable problem: "how to write about a world that challenged the ideology embedded within the literary conventions they used."

Added to this utopian literature of estrangement in the nineteenth century, however, was a version of the gothic romance, the scientific romance. Originating in Mary Shelley's *Frankenstein* (1818), and further developed in Shelley's *The Last Man* (1826), the scientific romance offered a critique of the results of science and technology as evidenced in the Industrial Revolution, and as filtered through the horror story: *Frankenstein* maps the archetypal modern tragedy, endlessly repeated in science fiction as well as in life, of the results of research science out of control of the scientist, while *The Last Man* creates a near-future world to explore the limits of science and human industry when faced with the natural force of mortality—in this case, a plague. In chapter 12 in this volume, Naomi Jacobs suggests that *Frankenstein*, "perhaps the single most influential work of speculative fiction by a woman," critiques not only the "scientist narrator, [but also] . . . [Shelley's] own desire to enter that frozen world of freedom and power, which ultimately destroys both parent and child."

The women writers of the early twentieth century, especially those publishing in the pulp magazines, turned again and again to these nineteenth-century traditions of the feminist technological utopia and

Shelley's scientific romance. Gertrude Barrows Bennett, Minna Irving, and Lilith Lorraine published versions of the feminist technological utopia, while Clare Winger Harris, Sophie Wenzel Ellis, L. Taylor Hansen, Kathleen Ludwick, and C. L. Moore borrowed the conventions of Shelley's *Frankenstein* to validate their authorship. Indeed, women writers throughout the century cite Shelley as their muse, Joanna Russ's narrator Joanna in *The Female Man* (1975) shouting "I am a poet! I am Shelley! I am a genius!" (151), and Phyllis Gotlieb including a poem on "ms & mr frankenstein" in her collection of short stories, *Son of the Morning* (1983).

Women writers in the early pulps also indicate the influence of early twentieth-century feminism in their visions of revised gender roles, promoting a system of separate spheres of influence in which women take over government (e.g., Lilith Lorraine or Minna Irving), or imagining a future or an alternate world where women are equal, even similar to men (e.g., L. Taylor Hansen and C. L. Moore). In chapter 9 in this volume, Jane Donawerth explores the "utopian transformation of domestic spaces and duties through technology, [the] revision of gender roles, and [the] reliance on male narrative voices" in women's science fiction in the 1920s science fiction pulp magazines. Such transformation suggests that these women writers form a bridge between the nineteenth-century technological utopian and later science fiction by women. Recently published essays on C. L. Moore have traced her dependence on Shelley as a model and her resistance and subversion of masculine science fiction in the 1930s and 1940s (see Gubar, "C. L. Moore"; and Gamble). From the nineteenth century on, a clear and traceable tradition of women's writing often derives its permission for women's writing from the example of Mary Shelley and its techniques of revising gender from the feminist technological utopia. Indeed, after World War I, most feminist utopias have been published as science fiction.

Although editors published fewer works by women in the 1930s, women writers returned in numbers to the pulps after World War II, and their presence changed the literature. Judith Merril, as editor and writer, helped shaped the new realism of postwar science fiction, and Merril's work epitomizes the advantages and disadvantages of realism for women. The advantages include realistic exploration of women's lives, as well as critical analysis of the effects of gender differences: for example, in her short story, "That Only a Mother" (1948), Merril explores the effects of atomic weapons on women's lives, and critiques parents' gendered responses to mutated children. The disadvantages include uncritical presentation of racism and of women limited by their feminine roles, as well as inability to represent a female hero: for example, in her near-future dystopia about the atomic bombing of New York, *Shadow on the Hearth* (1950), Merril presents a white heroine too feminine to act, and a negative portrait of the black maid who holds the household together. In the 1950s, the women with androgynous names—Andre Norton, Leigh Brackett, Marion Zimmer Bradley, and J. Hunter Holly—who wrote near-future dystopias or space operas with macho male heroes for the paperback market, did not much change the literary conventions of science fiction, but they made a secure place for women writers in the science fiction publishing industry. And women did influence the genre in the 1960s. Judith Merril introduced United States fans to the pleasures of fragmented, psychedelic "New Wave" techniques from British science fiction. Andre Norton offered witches as heroes in her long-running Witch World Series. And Marion Zimmer Bradley began the Darkover Series, featuring male homosexuals as heroes and, later, Amazons and lesbians.

The development of a women's tradition continued, often in the 1960s and 1970s characterized by the presentation of the traditionally feminine trait of empathy as a special power. We may trace the tradition, for example, in the development of the female hero through literatures of estrangement, from Norton's Jaelithe (*Witch World* 1963) to Russ's Jael (*The Female Man*, written 1971, published 1975), to Bradley's Jaelle (*The Shattered Chain* 1976). By the late 1960s popular fiction by women was in continual conversation with feminist theory and political issues: in feminist critiques of dystopian patriarchies, as in the work of writers like Pamela Zoline ("The Heat Death of the Universe" 1967) and Alice Sheldon as James Tiptree, Jr. ("The Women Men Don't See" 1973), and in feminist utopias by writers such as Ursula K. Le Guin (*The Left Hand of Darkness* 1969, *The Dispossessed* 1974, *Always Coming Home* 1985), Monique Wittig (*Les Guérillères* 1969), Joanna Russ (*The Female Man* 1975), Marge Piercy (*Woman on the Edge of Time* 1976), Suzy McKee Charnas (*Motherlines* 1978), and Sally Miller Gearhart (*The Wanderground* 1979). Indeed, Piercy's novel, in which the future feminist utopia of Mattapoisett was interwoven with the dystopian story of mental patient Connie Ramos, became a kind of scripture for the women's movement in the United States. These works advanced feminist critiques of much of Western culture, rather than limited criticisms of particular social or domestic practices: the utopias, especially, offered minority female heroes, gender equality, alternatives to the nuclear family, anarchic governments, revised sciences, and a debate on the use of violence to achieve change.

Some critics have hypothesized a midcentury break in the tradition of women's writing about a better place, but a writer like Naomi Mitchison, who wrote nonfiction feminist utopian newspaper pieces during the 1920s, and utopian science fiction after 1960, indicates the continuity that exists between feminisms of the 1920s and the 1960s and 1970s, and throughout these literatures of estrangement by women. In 1929, Mitchison, who was deeply involved in the feminist campaign for birth control, wrote that women will find contraception unnecessary only "when women have sufficient control over their external environment to ensure that their work will be compatible with having babies, or when the whole business of having babies becomes a real job in itself, carrying with it social respect and economic independence, . . . [or] when women have sufficient control of their internal environment to ensure that their bodies will not suffer during pregnancy or parturition, and also perhaps when . . . they can at their own will be fertile or not fertile" (Caldecott 23–24). These were still radical ideas half a century later, when Mitchison embodied them in *Memoirs of a Spacewoman* (1962), in Mary who chooses to have or not have children at her will, and in *Solution Three* (1975), where mothering is a career supported by state funds. But, as Sarah Lefanu points out in chapter 10 in this volume, in *Solution Three*, "there is no place in this perfectly planned world for sexual reproduction, with its cell divisions, reassortments of genes and resultant unpredictable mix of chromosomal material"—this is a world of "compulsory homosexuality."

What Mitchison's *Solution Three* suggests, and what much of Octavia Butler's fiction, as well as many of the 1970s feminist utopias grapple with is the imperfectibility of utopian—even feminist—desire. As many critics have pointed out, the science fiction by women and the feminist utopias after 1960 offer critiques of the process of utopia, as much as dreams for the future. This process of critique intensifies with the second generation of late-century feminist writers, who in the last decade have continued former feminist trends, with female heroes in adventure stories (such as Janet Kagan's 1988 *Hellspark*), critiques of patriarchal society (such as Suzette Hayden Elgin's 1984 *Native Tongue* and Carol Emshwiller's 1990 *Carmen Dog*), and utopias (such as Joan Slonczewski's 1986 *A Door into Ocean* and Fay Weldon's 1990 *Darcy's Utopia*). However, contemporary writers have also challenged the assumptions of the 1970s feminist utopias: in critiques of lesbian separatism, as in Cynthia Felice's 1986 *Double Nocturne*, Pamela Sargent's 1986 *The Shore of Women*, and Sheri S. Tepper's 1988 *The Gate to Women's Country*; in Margaret Atwood's exploration of the failure of feminist heroism in her 1985 *The Handmaid's Tale*; and in the exposure by African-American writer Octavia Butler of the racism and imperialism in the scenario of feminist utopia, in her Patternist Series. As Michelle Erica Green argues in chapter 11 of this volume, Butler critiques "utopian feminists" who "ignore, erase, and oppress human difference"; while for Butler herself, "difference, disagreement, and diversity provide the life force of her utopias."

The final part of the design of this tradition of women's writing becomes clear as the essays in this collection unfold. We have placed these essays in historical order, from Lee Cullen Khanna's discussion of Margaret Cavendish's seventeenth-century *Blazing-World* to Michelle Green's essay on Butler, with Naomi Jacobs's essay as conclusion to provide a thematic overview of literatures of estrangement from Cavendish to Le Guin. In between are detailed discussions of specific texts (Linda Dunne's essay on Sarah Scott's 1762 *Millenium Hall*, Rae Rosenthal's essay on Elizabeth Gaskell's 1851–53 *Cranford*, and Sarah Lefanu's essay on Naomi Mitchison's 1975 *Solution Three*); analyses of the oeuvre of significant authors (Carol Kessler's essay on Charlotte Perkins Gilman, and Michelle Green's essay on Octavia Butler); an examination of feminist critiques of male utopian dreams (Jean Pfaelzer); and historical sweeps of women's writing of a better place in certain periods (Ruth Capasso's essay on seventeenth-century France, Carol Kolmerten's essay on turn-of-the-century United States, and Jane Donawerth's essay on the 1920s science fiction magazines.)

Taken together, these essays speak to common themes and common strategies in women's writing about their different worlds. Critics in this collection find that women fantasize about cooperative sisterhoods and collectivism instead of hierarchy, find places set apart from men or ways to convert their fictional men to traditional "female" values, and devise new myths central to women's identities. Women also eliminate binary oppositions that construct women as "others," while centering their fictions on women's lived experience, especially on motherhood and raising children.

With these paradigms set up for us, we can now see that the texts covered in this collection exist in conversation with one another, or even in argument: they are sites where issues crucial to women are contested. They allow us to begin to examine how these women writers use different strategies for the same goal, where they agree, and where they come into conflict.

These essays allow us to see that the writers in this tradition depict women characters who need to create a world that nurtures them instead of one that silences them. The essays also allow us to see that, within this tradition, the means of creating such a world becomes a contested area. Some writers take an unambivalent position, creating women's-only communities. The benefits, as Linda Dunne and Rae Rosenthal demonstrate, are spaces where women are not monsters, where society may be reordered to include rather than to exclude. Other writers call such communities into question as escapist or even harmful in their suppression of difference. As Sarah Lefanu and Michelle Green point out, Mitchison and Butler celebrate difference, at both biological and social levels. Yet other writers incorporate this issue in their works, making it a basis for their narrative structure. As Carol Farley Kessler and Naomi Jacobs argue, Gilman alternates exclusion and inclusion of men in the society of *Herland,* while Ursula K. Le Guin relocates the contest within an androgyne.

Women writers of estrangement also share the task of refuting the ideology of romance, usually through their plot structures validating partnerships over romance (see Dunne, Kessler, and Green). Jean Pfaelzer furthermore argues that when women construct the future they challenge the simple automatic synthesis of utopianism and romanticism. Such strategies bring the women writers of this tradition into conversation in another contested area: women's sexuality. In some science fiction, women writers suggest that heterosexual romance must remain with us because it is linked with reproduction; they want the possibility of "limerance" but seek elimination of its constraints on women through technology (see Donawerth, Lefanu, and Jacobs). Heterosexuality is often challenged in these writings throughout the centuries, but pre-twentieth-century women's utopias often eliminated men in order to repress sexuality and the dangers of romance, while more recent narratives of all-women worlds often celebrate lesbian sexuality.

Finally, this tradition allows us to see not only that the writers question the binary oppositions that infuse much of the popular literature written by men, but also that they revise generic forms to generate means other than opposition or conflict to structure a story. For example, women writers employ narrative strategies that get rid of women as foils; they eliminate the one good and one bad woman of the sentimental romance (see Dunne, Kolmerten, and Donawerth). On another level they play down antagonistic dialogue. From Margaret Cavendish to Ursula Le Guin, women writers create multiple worlds in relation rather than in opposition; we hear multiple voices especially in recent utopian writing by such women as Marge Piercy, Joan Slonczewski, and Octavia Butler.

The more we have read, the more we have become convinced of a radical tradition of women writers who crossed generic and publishing boundaries, developing their own variegated tradition. This volume is a step toward a recovery of this radical tradition.

2

The Subject of Utopia
Margaret Cavendish and Her Blazing-World

Lee Cullen Khanna

argaret Cavendish's seventeenth-century text, A New Blazing-World, makes room for a discourse of difference in the utopian genre.[1] By constructing varied subject positions for women, her fiction releases the utopian genre from conventional binary oppositions in the depiction of the desire for the good life. Like later utopian fiction by women, Blazing-World tends to close the gap between the vision of utopia as natural paradise in arcadian settings and that of cultural construct, set in the city. Correlatively, her work also narrows the distance between representations of "the good life" as the gratification of sensual pleasures, and representations that focus on the predominance of reason in ordering moral life and the good state.[2]

Indeed, Cavendish's text makes clear that the transformation of subject positions changes utopian constructs. In other words, the point at which genre and gender intersect in the representation of utopian desire is in the locus of discursive authority. When Socrates and Thrasymachus debate the nature of justice, or Thomas More and Raphael Hythloday argue about the role of philosophy in political practice, the ideal social orders that emerge in the text differ dramatically from those arising from the conversation of the Empress of the Blazing-World and "Honest Margaret Newcastle" or the conversations of Connie and Luciente in Marge Piercy's Woman on the Edge of Time, to cite just one contemporary example.

A transformed subject position alters utopian constructs in a number of interesting ways, all of which are anticipated by Cavendish, although with varying emphasis and development. First, nature is valued and represented as a vast, complex, interactive system. Depictions of utopia, therefore, must work with this "web" of nature. Second, the idea of justice, so important to utopian thought, becomes substantially more inclusive than it is in the dominant tradition. Not only gender, but race, class, and other forms of life begin to find a place in such societies. Third, the pleasures depicted include the intellectual, moral, sensual, and aesthetic. Fourth, utopian desire is depicted as dynamic process as much as an achieved state. As a result, figurations suggesting movement such as imagery connected to the natural cycle, or mundane rites such as cooking and eating, or such symbolism as the journey or the dance assume greater importance. Fifth, the depiction of intimate relations becomes as or more important than the discussion of laws and social institutions. As private and public worlds are shown to intersect, these texts often render problematic such categories as individual and society, or even history and fiction. Sixth, art and creativity seem central to cultural life and to individual well-being. Finally, these representations of plenitude, multiplicity, and diversity tend to be found in new sites. This altered location may serve as initial sign of difference. For example, in *Blazing-World*, as in some recent utopias, a wintry polar landscape is the locus. A blank white space, largely uninhabited in history or fiction, seems an apt location for the inscription of new dreams.[3]

Utopian fiction exploring these points of difference is plentiful in the late twentieth century.[4] That Margaret Cavendish, writing a utopian fantasy three centuries earlier, addresses these issues as well, grants historical precedent to this intersection of genre and gender. In fact, her work may be seen to initiate an alternate utopian tradition in English. Although the Duchess of Newcastle clearly wrote out of an elitist seventeenth-century culture and a royalist commitment, her double marginalization, as exile during the Civil War and an ambitious woman in a world of male power, became an epistemic advantage in constructing a utopian world. The dislocation of her class during the years of the Republic (1649–60), as well as the estrangement from traditional sources of power and meaning caused by gender, must have fueled her vast literary output.[5] Additionally, the challenge to traditional philo-

1. Engraving of Margaret Lucas, Duchess of Newcastle, opposite p. 1 in *Letters from the Originals at Welbeck Abbey*. 1909. Roxburghe Club 141. Courtesy of the Bodleian Library, Oxford.

sophic ideas by the discoveries of the "new science," particularly the work of Bacon, Hobbes, and Descartes, enlarged the space for speculation in "natural philosophy."[6] No doubt such a changing intellectual climate also encouraged Margaret Cavendish. *Blazing-World* is but the most obvious example of her drive to build new worlds in the realm of discourse. Indeed, much of her writing relocates "utopia" at the borders of feminine desire and masculine models of meaning.

Her project was all the more remarkable, because the prohibitions against women's speech at the time were so substantial. The ideals of chastity, silence, and obedience as well as the traditional roles of maid, wife, mother, and widow remained normative for women, particularly English women, during the seventeenth century.[7] Even by midcentury very few women dared to publish their work, in spite of historic conditions that created some greater latitude in prescribed behaviors. Nevertheless, as a member of the royalist elite, Cavendish experienced firsthand the dislocations of traditional power during and after the Civil War, including the beheading of a king, exile, and the devastation of her family estates. Paradoxically, such losses may have contributed to her literary production. The collapse of long-standing sources of power and security may have opened a space for the expression of female desire. In fact, it may well be the case that the disintegration of external political and social order fueled Cavendish's insistent attention to the world within, particularly her attention to subjectivity in her most explicit utopian project, *Blazing-World*.

Indeed, I believe that *Blazing-World* is structured by its representation of the struggle for discursive authority and its figurations of female power. Once these issues are foregrounded, the text's shape becomes more apparent. Interestingly, too, women's power, variously represented in active roles and in discursive practices, does not remain singular. In *Blazing-World* figurations of female power and creativity are multiple and include depictions of shared power and the generative potential of a relational self.

A textual summary may clarify these contentions. The work begins with a deconstruction of the romance plot and the image of woman as simple object of male desire. In fact, the invocation of such a plot, and its undoing, may be a necessary precondition for utopian vision here. The text opens as follows: "A merchant, visiting a foreign country, fell extremely in love with a young lady" (*B-W* 1). Unable to obtain the lady's hand, because of his lower social status, the merchant abducts her, with the aid of a few sailors and a small boat. The little boat sails on for days, eventually negotiating a narrow passageway near the North Pole, and enters a new world. At this point all the men in the boat freeze to death. Yet, the young woman, warmed by the light of her beauty and favored by the justice of heaven, survives. Stranded in her boat, with the dead men around her, the unnamed protagonist is then greeted by strange creatures coming across the ice. These "bear-men" are the first of a multitude of hybrids the protagonist encounters in this new world. In fact, multiplicity characterizes both macro- and microcosmic figurations from this point on in Cavendish's text. The bear-men take the young woman over countless rivers and kingdoms, where she meets ape-men, fish-men, bird-men, and many other combinations before reaching the capital city, called Paradise.

Throughout this journey Cavendish's female hero is impressed with the utility of the architecture and, finally, the magnificence of the palace compound. Most buildings are low, practically constructed, thickly walled, and spacious. Much attention is given to the Emperor's palace, with its arches and columns and the enhancement of royal magnificence provided by the decorative use of gold and many-colored diamonds. The variety, abundance, and colors of the diamonds figure difference as do the many-colored hybrid citizens. The narrator observes that the residents of this new world:

> were of several Complexions; not white, black, tawny, olive or ash-coloured; but some appear'd of an Azure, some of a deep Purple, some of a Grass-green, some of a Scarlet, some of an Orange-colour, etc. . . . [and] were men of several different sorts, shapes, figures, dispositions, and humors . . . some were Bear-men, some Worm-men, some Fish- or Mear-men . . .; some Bird-men, some Fly-men, some Ant-men, some Geese-men, some Spider-men, some Lice-men . . . some Magpie-men, some Satyrs, some Gyants, and many more which I cannot all remember. (B-W 14–15).

When the protagonist is introduced to the Emperor of all that world, he promptly falls in love with her and worships her as a goddess. She assures him that she is mortal, and "the Emperor, rejoycing, made her his Wife, and gave her an absolute power to rule and govern that world as she pleased" (B-W 13).

Her authority thus neatly established, the new Empress then turns her attention to government. Her first acts concern learning and education. She organizes the citizens into professional "Schools" and founds learned Societies. Thus the Bear-men become her Experimental Philosophers, the Bird-men her Astronomers, the Fly-, Worm-, and Fish-men are her Natural Philosophers, etc. Subsequently, the Empress converses with her learned citizens, and these conversations occupy many pages of the text. These exchanges clearly allow Cavendish to pursue her interests in science, and these lengthy disputations reveal a view of nature as a vital, interdependent system (a view Cavendish explores in other writings as well).

Interestingly, the investigations of nature often undercut the centrality and importance of homo sapiens. Indeed, such creatures as the "Worm-men" prove to be indispensable to the Empress's scientific inquiry and are among her most brilliant servants. Conversations range from depictions of fantastic Blazing-World technologies such as the "Immortality Gum" and rocks that burn when wet, to satiric and witty attacks on rhetoricians and logicians, to metaphysical speculation on the existence of evil. These passages of "natural philosophy" reflect Cavendish's own preoccupations in many of her other works. Important, too, this lengthy discourse in "Paradise" represents an interesting process of intellectual exchange. In other words, although the Empress reproves and reforms some of her people's ideas and practices, she also learns, accepting the authority of various professional insights with admiration. Finally, at the close of these disputations, the Empress declares herself satisfied with the intellectual foundations of the state. She then turns her attention to religious reform.

Thus this woman, in utopian figuration, is seen first as Empress, then as scholar/scientist, then as religious leader. As she turns to the revision of current religious practice, the Empress asks why, although these people identify themselves as neither Jew, Christian, nor Muslim, there are no women in their places of worship. She is informed that women cause trouble in public places of religion or politics and that therefore they pray at home in their "closets." The first thing the new Empress does, as religious leader, is establish a Convocation of Women who will worship together. "The women," as the narrator says, "generally had quick wits, subtle conceptions, clear understandings, and solid judgments" (B-W 60). These women soon contribute to the general devotion of the citizens, and all are led by the Empress, who had the "gift of Preaching." She ensures their continued adherence to her Christian reformation by building two extraordinary chapels that combine spiritual enlightenment with the most interesting technologies of the new world. The Chapel of Terror is an emblem of Hell, built with Firestone obtained by the Bird-men from a special distant mountain. This stone burns when wet and is fired, when the Empress addresses the people, by means of an underground water supply. There she invokes the fear of damnation. In the other chapel, an emblem of Heaven, constructed above the first chapel, she preaches comfort and the mercy of everlasting life. This chapel is lined with starstone, which gives off perpetual light, but without heat. The narrator adds,

> And thus the Empress, by Art, and her own Ingenuity, did not only convert the Blazing-World to her own Religion, but kept them in a constant belief, without inforcement or blood-shed; for she knew well, that belief was a thing not to be forced or pressed upon the people, but to be instilled into their minds by gentle persuasions; and after this manner she encourages them also in all other duties and employments: for Fear, though it makes people obey, yet does it not last so long, nor is it so sure a means to keep them to their duties, as Love. (B-W 63)

After thus figuring the effects of female power in religion, the academy, and the state, the text presents an interrogation and revision of dominant discourse. It begins, interestingly enough, with the domestic and the local. The Empress longs to learn something about her own native land and seeks "immaterial spirits" to inform her. Through the investigations of her "Virtuosos," a gathering of the most brilliant of each of her societies, she is able to invoke and question these spirits. She begins by asking about "cabbalas," and an interest in cabalistic knowledge undergirds the many pages of questions that follow. The thrust of this extensive dialogue is satiric, as the pretensions of past discourses on the nature of truth are exposed. Interestingly, too, the supremacy of "Man" is punctured again, as when "The Empress desired the Spirits to tell her, Whether Man was a little World?" They answered, "That if a Fly or Worm was a little World, then Man was so too" (B-W 71). Later the Spirits confess ignorance about the many distinctions of intellect, soul, spirit made by earlier philosophers and add,

"Many, both of your modern and ancient Philosophers . . . endeavour to go beyond Sense and Reason, which makes them commit absurdities" (*B-W* 76).

The Empress's quest for knowledge seems a figure for a woman's quest for authority in a world conditioned by men's words. In pursuit of a different power the Empress then tells the Spirits, "I have a great desire . . . to make a Cabbala" (*B-W* 85).[8] This confession is marked with drama since the Spirits suddenly disappear and the Empress is so startled that "she fell into a Trance, wherein she lay for some while" (*B-W* 86). Upon awakening she is exceedingly troubled by the disappearance, fearing the Spirits committed some fault in their answers and so have been banished to the depths of the earth because of her queries. She is assured by her people that the depths of the earth are not so bad in any case, for "not onely all Minerals and Vegetables, but several sorts of Animals can witness, that the Earth is a warm, fruitful, quiet, safe, and happy habitation" (*B-W* 86). Eventually the Spirits are located by the Worm- and Fly-men, at the antipodes, and agree to return and aid the Empress with her desire to create a Cabala. The interrogation and play with earlier philosophic traditions, which preceded and made possible the Empress's expression of desire for authoritative speech, is continued in the following, most intriguing, section of *Blazing-World*.

First, ancient and modern scribes, from Aristotle to Descartes, are invoked, only to be rejected as inadequate or hostile to the Empress's project. Once again, then, the text foregrounds the issue of revision as a necessary precondition to expressions of feminist desire. Then, at last, the Spirits suggest one "honest Margaret Newcastle" as a suitable scribe. The soul of the Duchess suddenly appears to serve the Empress's discursive project. Interestingly, she advises the Empress to create, not a theological, philosophical, or political Cabala, but a poetical one. Then, she adds, you can use "Metaphors, Allegories, Similitudes, etc. and interpret them as you please" (*B-W* 92).

Although this provocative suggestion seems met with agreement, it is not explicitly pursued in the narrative. Instead, the friendship of the two women is foregrounded. The supportive interchange between them is depicted as spiritual, intellectual, and "romantic" in the Platonic fashion. The narrator says, "truly their meeting did produce such an intimate friendship between them, that they became Platonick Lovers, although they were both Femals" (*B-W* 92). Earlier, when the Empress welcomed the soul of the Duchess, she told the Spirits that her husband would have no need to be jealous, because her scribe would be of her own sex. Yet the Spirit responds, "In truth, Husbands have reason to be jealous of Platonick Lovers, for they are very dangerous, as being not only very intimate and close, but subtil and insinuating" (*B-W* 89).[9]

Indeed, the two women become so close that the Duchess confides her "extreme ambition" to the Empress. What are the reaches of your desire, her friend asks, and the Duchess responds that its utmost reaches cannot be known but her "present desire" is to be a princess. After some discussion of the niceties of titles, the thrust of Margaret Newcastle's desire is revealed—and that is to rule a kingdom as her friend, the Empress, does. Fully supported in her desire by her confidant, the Duchess consults the Immaterial Spirits about the existence of other worlds she might command. She is assured that there are indeed many worlds—as many as stars in the one we inhabit now—but they all have rulers. Rather than pursue her ambition by conquest, she is urged to create her own world, an immaterial world which she can design and possess absolutely. Margaret consents to this course as preferable to conquest and warfare. Then she begins to create her new world by invoking the models of the ancient philosophers: Pythagoras, Plato, Aristotle, etc. Yet they all prove insufficient to her purpose. Then she calls upon the "moderns" such as Descartes and Hobbes, and they too fail her. She dissolves the worlds created under their influence and invents her own, strictly according to her own desire.

When she has completed her project, she shows it to her friend, and the Empress is so enchanted with this newly minted utopia that she wishes to live there. The Duchess, however, encourages her to make her own. And so the Empress then destroys and creates "worlds" until she, too, is satisfied with her utopian construct. At this point she acknowledges her delight in being a ruler both within and without, for she enjoys both material and immaterial worlds of her own.

This surprising central section of Cavendish's text addresses several aspects of utopian fiction that speak to the intersection of genre and gender. Instead of the opposition of unsatisfactory "reality" to a better or perfect new society, characteristic of the dominant utopian tradition, the reader discovers a continuous process of making and unmaking worlds. Multiplicity, not binary opposition, constitutes the utopian methodology. Instead of a frame of contestatory dialogue, the reader discovers the intimate conversation of women friends who share many pleasures and support the attainment of each other's desires. Additionally, the distinction between reality and illusion is vastly complicated by the *mise en abîme* technique Cavendish explores here, and by her deliberate confusion, not only of author and character, historical and fictional subjects, but also material and immaterial societies, inner and outer worlds.

In fact, this crucial portion of *Blazing-World* seems to inscribe female friendship, relationship, and intimacy as the context for utopian visions. This context may also be understood as the ingenious inscription of a relational subjectivity. In its refusal of a fixed point of reference for the reader, this text establishes permeability and creativity as textual strategies for empowerment. The principle of permeability blurs those very categories taken as normative in dominant discourse. Unsettling as this may be for a reader, this technique works to transgress borders often used to exclude women and eliminate difference. Additionally, the representation of creativity in Cavendish's text empowers female characters and gestures toward the potential agency of readers as well.

After this provocative section, in which the two female characters realize their collaborative utopian projects, the reader is returned to the specificity of history. The Duchess and Empress decide to journey to the Duchess's world. As the narrator says, "Thus those two Female Souls travelled together as lightly as two thoughts into the Duchess her native World" (*B-W* 103). They were able in this form to view all parts of it at once and

> especially did the Empress' Soul take much notice of the several actions of humane Creatures in all the several Nations and parts of that World, and wonder'd that for all there were so many several Nations, Governments, Laws, Religions, Opinions, etc. they should all yet so generally agree in being Ambitious, Proud, Self-conceited, Vain, Prodigal, Deceitful, Envious, Malicious, Unjust, Revengeful, Irreligious, Factious etc. She did also admire, that not any particular State, Kingdom or Common-wealth, was contented with their own shares, but endeavoured to encroach upon their Neighbours, and that their greatest glory was in Plunder and

Slaughter, and yet their victory's less then their expences, and their losses more than their gains. . . . But that she wondered most at, was, that they should prize or value dirt more then mens lives, and vanity more than tranquility. (B-W 103–4)

The corruption of seventeenth-century politics is occasion here for the satire so typical of utopian literature. Not so typical, however, is the breaking of the fictional frame yet again by Cavendish, as she compliments her monarch by taking her characters to his court. The Empress voices an elaborate compliment to the grandeur of both Charles II and Queen Catherine and then is transported to Nottinghamshire and the Cavendish estate, Welbeck Abbey.

The visit to Nottinghamshire also allows an interesting expansion on the figuration of intimacy established earlier in the text. The friends watch the Duke emerge from the house to demonstrate his horsemanship and skill at the art of "manage." The Duchess, however, becomes alarmed at so much exercise before her husband's dinner, and her soul flies into his body. The Empress's soul soon follows, and then the three souls converse together within the Duke. In fact, the Duke and Empress so delight in each other's conversation "that these two souls became enamoured of each other; which the Duchess's soul perceiving, grew jealous at first, but then considering that no Adultery could be committed amongst Platonick Lovers, and that Platonism was Divine, as being derived from Divine Plato, cast forth of her mind that Idea of Jealousie" (B-W 110). The relation of female friends is here multiplied to include the "other" as the souls of the Duchess, the Empress, and the Duke converse in his head. Cavendish's startling invention of multicolored hybrid utopian citizens is here matched by a similarly fantastic invention in the depiction of intimate relationships. The satiric play at Plato's expense is both witty and subtly erotic. The bare hint of a lesbian connection earlier is matched by an allusion to adultery here, complicating gender relations and figuring a surprising ménage à trois.

The last scene in Part 1 of *Blazing-World* takes the reader out of the Duke's head and into a courtroom or, at least, to an allegorical trial. Up until this point the text has presented varying positions of female power: ruler, scholar, religious leader, and cabalist. The final role adopted in Part 1, this time by Margaret Newcastle, is that of barrister.

In effect, the Duchess becomes her husband's advocate in this trial. A court of law, presided over by Truth as judge, would seem the setting most appropriate to the theme of justice so prevalent in utopian literature. And if justice means, as Plato claimed, that each person be accorded his due, then Cavendish's preoccupation with the unjust rewards meted out to her husband for his political and military service to Charles II seems a relevant topic. Of course, utopian texts generally afford a larger purview of justice, moving beyond the particular case to the establishment of "just" institutions for the human community.

Interestingly, not only does Cavendish's trial scene not go beyond the specificity of her husband's case, but it seems to deny the possibility of justice and truth altogether. Although the Duchess is eloquent and is supported by Honesty and Prudence, while Fortune's case is badly presented by Folly and Rashness, there is no verdict. Outraged by Honesty's presentation, Fortune flees the court and Truth refuses to rule. The irresolution about the nature of justice and truth, like the multiple figurations of female subject positions, reflects the absence of any ultimate referent in the text's appeal to meaning. Truth is not absolute, but relational, as depicted in Cavendish's construction of subjectivity and construction of alternate worlds. Correlatively, a trial may present arguments, but any clear representation of one just verdict is necessarily avoided.

After this inconclusive trial, the Duchess breaks down in tears. Having failed to win her husband's case, she is upbraided by Honesty because she cares too much about Fortune. When she weeps, she invokes all the familiar stereotypes of the vulnerable woman, guilty only of being victimized. It is the one time in the text that the subjective stances adopted by the significant female figures, the Empress and the Duchess, seem to fail them.

The final dialogue of Blazing-World, Part 1, qualifies the construction of the social order just as the construction of an efficacious subject position has been qualified. After comforting the weeping Duchess, the Empress solicits her advice as political counselor. She admits doubts about her changes in the constitution of the Blazing-World, because her introduction of learned societies and religious changes may have introduced factionalism. The Duchess advises her to restore the original constitution, even if it means altering her own proclamations. Far better to admit error, she adds, than to persist in your own opinion to the detriment of public welfare. Such flexibility in a leader seems admirable, and in the spirit of personal and public motility so often figured in this utopian project. Yet, on reflection, the reversals contemplated by the Empress might also be seen as a recuperative gesture, similar to the depiction of the contrite and vulnerable Duchess after the trial. In other words, there may be a certain slippage here from a project of multiplicity and difference, pervasive up to this point, in the representations of both subjectivity and society. If the revoked decrees curtail the power of disparate groups, including the convocation of women, they qualify the gains made. Thus, the end of Part 1 seems to draw back from the revisionist daring of the preceding section.

However, if the end of the first section of *Blazing-World* suggests authorial anxiety about the new powers figured in Cavendish's creation of utopia, Part 2 returns the reader to the creative energy of female friendship and a fresh celebration of female power. It begins in a domestic and familial setting as the Empress worries about her native land. Because the Immaterial Spirits have brought her news of attacks on her former kingdom, she grieves at her helplessness. The Emperor suggests various ways of transferring forces to aid the besieged kingdom, but in a lively interchange, the Empress proves the inadequacy of all his ideas. Finally, he effectively throws up his hands and suggests that she call upon her good friend, Margaret Newcastle, for help. The soul of the Duchess appears on call, and she proves a most effective military strategist. She organizes the Fish-men to explore the tiny passage through which the Empress originally arrived and so determines that it might be negotiated by submarine. Although the Blazing-World has no such vehicle, the Duchess instructs the naval architects in its design. Subsequently, she and the Empress are able to travel back through the passage in golden submarines, pulled by Fish-men.

The underwater journey to the kingdom of ESFI revises the opening voyage of the text. In contrast to a vulnerable abducted maiden, sailing with foolish men, the reader now encounters an Empress, sailing in full regalia (even when submerged) and advised by her supremely confident and brilliantly competent female friend. This is, in fact, the third notable journey in a utopian text quite filled with travel of various sorts. The prominence of the journey motif here anticipates the importance of this figure when utopia is inflected by gender. Travel to different locations is obviously a convention of utopian fiction generally, but it is both varied and emphasized in utopian literature by women.[10]

This journey not only allows a dazzling display of royal female power, but revises the role of woman as ineffective defender of the right in the allegorical trial at the end of Part 1. In this section a besieged king is rescued by a woman and restored to his throne. It is easy to imagine the historic sources of this desire to figure a female general and savior. In Cavendish's utopian world, a woman accomplishes what no man could do for the exiled Charles II during the Civil War in England. Indeed, not only the historic situation of the Stuart dynasty in the seventeenth century, but Cavendish's desire to "save" her husband from unjust Fortune may underlie this depiction of female power and generosity.

Yet the significance of this section is not simply self-indulgent wish fulfillment. It speaks to the connection between the realization of subjective power and a movement outward toward a sharing of that power. In fact, a nexus of relations ranging from self-empowerment to the empowerment of others is crucial to Cavendish's utopian vision. For example, the Empress readily hands over the spoils of victory to her former king. Her own display of magnificence is central to this episode, and suitable to Early Modern conceptions of royalty. Yet such magnificence, notably relished and displayed, still reaches out. The Empress not only gives power to the King of ESFI, but returns to her Blazing-World to adore and be adored by her husband and to cherish her friend, Margaret Newcastle.

The three characters then discuss another creative project. The Emperor wants to establish a theater in Blazing-World and consults the Duchess about it. Although she disclaims any knowledge of stagecraft and stresses the unpopularity of her own drama in her native land, she agrees to help to establish this new national theater and even to write plays for it. She is assured her productions, concentrating on significant content as well as wit, will be welcomed in utopia. The Duchess mentions that the citizens of Blazing-World—Bird-men, Fly-men, and so forth—will be wonderful actors in a farce.

Again, this witty interlude in the new world clearly satisfies the author's own fantasies of fame, but signifies as well the importance of art and creativity in the utopian project. This attention to the artist, the embrace of the imaginative principle in establishing positive societies, sounds a striking new note in the utopian genre at this point in its history. The fear of the artist pervasive in dominant utopian thought is tied to a perceived threat to social order, truth, and discipline. Women's utopian fiction, on the other hand, may empower the imaginative principle for the same dangerous reasons.

The playwright, and friend of the Emperor and Empress of a Blazing-World, is eventually permitted to return to her own land. Once there, she tells the tale of utopia to her beloved husband and to her friends. She has been empowered by her vision of utopia, but this newly discovered efficacy results in a sharing and sense of community in the representation of history. Her friends inquire what the Empress does during her day. The Duchess says she spends most of her time studying and conversing with the learned, but for amusement also rides in the brilliant starlight of the night air. Royal magnificence is duly celebrated with elaborate descriptions of her bejeweled chariots. Finally the Duchess describes the recreation of the Empress and her court as they enjoy banquets and delicate "collations" of exotic fruit. Then the company listens to marvelous music of water and wind instruments. The concluding moments of the text center on the music and remarkable dance of that utopian court. After eating, the Duchess says, the entire company is wont to dance on the water, wafted not only by strange musical strains, but by the multitudinous backs of Fish-men. As the diversity and plenitude of nature support this final textual figuration, utopia becomes a dance of difference.

The beauty, harmony, and motion of this moment of communal interaction underscore the dynamism so typical of the utopian projects of women. That the dance is pleasurable, and follows upon a feast signifies the sensuality commonly valued when the utopian genre is inflected by the female gender.

Finally, the doubled images the text affords here, as the Empress and her court eat and dance by virtue of the Duchess's storytelling, aptly frame the text's repeated conflation of history and utopia. Readers may see the community at Welbeck Abbey, created by the Duchess's taletelling, even as they envision the marvelous dancing in a "Blazing-World."

Such permeable borders, between ideal worlds and idyllic historic moments, extend the permeable subjectivities that condition this text. For the focus of Cavendish's utopian project is necessarily the fashioning of subjective stances that create the possibility of entering the realm of public discourse.

In her afterword to the reader, the Duchess of Newcastle alludes to her undoing of dominant discursive patterns when she says,

> By this Poetical Description, you may perceive, that my ambition is not onely to be Empress, but Authoress of a whole World; and the Worlds I have made . . . are framed and composed of the most pure, that is, the Rational parts of Matter, which are the parts of my Mind; which Creation was more easily and suddenly effected, than the Conquests of the two famous Monarchs of the World, Alexander and Cesar. Neither have I made such disturbances, and caused so many dissolutions of particulars, otherwise named deaths, as they did for I have destroyed but some few men in a little Boat.(B-W 159)

Just as many a male artist's success has arisen from the bodies of beautiful dead women, it might be argued that Cavendish, in simple gender reversal, kills off men in order to create. Yet her brief, if shocking, elimination of the men at the beginning of her text seems rather to represent the deconstruction of discursive patterns that limit women to roles as simple objects of men's desire. As students of utopia we may cheer such a symbolic act, because it cleared the space for the figuration of a woman as ruler, scholar, scientist, religious reformer, aesthetic cabalist, military general, and generous friend. The importance of these shifting positions in *Blazing-World* is the testimony they bear to a struggle for discursive authority. Without an autonomous place to stand, without subjective power, no access to desire and utopian vision is possible. Therefore, with all its anticipation of difference in the description of a better world, the most vital aspect of Cavendish's early utopia is this attention to subjectivity.

In addition to affording multiple figurations of female power, *Blazing-World* explicitly explores a fluid subjectivity in three notable ways: the central *mise en abîme* episode in which the Empress invokes Margaret Newcastle as a scribe, the elusive narrative stance throughout the text, and the direct addresses to the reader before and after the "utopia" proper. All of these textual tactics serve to disguise the locus of discursive authority and undermine such categories as author, narrator, protagonist, character, history, and utopia, material and immaterial worlds, even representation and referent.

Although Cavendish's refusal to demarcate self and others consistently in her text has troubled some recent critics, a different approach may suggest its value.[11] Instead of condemning her solipsism or indecisiveness, we may see her depiction of internal difference as a route to imaginative energy and empathy. Cavendish saw her mind as capable of creating not only innumerable worlds, but innumerable subjective stances. Her Empress might delineate her own discursive space and yet enter other selves at will. Cavendish's authorial stance might be complicated not only by the sudden appearance of "Honest Margaret Newcastle" as scribe to Margaret Newcastle's protagonist, but the apparently separate first-person narration might slip into an identification of protagonist and author or elide narrator and author.[12] Such motility, however disconcerting to a reader, figures a relational subjectivity crucial to the issue of gender and utopia.

Cavendish's perspective suggests that assumptions of identity and particular positions of power need not prevent other discursive roles or relational positions. Therefore, the elusiveness of narrative strategy in *Blazing-World*, like the multiple figurations of subjective power, bespeaks a concern for both individual authority and community—or the desire both to assume power and share it.

Certainly a reader may see the self-referentiality of Cavendish's *Blazing-World*, but one might also, I believe, attend to its concern for connectivity. The allusion to multiple utopian visions, within a given utopian construct, surely arises, in part, from the generative power of female friendship. Nor is this friendship exclusive, since "the Empress" and "Honest Margaret Newcastle" at least make gestures toward satisfying relations with the opposite sex, in the form of both the Duke and the Emperor of Blazing-World. Additionally, when female authority is most grandly figured in the dazzling military victory depicted in Part 2, it is instantly shared with the King of ESFI. The text concludes, as I have said, with visions of expanded communities.

Moreover, the generative and generous impulse toward others spills over the textual frame (permeable as that frame already is) to include readers. In a prefatory letter, the Duchess says that she appends the *Blazing-World* to her *Observations* in order to "recreate" her mind and to delight the Reader with variety . . . if it add any satisfaction to you, I shall count myself a Happy Creatoress. . . . I cannot call it a poor World, if poverty be onely want of Gold . . . and Jewels. . . . As for the Rocks of Diamonds, I wish with all my soul they might be shared amongst my noble Female Friends, and upon that condition, I would willingly quit my part; and of the Gold I should onely desire so much as might suffice to repair my Noble Lord and Husbands Losses: For I am not Covetous, but as Ambitious as ever any of my Sex was, is, or can be; which makes, that though I cannot be Henry the Fifth, or Charles the Second, yet I endeavour to be Margaret the First. And although I have neither power, time nor occasion to Conquer the World as Alexander and Caesar did; yet rather then not to be Mistress of one, since Fortune and the Fates would give me none, I have made a World of my own: for which nobody, I hope, will blame me, since it is in every ones power to do the like. (*B-W* a5)

In the concluding remarks of her preface, the author confesses her ambition for fame and power, much as does "Honest Margaret Newcastle" to her friend the Empress. She argues here, too, that the desires of Women can best be achieved by claiming discursive rather than material power. Also of importance, she conceives a golden world, both literal and figural, only to give away all its jewels to her female friends. And if she exults in her own discursive accomplishment, she reaches out to remind her readers, in her concluding phrase, that they may share that power.

Cavendish's interesting preface is matched by her epilogue. This final playful and provocative address to the reader moves so gracefully among its varied subject positions that it deserves substantial quotation.

In the formation of those Worlds, I take more delight and glory, than ever Alexander or Cesar did in conquering this terrestrial world; and though I have made my Blazing-world a Peaceable World, allowing it but one Religion, one Language, and one Government; yet could I make another World, as full of Factions, Divisions and Warrs, as this is of Peace and Tranquility; and the Rational figures of my Mind might express as much courage to fight, as Hector and Achilles had; and be as wise as Nestor, as Eloquent as Ulysses, and as beautiful as Hellen. But I esteeming Peace before Warr, Wit before Policy, Honesty before Beauty; instead of the figures of Alexander, Cesar, Hector, Achilles, Nestor, Ulysses, Hellen, &c. chose rather the figure of Honest Margaret Newcastle, which now I would not change for all this Terrestrial World; and if any should like the World I have made, and be willing to be my Subjects, they may imagine themselves such, and they are such, I mean in their Minds, Fancies or Imaginations; but if they cannot endure to be Subjects, they may create Worlds of their own, and Govern themselves as they please. But yet let them have a care, not to prove unjust Usurpers, and to rob me of mine: for, concerning the Philosophical-world, I am Empress of it my self; and as for the Blazing-world, it having an Empress already, who rules it with great Wisdom and Conduct, which Empress is my dear Platonick Friend; I shall never prove so unjust, treacherous and unworthy to her, as to disturb her Government, much less to depose her from her Imperial Throne, for the sake of any other, but rather chuse to create another World for another Friend. (*B-W* 159–60)

Again, of course, the reader may see that the locus of utopian desire for Cavendish is discursive power and a continuous generativity. Inextricable from this achievement as Margaret the First, however, is the figuring of a relational self: the ruler who invites "subjects" into her utopian world; the friend who rushes to subvert any potential threat to the Empress of the Blazing World. Yet, lest readers feel excluded from this playful and elitist friendship, Cavendish urges them to similar achievement. Implicitly she acknowledges that this apparent aristocracy is available to all—if they but dare to enter the realm of discourse.

Nor does this concern for the connection between self-assertion and power-sharing, discursive authority and a disguised locus of identity, speak only to women. Although Cavendish's *Blazing-World* clearly highlights the intersecting of genre and gender, by demonstrating the difference made to utopian projects by way of a gendered subjectivity, it also speaks to problems faced by men and women. Today, as marginalized peoples, of both sexes, different races, classes, and ethnicities, struggle into speech and declare their desires, the problems generated by conflicting needs proliferate. At this point in world tensions, we could do worse than attend to texts that figure, as does *Blazing-World*, a multiple subjectivity and connections between self-assertion and sharing. The exploration of such complex connections

not only illuminates stubborn binary oppositions in the dominant discursive tradition but some troubling paradoxes in current political realities as well. For example, we may see the need for new definitions
of "self," no matter our gender, as maps of our world shift before our
eyes. As the Soviet Union and East European nations disintegrate,
people are apparently freed from oppressive states only to embrace re-
ductive tribalisms. To promote "civic culture" in the face of fluctuating
national boundaries and ethnic migrations requires fresh attention to
our processes of self-fashioning.[13]

In fact, some recent political theory suggests that the flexible identity of individuals—the ability to create and sustain multiple points of
subjective authority—may be essential to our social survival.[14] Interestingly, a work written in the seventeenth century, the largely unread
Blazing-World by Margaret Cavendish, sheds light on this urgent utopian project, even as it makes room for expressions of women's desire.

3

Islands of Felicity
Women Seeing Utopia in
Seventeenth-Century France

Ruth Carver Capasso

In 1690, Mme. d'Aulnoy described an idyllic world, which she called the "Island of Felicity." In its natural beauty, its peaceful, amicable society ruled by women, and its protection from the violence of the outside world, the island illustrates elements of a dream present in the works of two other important women of the period, Mlle. de Scudéry and Mlle. de Montpensier. Conscious of the limits to a woman's freedom in seventeenth-century France, each of these women dreamed of the creation of other worlds, where alternate values could be enacted and individual choices respected. Their sense of the obstacles preventing the realization of their dreams led them to imagine utopias, worlds of "nowhere."

It is perhaps not surprising that these three writers created images of new worlds; each had been influenced by a strong movement to reform contemporary society, a movement now known as preciosity. Its leaders were women, for although there were male *précieux*, the values and style of the movement appealed primarily to women. The goals of preciosity were aesthetic and moral reform: its members wished to purify language and manners, to practice and appreciate the arts, to assert women's rights to education, and, in some groups, to advocate radical social changes, such as divorce, trial marriages, and celibacy. Friendship was the most prized relationship, at least in theory, both be-

35

tween the sexes and between members of the same sex. Jealousy and division among women were evils to be banished. Even the desire to reshape one's physical environment found expression: women, following the example of the marquise de Rambouillet and her *chambre bleue*, redecorated their homes for greater comfort, convenience, and aesthetic pleasure. As Dorothy Backer wrote, "the seventeenth century *précieuse* was a new kind of woman. No longer content to be the passive object of masculine sentiments, she wished to experience and express feelings of her own. She would take hold of her environment and make it habitable; she would go further and reshape her own identity therein and force it on the world" (10).

The salon was the focal point of the precious movement and hostesses such as the marquise de Rambouillet, Mlle. de Montpensier, and Mlle. de Scudéry attempted to create atmospheres in which conversation and courtesy could flourish. Although the most famous figures were aristocrats, women of the bourgeoisie and even of common origins were accepted on the basis of individual worth; "we can actually speak of a leveling spirit as one of the characteristics of *préciosité*" (Backer 12).[1]

The movement was at its height in the 1650s; according to Backer, "there was a moment in the 1650s when virtually every literate woman in France was in some wise a *précieuse*" (10). The excesses of some of its members were attacked by Molière in his play *Les Précieuses ridicules* (1659), but preciosity continued to exert a profound influence on the language and ideas of educated women through the end of the century.[2]

In this atmosphere of social debate and attempted reform lie the seeds for the utopias I shall discuss here. Mlle. de Scudéry, Mlle. de Montpensier, and Mme. d'Aulnoy all participated in the phenomenon of preciosity in the social arena (each hosted a salon) and in their writing. By the very genres they chose—the novel, the literary fairy tale, and the letter—they appealed to a feminine readership and modeled the forms of social exchange which the salon aimed to promote.[3]

Throughout her prolific career, Mlle. de Scudéry (1608–1701) created characters that expressed her ideals of virtuous love and sociability.[4] She imagined communities where social intercourse, represented above all by the art of conversation, was governed by reciprocity and politeness.[5] Thus her fictional utopian societies embellish and idealize the behavior attempted in actual salons. Her works were greatly successful during her lifetime and well into the eighteenth century.[6] Critics today acknowledge her importance to the period; Joan De Jean speaks of her as "the 'founding mother' of the female tradition of prose fiction in the seventeenth century" (4).

Mme. d'Aulnoy (1650 or 1651–1705), although of a later generation, was also influenced by preciosity in her language as well as her ideals of love and social intercourse.[7] The author of memoirs, novels, and novellas, she is best known for her fairy tales, which play with the limits of language, sexuality, and gender roles.[8] D'Aulnoy's life, which was at the time and to some degree remains as much an object of critical attention as her works, also pushed the limits of accepted behavior. Wed at an early age, she may have been involved with her mother in an attempt to have her husband arrested for treason. Although nothing was ever proved, the scandal shook her reputation, and she dropped out of Paris society for twenty years, possibly spending part or all of this time abroad. Having returned to Paris, she began a highly prolific and successful writing career that lasted approximately fourteen years. Yet once again, in 1699 scandal touched her life: a woman was accused of arranging for her husband's murder, and because she had spent the day of the murder visiting Mme. d'Aulnoy, the writer's reputation was damaged. She retreated from Paris society, and we know very little of the last years of her life.[9]

Unlike Mlle. de Scudéry and Mme. d'Aulnoy, Mlle. de Montpensier (1627–93) was not a writer by profession. Although she did write literary portraits and her memoirs, which provide a fascinating view of court life, she is primarily remembered for her conflicts with the king. Known simply as "Mademoiselle" or "la grande Mademoiselle," she was cousin to Louis XIV. Her high social position and her delighted participation in the activities of court life led her to dominate her society. Yet she spent much of her life in exile from the court because of offenses against the king.[10] These periods of solitude forced her to create her own world, first in the half-ruined château of Saint-Fargeau, then at Choisy. Her constructions gave her firsthand experience in rebuilding a castle and reshaping a society to suit her needs. Despite her desires for marriage, particularly for one that would allow her to satisfy her personal ambition to reign, Mlle. de Montpensier was never permitted by the king to marry, and her passion for a simple gentleman late in her life made her an object of public discussion.[11] This enforced restriction of her life, this marginalization, may have made Mlle. de Montpensier dream of rework-ing society on a grander scale.[12] Raised in the salons of Mme. de Ram-bouillet, when she tried to make her own world, she made it to the pattern of precious society. When, at the age of sixty-three, she dreamed of a new world with her friend, Mme. de Motteville, the ideals of the preciosity of her youth remained as guidelines.

These three writers dramatize needs and desires that recur repeat-edly throughout the history of feminine utopian writings, yet the ex-pression of these needs is shaped by their historical moment and by the economic and social class of the aristocratic writers and their au-dience. Thus it may be best for me to acknowledge that I am using the term "utopia" in a broad sense. As will become clear from my discus-sion, several of the works analyzed make no attempt to present the de-tailed blueprint of a complex society, such as one finds in More's *Utopia*, or even of a small community, such as we see in Sarah Scott's *Millenium Hall*. Indeed, the term "utopia" was not used in the period, appearing first in the dictionary of the Académie Française in 1762.[13] Although several utopias had been written by men by 1690, the year of Mlle. de Montpensier's and Mme. d'Aulnoy's works, there is no way of know-ing whether the women writers I shall discuss had any familiarity with these texts.[14] The works of Mlle. de Scudéry, dating from the 1650s and 1660s, are clearly independent of any immediately contemporary influence. Thus the visions of these writers appear to be formed less from the tradition of the utopia as a genre, than from the growing body of work by women who questioned and attempted to revise their soci-ety, particularly in terms of individual happiness and fulfillment.[15] It is therefore not surprising that economic and political issues are frequently neglected in order to allow a focus on the psychological and interper-sonal. Yet, despite this limited focus, the works are fundamentally uto-pian in their impulse to imagine better worlds and, even if the visions may seem incomplete or simplistic from contemporary perspectives, I believe it is worth stretching the canon to include these early dreams.

Mlle. de Scudéry's first great success, the novel *Artamène, ou le grand Cyrus* (published in ten volumes from 1649 to 1653), reflects closely the *précieuse* society of the time and is read as a roman à clef, with numerous characters representing members of the marquise de Rambouillet's circle. In its reflection of aristocratic life, it adopts val-ues of the period, including ambition, in the form of the desire to distinguish oneself in society, and admiration for military valor. The hero is Cyrus the Great, conqueror of Persia, and his prowess in battle fills many pages. But his value system is challenged by the heroine, Mandane, who abhors war and refuses to allow him to speak of his battle: "I feel such an aversion to war, that I do not even like to hear anyone speak often of the glorious advantages that the king my father has won through your valor" (1:371). War is equally absent from the idealized island of Cyprus, setting for two intercalated tales; men who wish to excel in military endeavors must join the forces of other countries. The island is a place of both natural and manufactured beauty: "this beautiful island . . . for its size, location, fertility, beautiful and great cities, and its magnificent temples, is considered the most famous and the most considerable of all those in the Aegean sea" (2:560–61). Although Cyprian society is not portrayed as perfect (infidelity can occur to mar love and families are still capable of sacrificing their children for profitable marriages), the basic values of this orderly society (established by a queen and dedicated to Venus) anticipate the later work of Mlle. de Scudéry as well as that of Mlle. de Montpensier and Mme. d'Aulnoy:

> We are taught, then, that we must love our goddess, that we must love our princes, that we must love our laws, that we must love our homeland, that we must love our citizens, that we must love our fathers, brothers, wives and children, and after all that, that we must love ourselves, so that we may do nothing shameful. We are also told that we must love glory, the sciences, and the fine arts, that we must love innocent pleasures, and that we must love beauty and virtue more than all that I have just said. . . . Public festivals are very frequent there, conversations are fairly free and very witty; competitive games are quite common; balls are very entertaining; the music is quite charming (2:562–64).

With this emphasis on beauty, virtuous love, and the tranquil pursuit of individual fulfillment through learning and artistic expression, Mlle. de Scudéry sketches the outline of a society, whose ideals she will continue to develop throughout her works and which will influence later writers.

With the story of Sapho, in volume 10 of the same novel, Mlle. de Scudéry returns to the image of an ideal land. The "new Sauromates" inhabit a lovely country that was, significantly, a product of internecine war. Greek immigrants formed a community within the lands of the less civilized Sauromates (identified by the narrator with the Scythians). To protect his enclave, their leader ordered the lands around them to be devastated, so that "there are at least three long days of desert to pass through, from whatever side that one arrives" (10:569). This society, compared to an island, is governed by strict rules of access: guards watch the borders, inhabitants must be screened before they are allowed to leave and then undergo three months of scrutiny before reentering, and no stranger who enters may depart. This severity resulted in revolt within the community and banishment of the rebels. Nevertheless, the current society is represented as benevolent, ruled by a young queen (although her heir, a son, shows that the rule is not matriarchal.) The community is graced by "all the arts and all the sciences" (10:573). Faithful love is the greatest value, but while the inhabitants of Cyprus seemed to rely primarily on education to ensure fidelity, here a formal judicial system legislates stable relationships: "we have even made particular laws for Love; and there are punishments for unfaithful lovers, as there are for rebellious subjects" (10:573). Clearly Mlle. de Scudéry regarded such a society as vulnerable both to external and internal attack and imagined mechanisms to defend the values of peace and faithful love that she could not hope to see universally embraced.

Yet another society dedicated to the pleasures of the arts and of chaste love appears in her novella *Mathilde* (1667). Once again, the ideal community is radically separated from the violent patriarchal world that surrounds it. A historical tale set in Avignon, *Mathilde* does not superficially conform to what is usually considered a utopian novel. The narrative traces the adventures of a young woman who, raised in the company of Petrarch and Laura and imbued with Laura's ideals of independence and platonic love, rejects romance and fights off unwanted suitors until she finds a love that answers her needs. The plot, in itself, is not greatly different from other adventure romances of the period, many written by Mlle. de Scudéry. But running through the novella is the theme of the ideal society, present to the girl in her youth, lost during a time of conflict in patriarchal society, and reclaimed at the end as Mathilde shapes her own life.

The ideal society has been formed by a woman: Laura. It is Avignon, a politically neutral state that welcomes the young Mathilde and her family, in exile after her father's political difficulties. Mathilde is more or less adopted by Laura, and her life is spent in enjoyment of elegant games, conversation, and above all, the respectful attentions of Petrarch and other gentlemen. It is highly significant that the platonic love, so often associated with Petrarch in literary history, is here presented as the philosophy of the woman, Laura. It is she who explains to Mathilde the values of emotional neutrality and the dangers of marriage:

> When people are free, they can hate each other and never see each other, they can even sometimes revenge themselves without shame; but when they are married, honor demands that they still love one another, although their hearts no longer want to; they must be inseparable when they would like never to see each other again, and they must experience the pain of seeing an extinguished love, or, more properly speaking, a love changed into indifference or hate. (43)

It is worth noting that the even-minded Laura sees marriage as an alienation of liberty and a source of emotional suffering for men as well as women: the "they" of her imagined unhappy marriage includes the man also.

In agreement with these sentiments, Mathilde determines to have nothing to do with marriage. But her happy life is threatened when her father exerts his authority to bring her back to Madrid, where she is persecuted by the violence of several suitors, including the king and his cruel son. The prince Pedro can be seen as a male counterpart to Laura, establishing his own society according to his rules. While her politically neutral Avignon is a realm of peace and a haven for refugees, his Madrid is a city of ambition and violence, where freedom of any sort is precarious. Mathilde's final escape from the city thus takes on a wider political significance, as she demands that Alphonse, the one man she has found who seems worthy of living the life of Laura and Petrarch, abandon his political ambitions and leave the court. He agrees, and the couple voluntarily exile themselves to Avignon. Happiness is possible because it has been founded on the woman's terms.[16]

At the end of Mlle. de Scudéry's novel, utopia has been achieved as the two lovers go to live near Laura and Petrarch. Yet their utopia is limited and highly personal, founded on individual love and enacted in a purely aristocratic setting.

A somewhat broader view of utopia is presented by the writings of Mlle. de Montpensier. Her work is unique among those I have chosen to discuss, for it is not a fictional work, but plans laid out in a number of letters sent to her friend, Mme. de Motteville. No complete collection of the letters has been printed, although Mlle. de Montpensier assures the reader of her *Mémoires* that such a collection would make "a fairly thick volume" (452–53). Two letters were published in a collection entitled *Oeuvres galantes*, while four were published in 1735 with the *Mémoires*.[17]

Mlle. de Montpensier's utopia was to be established in the country, on a spot chosen to offer the beauty of a river and a woods. "One would arrive there by great highways where the sun could hardly be seen at high noon" (6). Inhabitants would enjoy fertile gardens: "I would take great pleasure in planting and seeing grow all these different trees" (7). Fountains and streams would delight the senses. Architecture would be important, and members would live in pavilions designed to suit their own tastes: "each would have a house built to his fantasy" (7).

Visits within the community, music, painting, and reading would pass the time. Physical activity would not be forgotten; one would play at pall-mall, a seventeenth-century game in which a boxwood ball was struck with a mallet to drive it through an iron ring suspended at the end of an alley: "it is an honest game and a fitting exercise for the body, which it is good not to forget, while thinking of the exercise of the mind" (9). To avoid becoming ignorant provincials, members would keep in contact with the outside world through reading the latest literary works and through letters. Such letters would teach those still living conventional lives to envy the reformed community: "We wouldn't break off the commerce we'd have with friends at court or in society, but I think that we would become such that it would be more glorious for them to write to us, than for us to respond to them" (8).

Even a limited element of pleasurable work would be available to those who desired it. If anyone wished to play at being a shepherd, the beautiful prairies would support flocks of sheep. "I wouldn't disapprove if people milked cows or made cheeses and cakes, since one must eat, and I do not intend that the plan of our life be fabulous, as it is in those novels where one observes a perpetual fast and such a severe abstinence" (11–12). The influence of *L'Astrée*, a highly popular pastoral novel (published in four parts from 1607 to 1624) is obvious in this picture of work as amusement.[18]

A unique feature of Mlle. de Montpensier's pastoral utopia is the provision for religious observances. Although Mlle. de Scudéry spoke of love for the goddess Venus on Cyprus and made her characters show proper respect for religion, her vision nevertheless remains predominantly secular. As will be clear in the discussion of Mme. d'Aulnoy, religion is not even mentioned in her tales. But Mlle. de Montpensier felt that a concern for one's religious development and for one's salvation was necessary for moral living. She wished to establish a Carmelite convent, where community members could pray and hear "excellent sermons." She also wished to build "a beautiful church served by secular priests who were able and zealous and who would instruct neighboring villages" (13–14). Her desire to spread the benefits of utopia to neighboring communities (she even thought of constructing a hospital for the ill and for poor children) adds a dimension to her plans that is evidently lacking in the works of Mlle. de Scudéry and Mme. d'Aulnoy. Mme. de Motteville goes a step further, suggesting that within the ideal land there should be room for those who appear less than perfect: "In a well-refined state, the crippled, the blind and the deformed must find sustenance and protection as well as the more perfect" (45).

Mme. de Motteville was generally supportive of her friend's idea, although she expressed some amusement at the idea of playing shepherd. However, on the issue of the relations between the sexes, the two women disagreed. Mlle. de Montpensier was quite willing to open the community to both men and women, but admittance would be denied to married couples, and falling in love would be cause for expulsion: "I would be of the opinion that there should not be married people there, and that everyone should be widowed or have renounced this sacrament" (5–6). When Mme. de Motteville questioned the wisdom of such a measure, Mlle. de Montpensier defended her position in stronger terms: "You will permit me to say that what has given men superiority has been marriage, and that what has caused us to be called the weaker sex was this dependency in which men have subjugated us, often against our will, and for reasons of family, of which we have often been the victims. Well, let us pull ourselves out of slavery; let there be a corner of the world where one may say that women are their own mistresses" (35). Mme. de Motteville, herself a victim of a less than happy marriage, nevertheless felt that her friend's plans would not be practical: "I think that finally you would be obliged to permit that so common error which an old custom has legitimized and which is called marriage" (22). Indeed, she suggests that marriage may be necessary for the happiness of some individuals: "If this severe law is established in your solitary republic, it is to be feared that your virtue may work to make unhappy people" (44). Mlle. de Montpensier may have hoped to skirt this danger by peopling her land with mature individuals who would be less likely to suffer from the passions of love; this was her solution to the problem of ambition: "one can find oneself at an age where ambition is less keen and where very reasonable people can cure themselves of it easily" (5).

The essential factor in this utopia, aside from the beauty of the setting and the pleasures of a society that recalls the best of the salons,[19] is the sense that in this world, apart from the pressures and conflicts of court life and the demands of marriage, one would be free to develop spiritually, emotionally and socially. Mme. de Motteville summarizes the philosophical background to this ideal as she writes: "I had thought that this life would be happy if one could add to Christian piety the wisdom of the philosophers and the civility of the famous shepherds of the Lignon [the river in the novel *L'Astrée*]" (16).

Writing in the same year as Mlle. de Montpensier (1690), Mme. d'Aulnoy reexamines the idea that love is a threat to a perfect society. Her "L'Isle de la Félicité" is a tale recounted by a character in a larger work entitled *Histoire d'Hypolite, comte de Duglas*. It describes the perfect home of a princess, Félicité, and the changes wrought in her life when the island's isolation is broken by the intrusion of a man. The fact that d'Aulnoy creates an island, a locus traditional in utopian writing, is particularly significant for a woman writer, for it is thus a world apart, apparently offering safety from intrusions that might threaten the fragile autonomy of the inhabitants. In a time when women had little control over their own mobility and privacy, an invulnerable world apart was a dream.[20] The Island of Felicity is safe, for no one knows its location: "no one, my lord, may enter there. People do not tire of seeking it, but human fate is such that no one could find it. One travels all around it in vain" (2:107). Should anyone find the island, monsters prevent entry: "if the guardians of the island, who are terrible monsters, see you, however brave you may be, you will succumb, and the greatest misfortunes will befall you."[21] Time itself is no threat, for the inhabitants live forever: "they were never ill, they did not even have the slightest indisposition. Their youth was not changed by the course of years; it was in this delicious place that one drank deeply of the fountain of youth" (2:117).

The beauty of the island arises from the harmony of art and nature. The palace and gardens of the Princess Félicité are set in a bountiful and temperate land: "the rain was scented with orange blossom, fountains rose up to the clouds, the forests were made up of rare trees, and the flower beds filled with extraordinary flowers; streams clearer than crystal ran on every side with a soft murmur. There the birds gave concerts more charming than those of the best masters of music. Fruits came naturally, without being cultivated, and one found everywhere on the island tables set and delicately served as soon as one wished" (2:110).

The isolated women are by no means leading a rustic or ascetic existence; their palace is constructed out of precious jewels and gold: "the walls were of diamond, the floors and ceilings of jewels which formed compartments; gold was more abundant than the jewels" (2:110). The overall effect is harmonious: "it seemed that all the arts had competed with an equal success to contribute to the magnificence and perfection of this building" (2:112). The gardens are designed for pleasure and decorated with charming statues, as a visitor discovers: "he passed through a few lanes; he saw grottoes made especially for pleasure and he noticed in one of them a Cupid of white marble, so well made that it must have been the masterpiece of an excellent workman" (2:111). These details imitate the contemporary apogee of taste and style: Versailles. Modern readers may associate Versailles with an ever-increasing centralization of government and with the restrictions and conflcts of monarchy and patriarchy, and we have seen that women utopian writers of the period rejected these values. But in this context, the palace also functions as a model of intellectual and sensual pleasures, pleasures Mme. d'Aulnoy claims for her heroine. In this text, then, as in the works of Mlle. de Scudéry and Mlle. de Montpensier, the imagined utopia retains the best material features of the contemporary society.

The essential feature of this world is, of course, the absence of men. The rejection of men from a woman's utopia is by no means unique to the seventeenth century; it is a feature of many other women's utopias. Men are rejected in female utopias for various reasons, but chief among them must be the desire to imagine a society freed of patriarchal authority and values, however these may be understood. In Mme. d'Aulnoy's work, a world without men is a world of peace.

The princess rules the island, although there is no indication of her exertion of authority, nor any need for political or social control. This depiction of court life is the antithesis, and an implicit criticism, of contemporary political reality, in which the court of Louis XIV was dominated by an uneasy jockeying for favor, and in which increasing centralization extended the king's control throughout the country. Mme. d'Aulnoy's imagined world is a manageable community where relations are based on intimacy rather than hierarchy. The inhabitants peacefully pass their days in making music, playing games, and reveling in the sensual pleasures of their peaceful land. Zephire, the breeze, describes one of his visits: "I was in the gardens of the Princess Felicity; she was walking with all of her nymphs. One was making a garland of flowers, another, lying on the lawn, uncovered her breast a little to allow me more freedom to approach and kiss her; several danced to songs" (2:104–5). The inhabitants are united in clear ties of affection, and the nominal hierarchy indicated by the existence of a princess is less a reflection of political theory than a construct of the story. Mme. d'Aulnoy is not particularly advocating monarchy as an institution; Félicité's superior title merely serves to match her superior beauty, which is necessary for her position as heroine (in this genre and this period). Nevertheless, the society is not completely egalitarian: in an early scene a nymph commands a (female) gardener to fill a basket with flowers for the princess (2:112). The gardener's quick response suggests her devotion and affection for the princess, but it may also mean that in a perfect world, servants are perfect and free of class consciousness or resentment.

The tranquility of this society and the happiness of its princess are jeopardized when a male intruder enters the closed world. A Russian prince loses his way on a hunting trip and takes refuge in a cave. There he overhears Zephire speaking to the other winds about the island. He persuades Zephire to carry him there, so he may see the lovely Félicité.[22] The princess, having never seen a man before, is awestruck, and the couple quickly fall in love. (Mme. d'Aulnoy never exhibited the rejection of sexuality that some critics attribute to the precious writers of the earlier seventeenth century.) They live together in joy until the prince discovers that he has been idly happy with her for three hundred years. Shocked to learn that he has let his political reputation languish for so long, he leaves the island to make his name through glorious military deeds: "he reproached himself for having spent so much time with a mistress and for having done nothing that could put his name among the ranks of the heroes" (2:120). Of course, once he has left the protection of the island, Time catches and kills him. Zephire, returning the body of the prince to the feminine world he had rejected, piles up his arms in silent and ironic tribute to the values which cost him his life. The heartbroken princess closes the doors of her palace, and the tale ends with the commentary that there is no perfect felicity.

The tale encourages an allegorical reading, with their princess representing the vulnerability and tenderness of all women, while the prince reveals the cost to both men and women of the patriarchal values of ambition and violence. The story is not meant to condemn the individual male protagonist, for it is his willingness to help an old man that leads to his death, but rather to point out the inevitable dangers of a life devoted to the values of reputation and power.

"L'Isle de la Félicité" ends pessimistically, with the suggestion that utopia cannot exist between men and women so long as fundamental gender differences lead them to dream such different dreams. Yet Mme. d'Aulnoy continued to play with the idea of "happily ever after" through her volumes of fairy tales, published from 1697 to 1698. In the story "Le Prince Lutin," we see a reworking of Félicité's adventure, with a more optimistic ending. Once again the setting is an idyllic island of women, dedicated to pleasure and forbidden to men. It was founded by a fairy who had been deeply wounded by a man's infidelity. "She transported her palace; she drove away the guards and officers: she took women of the Amazonian race; she sent them around her island to keep a close guard, so that no man could enter. She called this place the Island of Tranquil Pleasures; she always said that one couldn't have true pleasures when one had any society with men: she raised her daughter in this opinion" (1:162). Despite her precautions, the island's isolation is broken by a young man, the prince Lutin, endowed by another fairy with invisibility and magical means of transport. He is struck by the beauty and luxury of the palace.

> The palace was of pure gold; above it rose figures of crystal and precious stones, which represented the zodiac and all the marvels

of nature, the sciences and the arts, the elements, the sea and the fishes, the earth and animals, scenes of Diana hunting with her nymphs, the noble exercises of the Amazons, the amusements of country life, troops of shepherdesses and their dogs, the cares of rustic life, agriculture, harvests, gardens, flowers, bees; and among all these different things, there appeared no men, no boys, not even a poor little Cupid. (1:165)

As on the Island of Felicity, the richness of the materials and their great variety indicate a desire to embrace all the pleasures that the world may offer.

[h]e passed through a great number of vast rooms; some were filled with beautiful pieces from China, whose fragrance, combined with the strangeness of the colors and figures, pleased infinitely. Others were made of porcelain so fine, that one saw daylight through the walls; others were of carved rock crystal. There were rooms of amber and of coral, of lapis lazuli, agate, and carnelian; and the room of the princess was made completely of great mirrors, for one could not multiply too much such a charming object. (1:166)

The Island of Tranquil Pleasures is a refuge from the world, yet it shows some awareness of it, as in the pictures of idealized work, and in the conscious avoidance of men. (In d'Aulnoy's earlier tale Félicité did not even know that men existed; when she first saw the Russian prince she thought he was a phoenix. The princess of Tranquil Pleasures has a more complete understanding of the dangers—physical and emotional—that men may pose.)

The prince is charmed by the inhabitants of this realm: "He saw on all sides young girls with a sweet air, innocent, laughing, and beautiful as the beautiful day" (1:166). He begins a patient, respectful, but persistent courtship of their princess. At first she is determined to preserve her peaceful, healthful way of life; indeed, she attributes her longevity, not to her fairy heredity, but to celibacy and the resultant emotional security, as she explains to a companion: "Do you think that if I led an unquiet and turbulent life, that I would have lived so many years? Only innocent and tranquil pleasures can produce such results" (1:173). Nevertheless, she finds herself increasingly drawn to the mysterious stranger, who contrasts in all ways with another suitor, Furibond, a repulsive creature who may be interpreted as representing all the evils of male aggression and cruelty. When Furibond launches a military attack against the island, Lutin defeats him, saving the princess and her island.[23] The grateful princess begs her fairy mother to allow her to wed, asserting that this man will be faithful. Her mother agrees and transports the entire Island of Tranquil Pleasures to the prince's kingdom. The end of female isolation is complete, for, like a Gilbert and Sullivan operetta, the female chorus weds the male, as the nymphs marry the men of Lutin's army. The tale's rapid ending gives no details of the fate of this society as it blends into a more traditional world, although the fairy mother promises to remain with them and assure their happiness.[24]

Once again Mme. d'Aulnoy has created an idyllic world, only to have it transformed through love. In this tale, the pleasures of the island are retained at the end, guaranteed by the female powers—the fairies—who establish it. Yet the island world's distinctive quality, its all-female society, has been abandoned, leaving the reader to wonder if it was no more than a temporary asylum, until a better solution could be found. Perhaps the final arrangement, moving the Island of Tranquil Pleasures into the "real" world, is meant to represent the ultimate utopia. If this is so, then Mme. d'Aulnoy seems to suggest that true happiness and union between the sexes depends on a male acceptance of female values and social behavior. The happiness of the women is assured only because they have found men willing to live life on their terms.

Mme. d'Aulnoy, Mlle. de Scudéry, and Mlle. de Montpensier focus their attention on aristocratic ways of life. They make no formal restrictions that would exclude members of the lower classes, yet few could meet their standards of taste or education. Needless to say, little or no mention is made of the labor required to support these communities, to feed and clothe the happy inhabitants. The pastoral pleasures depicted on the Island of Tranquil Pleasures or proposed by Mlle. de Montpensier translate a longing for a life free of social constraints and ambition. But while adopting the costume of a shepherd offered a temporary release from the structure and artificiality of contemporary court life, it should not be read as indicative of true egalitarian impulses.

The heroines, like the readers of these tales, are predominantly aristocratic. They are not new women making a new society, but rather fairly traditional figures, seeking refuge in a gentler, freer land. Furthermore, these works give no strong assurance that, having found the perfect world for their self-expression and development, the heroines do indeed change, discovering qualities and abilities that had been neglected in patriarchal society. (Such development is shown in the women of Herland, for example, as the inhabitants demonstrate power, agility, assertiveness, and other typically "male" qualities, required by their autonomous status.) In their defense, however, the idealized worlds of these authors—having barely existed beyond one generation—have not yet had time to produce a new breed of inhabitants.

Nevertheless, it is clear that these aristocratic women are not attempting to outline a complete reworking of their society; they have neither the social and political training nor, most likely, the motivation, to wish all aspects of their world to change. They focus primarily on the needs of individual women like themselves, rather than demonstrating what those women might offer the world. Only Mlle. de Montpensier and her correspondent, Mme. de Motteville, display a social conscience that embraces the needs of the less privileged.

Because of the emphasis on individual happiness, there is a timelessness about these worlds, a static quality that ignores the impulse toward progress and change that lies at the heart of much utopian thought. Children, whose education and care are usually important in female ideal worlds, barely exist except in the form of an occasional adolescent girl, such as Mathilde, preparing to enter the world of women. This absence is most probably the result of women's rejection of the patriarchal establishment that viewed them solely as potential mothers, whose value rested firmly on their ability to produce heirs. In contrast, male utopian writers of the late seventeenth century reaffirm this traditional viewpoint, depicting the female role in their ideal worlds as strictly sexual, focusing on reproduction and scorning infertile women.[25] The very real dangers of maternity in the seventeenth century, and the extremely limited methods of contraception, which made abstinence a form of self-protection, were additional reasons to pass over maternal pleasures. Furthermore, the desire for education and personal enrichment that fired the movement of préciosité made many women of the century long to establish their own worth as individuals, apart from their positions in the household. As can be seen in this contemporary description of a sophisticated woman, that sometimes meant rejecting the traditional maternal role. "One must not imagine, thus, that in speaking of this accomplished woman of whom we are tracing the image, we intended to paint a mother of a family who knows well how to give orders to her servants and who takes good care of her children. Music, history, instruments, philosophy, and other similar exercises are more in accord with our design than those of a good housekeeper."[26]

Thus these utopias of the seventeenth century must be classified as worlds made predominantly for the fulfillment of individual women, and not for the transformation of society, as havens rather than revolutionary nuclei and, while they are "feminist" in their insistence on women's needs for happiness, it would seem inappropriate to apply the term "matriarchal" to systems that make little or no provision for any establishment of familial relationships, or for the ordering of life for future generations.

Perhaps no plans were made for future generations, because the women utopists themselves had trouble believing in the dream. Nor did they make much effort to convince their readers. We see none of the conventions of the genre, designed to make fantasy seem real, such as the first-person narrator who observes and records his visit, thus providing a sense of credibility, or the details, maps, and documents meant to substantiate his accounts. Instead, we see utopias presented in the delightful but hardly grave genre of fairy tales by Mme. d'Aulnoy and in the conditional mood by Mlle. de Montpensier: "We *would* become. . . ."[27] Only Mlle. de Scudéry spoke more authoritatively: she utilized the form of a historical romance, a genre that was granted somewhat more credibility as history in the seventeenth century than in the present time, and her reference to historical figures such as Sapho and Laura may have been an attempt to establish a tradition of women's abilities and aspirations.

Yet if we can read Mlle. de Scudéry as being guardedly optimistic about the possibility of feminine utopias, it would seem that her optimism was not shared by the writers of the last decade of the century, Mme. d'Aulnoy and Mlle. de Montpensier. This may reflect a sense of disillusionment or at least caution arising from the failure of the *précieuse* experimentation to significantly transform society. It was perhaps this very attempted enactment of their dream that led women to sense its inadequacies and to address through their fictional heroines the fundamental problem that continued to trouble them: love. Whatever physical and social advantages their heroines possess in these ideal

worlds, they are nevertheless constantly vulnerable to emotional suffering through their relationships with men. Islands may offer a physical retreat, but cannot ensure inner tranquility, if love is permitted
within their borders. Yet, without love there would seem to be no story,
nothing to talk about in the harmonious society. Mathilde's story is
static until Alphonse enters the scene. Sapho takes her beloved Phaon
with her to the land of the new Sauromates. And the innocent women
of Félicité's island amuse themselves in a garden decorated by a statue
of Cupid bearing these words:

> Whoever is ignorant of the pleasures of Love
> Has never experienced true sweetness.
> It alone can fulfil our desires
> And make life agreeable.
> Without it the greatest wealth
> Is powerless to charm us
> And everything is lifeless.
>
> (2:111)

Indeed, Mlle. de Scudéry and Mme. d'Aulnoy seem to suggest that
love is inevitable, a part of the young woman's development: both
Mathilde and Félicité are young, and their period of independence from
men may symbolize little more than the young girl's latency period, certain to be altered as her sexual desires awaken. Mme. d'Aulnoy's tale
"Le Prince Lutin," would seem to trace sexual awakening, as she describes the young girl's innocence and her increasing preoccupation
with the man. On the morning when they finally meet, her sensuality
is evident: "the princess was dying of heat and restlessness; she got up
earlier than Aurora, and went down in dishabille to her lower apartment." She finds the sleeping hero and delights in her first true vision
of him: "she softly touched his hair, she listened to him breathe, she
could not tear herself away from him" (1:194). Mme. de Motteville
would seem to suggest that such desire must be permitted, despite its
dangers.

Regardless of their seeming independence, strong heroines of the
seventeenth century continue to express a need for heterosexual love.
Parthénie, the heroine of a tale by Mlle. de Scudéry and citizen of the
almost ideal world of Cyprus, having suffered terribly from the infidel-

ity of men, is determined to remain single and independent, rejecting a society that judges her on beauty alone. Yet she admits to a confidante that love alone can give her true happiness: "the felicity of life exists only in reigning sovereignly in the heart of someone and of making an agreeable exchange of pleasures and sorrows with a reasonable person" (6:152).[28] She adds wistfully: "an innocent and completely pure love would be the sweetest thing in the world, if it could last" (6:153).

Thus a fundamental ambiguity shapes these utopias: paradise is not paradise without a man, the single factor most capable of destroying the heroine's happiness. In the final analysis, it was not society, but passion that these seventeenth-century utopians longed to reshape, changing its violence into the safety of Laura's neutral land, transforming its pain into something enduring and nurturing, like Félicité's island.

4

Mothers and Monsters in
Sarah Robinson Scott's *Millenium Hall*

Linda Dunne

A s the feminist project of recovery and reevaluation of women's writing advances, certain key texts are emerging that contain elements that make them especially relevant to the construction of a social and literary history that can inform and reform the present. Sarah Robinson Scott's *Millenium Hall*, originally published in 1762, is such a book. As a utopian description of an idealized community of women, which is partially based on the personal life of the author, *Millenium Hall* also contains a compelling and bitter critique of eighteenth-century society, and presents an alternative to the traditional marriage plot of the eighteenth- and nineteenth-century novel. In addition, by incorporating the maimed and the monstrous into an idealized community of aristocratic ladies, the book appropriates and subverts the common phallocentric perception that all-female communities are inherently defective.

Very little is known about the life of Sarah Robinson Scott.[1] She was born in 1723 in Yorkshire to Elizabeth Drake and Matthew Robinson, well-educated but not wealthy members of the gentry. Both Sarah and her older sister, Elizabeth, who was to become Elizabeth Robinson Montagu, an acknowledged leader of the eighteenth-century Bluestocking Club, received unusually good educations, both at home and in boarding school.[2] Unlike her more famous sister, Scott chose to live a quiet and private life on the fringes of English society and, although she published nine books during her lifetime, all of them anonymously, she died in relative obscurity and her brief obituary failed even to mention her writing. At the age of twenty-eight, she was briefly married to George Lewis Scott, who was some thirty years older than she, a scientist, mathematician, and tutor to the Prince of Wales. But before she had been married a year, her father and brothers physically removed her from her husband's house, and the marriage was legally dissolved. We do not know specifically what happened, but no blame of Sarah Scott was suggested, and the divorce settlement left her with half of her fortune plus 150 pounds a year. Sarah Scott's closest relationship, however, was with Lady Barbara Montagu, daughter of the first earl of Halifax, known as Lady Bab. The two young women apparently met sometime before 1748, when Scott was in her midtwenties and, by all accounts, they were never separated until Lady Montagu's death in 1765. Lady Montagu accompanied Scott on her wedding trip and lived with her and Mr. Scott during their brief marriage.[3] Not long after the divorce, the two women moved to Lady Montagu's house in Bath and, sometime after, began to spend their summers in the nearby rural town of Batheaston where they engaged in charitable work, including a school for local girls that may have been a model for *Millenium Hall*. The two women supplemented their income with Scott's writing. After Lady Montagu's death, Scott remained in Bath for a couple of years and then wandered from place to place, apparently in poor health, finally spending her last years in the town of Catton.

Millenium Hall, Scott's most well-known and her only reprinted work, is assumed by most commentators to be at least partially based on the lives of her and Lady Montagu.[4] Published anonymously in 1762, the full title reads: "A Description of Millenium Hall, and the Country Adjacent: Together with the Characters of the Inhabitants and such Historical Anecdotes and Reflections, as May excite in the Reader proper Sentiments of Humanity, and lead the Mind to the Love of Virtue. By A Gentleman on his Travels."[5] Most simply described, *Millenium Hall* tells the story of a group of upper-class women who have developed an alternative community that is physically insulated from the dominant English society from which their members have escaped. This female community is discovered by accident by two male travelers, the elder of whom, identified only as "a gentleman on his travels," is the narrating persona who recounts his discovery, including a description of Millenium Hall and the stories he is told about its residents, in the familiar form of a letter to his publisher.

In an early essay about the common conventions of feminist utopias, focusing primarily on contemporary works of the 1970s, Carol Pearson wrote that "the most common plot structure of the feminist utopian novel is the conversion story in which a male narrator comes to see a feminist society as superior to a male-dominated one" (59). *Millenium Hall* presents us with a very early version of this plot structure, which is especially revealing as a comment on eighteenth-century England. Both of the male travelers who enter the utopia are products of a corrupt and unhealthy society. The narrator, who remains anonymous in this book, is a member of the dominant English male ruling class; he has just returned to his homeland after twenty years in Jamaica where he made his fortune as a plantation owner and slaveholder. We are told in the opening pages that the purpose of his journey is to restore his health, which had been ruined in the colonies where, in his words: "while I increased my fortune, I gradually impaired my constitution" (30). The metaphor of ruined health certainly stands for the health of the narrator's soul as well as his body, and the context provided by the book as a whole suggests that the metaphor extends to eighteenth-century England in general.[6] His companion, Mr. Lamont, is younger and less world-weary but no less corrupt. He is described even by the narrator, who is his friend and traveling companion, as a vain and dissipated "coxcomb" of twenty-five for whom "fashion, not reason, has been the guide of all his thoughts and actions," and whose poor education has left him both morally and intellectually deficient (31). Both men, then, are members of the privileged ruling class who have been, in different ways, weakened by their participation in a corrupt society. They are both prime candidates for a healing conversion to a way of life that is informed by both feminist and Christian values. It is understood that this conversion of the male visitors represents the potential for general societal reform extending beyond the boundaries of the female community and the book. This understanding is confirmed in a sequel, *The History of Sir George Ellison*, published in 1766, in which we learn that after leaving Millenium Hall, the narrator, now identified as Sir George Ellison, used the fortune he had accumulated in Jamaica to establish his own charity school for boys.

Also consistent with the tradition of feminist utopias that followed well into the late nineteenth and twentieth centuries, Millenium Hall is situated within an idyllic pastoral setting, which includes open pastures upon which sheep and cattle graze, wooded forests filled with wildlife, streams stocked with fish, and elaborate gardens and hedges—"a female Arcadia," whose resident ladies are "epicures in rural pleasures, and enjoy them to the utmost excess to which they can be carried" (177). The landscape is described in terms that clearly suggest abundant fertility and female sexuality. In *Literary Women*, Ellen Moers observed a distinctly female landscape based upon female anatomy in much literature by women. She proposed that as certainly as we can identify images of the phallus in male literature that are connected to issues of power, other kinds of landscapes, such as open fields, twisted lanes, streams and rivers, ravines, and enclosed gardens, are identified with female sexuality and are connected to issues of fertility and maternity (252–64). The landscape surrounding Millenium Hall is extraordinarily suggestive when viewed from this perspective. At its outskirts are rolling hills, then an avenue of oaks leading to broad pastures, followed by profuse and fragrant flower gardens surrounded by hedges and interspersed with streams. At the center of all is the "Primum Mobile" (6), Millenium Hall itself. In addition to natural landscape, the grounds hold a variety of structures that seem to be placed there only to designate specifically the gender identity of the landscape. A temple dedicated to Solitude, sacred to the virgin goddess Diana, is an obvious and literal example. A beautiful grotto that is nearby, with ivy and moss covering its walls and a rivulet cascading down its side, and which, in the words of the narrator, one might imagine as "the habitation of some devout anchoret," is even more graphically suggestive of female sexuality (43).

This female landscape provides a haven of safety to all creatures of nature. Women and girls go from place to place unharmed and unafraid. No one is near who poses the slightest threat to their persons. Even the animals, the narrator observes with wonder, "live so unmolested, that they seem to have forgot all fear, and rather welcome than fly those who come amongst them. . . . We there, 'walked joint tenant of the shade,' with the animal race; and a perfect equality in nature's bounty seemed enjoyed by the whole creation" (42).

The societal and economic structures that were carefully established by the residents of Millenium Hall are designed to extend this "perfect equality in nature's bounty" to all people and creatures. Although Scott was unable to imagine a classless society, the structure of Millenium Hall is surprisingly egalitarian within the rigid boundaries of the hierarchical class distinctions of the eighteenth century. In order to create a community based on "perfect equality," an alternative economic system has been developed based on communal sharing of resources. At the apex of the community are the residents of the Hall itself, six ladies who inherited considerable fortunes and have combined their resources not only to provide for their own well-being, but also to support a variety of charities for the protection and education of others. Once pooled, their financial assets are substantial, amounting to at least 86,000 pounds plus jewels, silver, and the property of Millenium Hall itself.

In a very concrete way, the ladies of Millenium Hall have taken themselves and their money out of the dominant male-controlled economic system that, we are shown throughout the novel, destroys and exploits both women and nature. They have done this by not marrying and by replacing the primary economic system that is built on the wealth of patriarchal families with an alternative economy that is based on communal feminist principles. This new economy appropriates financial resources not to build or maintain private family fortunes but to nurture and protect the poor and unfortunate, the creatures of the natural world, and, most importantly, other women. The following story from the novel symbolizes how this appropriation of resources works. One of the ladies' projects is the restoration of a mansion to provide a home for unmarried gentlewomen who, because of the inadequacy of their personal resources, are obliged, in an economic society that is based on marriages, to become dependents in the families of others and who therefore "suffer all the evils of the severest servitude and are . . . the most unhappy part of the creation" (80). The mansion that is under restoration had previously belonged to a miser. This miser let his home and grounds go to ruin while he gave all his attention to guarding his money. He was found one day in the heart of his decayed estate, his dead body thrown over his chest of gold. His property and fortune were inherited by an impoverished nephew, who quickly squandered all the gold in the chest through decadent living and was forced to sell even the mansion, now in a complete state of deterioration, in order to pay his gambling debts. Using a small portion of their pooled resources, the ladies of Millenium Hall bought the mansion and, in the present time of the novel, were in the process of restoring it as a residence for poor unmarried gentlewomen, thereby transforming what men had neglected and ruined into a useful alternative community for the protection of women who would otherwise have been fated to lives of ridicule, dependence, and exploitation in the patriarchal society beyond Millenium Hall (221–25).

Many other charities were initiated and supported by the ladies of Millenium Hall using their combined fortunes. These charities provide a means for women of all classes, who by choice or circumstances fall outside the normal world of heterosexual marriage, to live useful, free, and fulfilling lives. Each of these charities serve women and girls from a particular social class but each is organized on principles that are internally egalitarian. In the community mentioned above, a "sisterhood" of unmarried and impoverished gentlewomen live together in a society based on communal principles in which a comfortable standard of living is achieved by pooling the inadequate fortunes of each in order to maintain the house. Out of this common fund, each resident receives an equal allowance for her personal expenses. Each is also required to contribute equally to the everyday work of running the household. In another community, a group of old peasant women live in close proximity to each other in identical single-person cottages, which are described as "new and uniform," each contributing what she can to the well-being of all, but each receiving equal support regardless of her ability to work. In addition to these communal residences, the ladies of Millenium Hall support cottage schools for the children of the poor. The education offered to the girls in the cottage schools is limited only by interest and ability. Another group of young women being raised within Millenium Hall itself are taught service skills to enable them to support themselves without marrying if they chose; however, whether they decide to marry or enter into service, all are sent into the world with dowries. An interesting and unusual form of wage distribution in the interest of social welfare is practiced in the carpet factory that the ladies purchased and managed in a nearby town in order to provide employment for the local residents. There, instead of paying all workers at the same rate, regardless of their capacity to work, children and old people, whose production is not so great as the other workers, are paid at a higher piece rate so that their total wages will be more comparable to those of adults who can work at a faster rate.

The most valued activities at Millenium Hall are education and the cultivation of arts. Although the ladies help train and support people of the working and servant class who must work for economic survival, the girls and women who live at Millenium Hall are devoted to far nobler pursuits. When the narrator and Mr. Lamont first enter the main house, they are confronted with a scene that reminds them of the "Attick school."[7] Ladies and young girls are engaged in drawing, painting, sculpting, engraving, writing, reading, dressmaking, and embroidery. In another room, more girls are practicing musical instruments. Each is engaged in the activity that most pleases her and best utilizes her talents. Each evening, a concert is given with full orchestra and chorus. Original art is everywhere. In order to protect the devotion of the ladies to education and the arts, social intercourse is completely voluntary and, if a guest enters the room, it is understood that no one is under any obligation to stop what she is doing unless she chooses to do so. Similarly, everyone has the freedom to leave a social gathering if she likes, and "as no one is obliged to stay a minute longer in company than she chuses, she naturally retires as soon as it grows displeasant to her, and does not return till she is prompted by inclination" (85–86). At the same time, selfish inclinations that impinge on the rights of others are repressed for the good of the group and an inability to get along with others is reason for expulsion from the community.

By promoting the growth of the individual, the community at Millenium Hall functions like an idealized family. All relationships at Millenium Hall are modeled on the primary relationship between mother and daughter. As such, Millenium Hall stands in stark contrast to the dangerous and competitive world that surrounds it on all sides from which the ladies have escaped. This world is described in detail in four histories inserted within the utopian frame that are narrated by Mrs. Maynard, one of the residents of Millenium Hall who happens to be a cousin of the narrator. These histories provide a glimpse of each individual's previous life and tell how she escaped from a corrupt and hostile society that is, in every respect, the opposite of the community at Millenium Hall. In the male-dominated society described in the histories, women are victimized and powerless, and the options available are so limited that they are often forced to make choices that are self-destructive simply because no good alternative exists. The world described to the narrator—and in turn to the reader—by Mrs. Maynard is a world of fundamentally dysfunctional families, in which mothers are unable to protect their daughters. It is a world in which men are either evil or weak—the evil ones bent on destroying women in a power game of sexual conquest, the others contributing indirectly to their destruction by being too weak to love or protect them effectively. Because of the power imbalances in this essentially patriarchal society, heterosexual passion is almost always destructive for women. The world portrayed in the stories has no socially acceptable place for women who are unable or unwilling to assume their traditionally ascribed roles as married women.

Countering the forces of patriarchal power are loving, nurturing relationships between women that are modeled on the primary bond between mother and daughter. Women have only each other and their own virtue and wit to protect them against the abuses of men. The formation of these mutually supportive relationships between women is the primary plot of *Millenium Hall*, just as surely as the search for a suitable husband is the generic plot of the canonized novels of the eighteenth and nineteenth centuries. All of the histories told to the narrator by Mrs. Maynard involve the trials of a young woman who is, in each case, either a real or an apparent orphan; the intervention of a romantic friend or surrogate mother; and, not incidentally, the accident of a substantial fortune inherited, in all but one case, from a female relation. The trials all involve the cruelty or weakness of men.

A summary of the history of Miss Mancel and Mrs. Morgan, the two founders of Millenium Hall and the model for all other relationships, gives an idea of the way this antimarriage plot functions. The stories of these two women are told together, because, according to Mrs. Maynard, "from their childhood [they] have been so connected, that I could not, if I would, disunite them in my relation; and it would be almost a sin to endeavor to separate them even in idea" (48). They met, we are told, in boarding school when Miss Melvyn (Mrs. Morgan) was fifteen and Louisa Mancel was ten. In her earlier childhood, Miss Melvyn was one of the few children in the novel to have had the nurturing love of an ideal mother who taught her the principles of virtue and Christian love. Although she died when her daughter was only fourteen, Lady Melvyn left a legacy more valuable than all the fortunes that made Millenium Hall physically possible: she provided the soul of Millenium Hall, the memory of mother-love that gave Miss Melvyn the ability to love unselfishly and unconditionally, and so provided a model of good mothering that informs the entire project described in the rest of the book. In imitation of her mother, Miss Melvyn assumed a surrogate-mothering relationship with the orphan, Miss Mancel, although the two girls were separated by only five years. This love that was initially modeled on mothering was transformed, as the girls grew into young women, into a more equally supportive romantic friendship. However, their friendship was not allowed to flourish unchallenged by heterosexuality. The trials of the two young women included especially assaultive and cruel behavior on the part of much older men who put themselves in the ambiguous positions of both surrogate father and potential lover. Louisa Mancel's beloved and apparently benevolent guardian tried to seduce her as soon as she approached the age of sixteen, having pretended, all through her childhood, to be fatherly while really only waiting for the day she would be old enough to become another of his conquests. Torn between her duty to her guardian as a surrogate parent and her desire to be chaste, Miss Mancel was saved only by the timely death of her would-be seducer. Meanwhile, Miss Melvyn, as soon as she became twenty-one, was forced by her stepmother—with the concurrence of her father, who was tricked into distrusting his daughter—to marry Mr. Morgan, an elderly and debauched man, whom she detested. Her one hope for enduring this unwanted marriage was to be able to have a home in which she and Miss Mancel could continue their friendship, but Mr. Morgan refused to allow her friend to join the household because, in his words, "I will have no person in my house more beloved than myself" (96). In addition, he forbade the two friends to have any contact at all.[8] Finally, when Miss Mancel, left alone and friendless after her friend's marriage to Mr. Morgan, fell in love with the young son of her employer, the unsuccessful romance was thwarted by the weakness of the young man who, lacking faith and strength of character, died from what was in effect suicide just as it became possible for them to marry. But, not everything was bleak. On the side of good fortune, Louisa Mancel, who from her earliest childhood had thought her mother was dead, was reunited with her through happenstance and, upon her mother's death soon after, inherited a large sum of money that had been brought from the colonies. Meanwhile, Mr. Morgan, who turned out to be an abusive drunkard, finally died of paralysis and insanity, leaving Mrs. Morgan with a large fortune and property as a reward for her patient suffering. United by their love for each other, which had never wavered through their many trials and long separation, the two friends, now aged twenty-four and twenty-nine, combined their fortunes and founded Millenium Hall on the property that had once belonged to Mr. Morgan. By joining together and founding a community for women, Miss Mancel and Mrs. Morgan converted tainted money that been acquired through exploitation by corrupted men to a good purpose.

The other four residents came to Millenium Hall on different but essentially similar paths. All were orphans or thought they were. All suffered from the sexual advances, desired or not, of men. All were aided by a real or surrogate mother. And all inherited a fortune from an older female relative. One more history deserves to be described more specifically because in it the theme of motherly love as a model for all other relationships is developed in an especially explicit way. Miss Harriot Selwyn was "bred a philosopher from her cradle" by an intellectual widowed man who she had been told was her father (157). When she was seventeen, she formed a romantic friendship with her neighbor, Lady Emilia Reynolds, who was "upwards of thirty." When Harriot's apparent father died, she and Lady Emilia retired to the country where they lived so happily together that the younger woman rejected all suitors, preferring to live quietly with her friend. However, in a sudden dramatic twist of the plot, Lady Emilia became suddenly and fatally ill and, on her deathbed, revealed that she was Miss Selvyn's real mother. When she died, Lady Emilia left her daughter a considerable fortune, which she was then able to bring to the community at Millenium Hall. In this history, Miss Selvyn not only found her real mother in the form of a friend, but her mother, by posing as a friend, taught her daughter how to love. The story of Miss Selvyn is essentially happy; she rejected marriage only because she was so happy with her friend/mother that she saw no reason to change her situation. However, the story of her mother, told in a confessional deathbed letter, is tragic. The story of Lady Emilia is the account of a woman who rejected marriage only because she was unable to control her or her lover's passions. When she was a young woman, Lady Emilia and her betrothed submitted to their sexual passion prior to marriage, resulting in the conception of Miss Selvyn. Despite her pregnancy and the continued love of her betrothed, Lady Emilia refused his entreaties to marry him, claiming that their love had been fatally tainted by their sin. She gave their daughter to a childless couple to raise. Eventually, after years had passed, the parents were purged of passion and able to share a chaste friendship with each other. The conclusion with which the reader is left is that, in the world of this novel, all heterosexual passion, even that shared by two essentially good people, is evil and dangerous if it is not carefully controlled and, indeed, repressed.

The mother/daughter relationship and the creation of a functional home grounded on the nurturing relationships between women is the ultimate model for a good society presented by this idealized vision of a successful community of women. To create a functional home based on mutual caretaking and respect for the individual is to create an alternative society in which women are able to pursue their own self-development in an environment free from male oppression and danger. Like the fictional world portrayed in so many eighteenth-century novels, the society presented in the histories of the ladies of Millenium Hall is dangerous, cruel, and inhospitable, especially to women. But while the typical heroine of the canonized novel survives that world by finding a suitable heterosexual marriage and a country estate, the women in Scott's novel escape that world by finding each other and Millenium Hall.

In the course of constructing a book that provided a feminist utopian alternative to the corrupt and abusive world of society, Scott created an episodic narrative structure that provided an alternative to the linear marriage plot and she developed a collective character who escaped the individuality of the fictional heroine. Each of the histories told to the male narrator and his companion by Mrs. Maynard focused on a single protagonist (except that of Mrs. Morgan and Miss Mancel, which was told as one integrated history.) These histories, consequently, bear a structural similarity to the narrative tradition that was being established during the eighteenth century in which the trials and tribulations of a young, female heroine are resolved with an appropriate marriage. These histories also present each character as an individual, each with her own parents, trials, and personality. However, even in the histories, the characters begin to merge, for the names of the heroines bear a striking similarity to each other: three have surnames that begin with M, two have the given name Harriot, and two have rhyming names (Melvyn and Selvyn). This apparent merging of the characters becomes even greater within the narrative frame in which Millenium Hall itself is described. In the sections describing the utopian community, very little distinction is made between any of the ladies, and no single character emerges as the heroine. Passages that are spoken by one could just as probably be spoken by any other. The only details that differentiate one from another are that one lady paints while another engraves, or that one plays the harpsichord, another the violin. This dual structure of personal histories embedded within the description of the utopian community allows the author to present the isolation of each woman as the single heroine of her own story prior to her entering Millenium Hall where she becomes, in a sense, freed from the burdens of eighteenth-century heroism. Thus, the structure of the novel itself places it outside of and even in opposition to the more traditional romance novel with its single heroine in pursuit of a suitable marriage.

Millenium Hall is primarily the description of a utopian community for women who chose to reject the external patriarchal and heterosexual world, with its unbalanced power relationships and threats of violence to women, in order to pursue lives in which they were free to develop their whole intellectual and spiritual beings. However, contained within this utopian community is an enclosure that stands in apparent antithesis to Millenium Hall and the conditions and potential of its residents. In the very beginning of the novel, on his first morning as a visitor, the narrator is taken by his hosts on a walk around the grounds. As they walk, he sees a high green fence or pale, seven or eight feet high, lined with a hedge of evergreens. He asks what it is and, at first, his inquiries meet with no response. He guesses that perhaps the fence contains a zoo, but is told, in no uncertain terms, that the ladies do not believe in imprisoning wild animals or anything else for amusement. After pressing for an explanation, he is finally told that the fence encloses an asylum for dwarfs and giants or, as they were called at the time, monsters.[9]

This is a somewhat startling discovery, both for the narrator and for the reader. It is disturbing to find that, in addition to the proper ladies and their well-behaved students, Millenium Hall provides a home for some eight dwarfs and giants, most of them female, who, until being rescued, were doomed to lives of humiliation, exploitation, and physical abuse. Before coming to Millenium Hall, these unfortunates had been shown for exhibition by "monster-mongers" who "seem to think that being two or three feet taller gives them a right to make them a property, and expose their unhappy forms to the contemptuous curiosity of the unthinking multitude" (44–45). Their experience of being public spectacles has left them horrified of the possibility of being seen by strangers. The fence is clearly intended to protect the inhabitants from the outside world and not, as in a zoo, to imprison them, although the initial mistaking of the asylum for a zoo tends to conflate the two in the reader's mind.

Pressed by the two gentlemen to explain the nature of the asylum, Miss Mancel describes the pain that these "unfortunates" have suffered at the hands of society and relates their situation to that of the strangers entertained by the infamous classical villain, Procrustes:

> Procrustes has been branded through all ages with the name tyrant; and principally, as it appears, from fitting the body of every stranger to a bed which he kept as the necessary standard, cutting off the legs of those whose height exceeded the length of it, and stretching on the rack such as fell short of that measure, till they attained the requisite proportion. *But is not almost every man a Procrustes?* we have not the power of shewing our cruelty exactly in the same method; but, actuated by the like spirit, we abridge their liberty, and torment by scorn, *all* who either fall short, or exceed the usual standard, if they happen to have the additional *misfortune of poverty.*" (45; emphasis added)

In recalling the cruelty of Procrustes, Miss Mancel was not only warning her visitors not to make the mistake of insisting that all people be alike, in size or in spirit; she was also subtly contrasting the reception that they themselves had received as travelers and strangers at Millenium Hall, with the treatment they might have received from such a host as Procrustes. Having been so warned, the narrator is given permission to enter the enclosure, where he admires the landscaping as well as the noble characters of the inhabitants.

As he spends more time at Millenium Hall, the narrator discovers that the so-called monsters are not the only misfits to live there. First, he notices that the housekeeper has a maimed hand. She then tells him that "the cook cannot walk without crutches, the kitchen-maid has but one eye, the dairy-maid is almost stone-deaf, and the housemaid has but one hand" (130). The musicians who perform in the evening concerts are similarly disabled. In fact, he discovers that all but two of the entire household staff are physically disabled in some respect.

Disabled house servants, dwarfs, and giants—what are these symbols of aberration and disorder doing in an idealized community that is, in all other respects, a model of beauty, order, and harmony? What fictional and psychological purposes do these monsters serve? On one level, their presence can be seen as a measure of the degree of Christian charity practiced by the ladies of Millenium Hall, a charity that extends even to the most unfortunate members of the human family, like the biblical account of Christ and the lepers. But Miss Mancel's reference to the story of Procrustes suggests that there is more to it than that. If the majority of *men* are like Procrustes, and if all who deviate from the norm *without the protection of money* are imprisoned and tormented, we might suspect that, through the voice of Miss Mancel, Scott has intentionally extended the moral of the story to the situation of the ladies of Millenium Hall, all of whom had been exposed by their own poverty and powerlessness to the torments of men. The similarities between the exploitation of the "monsters" and the economic situations of women are made fairly obvious in the histories that immediately follow in the novel.

In almost every respect, the monsters function as a distorted mirror image of the ladies of Millenium Hall. The similarities between the persecution and exploitation suffered by the dwarfs and giants with the lives of the ladies as narrated in the histories are not difficult to see. The vivid image of the physical mutilation that is required to make the social misfit conform to society's norm draws a parallel between the pain experienced by the dwarfs and giants, and the pain suffered by the ladies in the outside world as the people around them tried to force them to fit standards of behavior for which they were not suited. Prior to being rescued, the dwarfs and giants had been put on exhibit and "exposed to the contemptuous curiosity of the unthinking multitudes." In much the same way, the young ladies portrayed in the histories were exposed to the lustful eyes of male admirers, whether or not they desired to be admired. To add to their discomfort, because of their size and afflictions, the dwarfs and giants were kept uncomfortably confined in small rooms. Similarly, in the world of society depicted in the histories, women are restricted to lives spent, for the most part, indoors, bounded by the walls of drawing rooms. Another set of parallels has to do with the responses of the monsters and the ladies to their oppressed status. Scott writes that when the monsters were first rescued from their lives of oppression, "their healths were much impaired, and their tempers more so." Some were even so afflicted with vanity that they maintained "pretensions of superiority" over their fellows, based on the amount of recognition they had been given as public spectacles (46). In much the same way, many of the women depicted in the histories had also been physically and morally co-opted by the male-dominated society, trading their own integrity for a share of male privilege. Finally, a parallel between the monsters and the ladies can be seen in the very existence of the novel itself, in which the stories of the women, told voluntarily by Mrs. Maynard, expose the lives of the residents of Millenium Hall to the visiting eyes of the gentlemen as well as to the reader, in much the same way as the visit into the asylum, made with the permission of the monsters, exposes them to the same eyes.

To underscore the relationship between the ladies and the monsters, the physical characteristics of the asylum are a microcosm of the estate. Both are enclosed, the asylum by an actual fence, the estate by an equally protective boundary. The asylum is a protected space of approximately six acres, containing a stream, chicken pens, flower gardens, an arbor of woodbines and jessamine, and a house. Millenium Hall is described as an estate of hundreds of acres, with streams, forests, pastures, a pigeon house, rabbit warren, and dairy, along with flower and vegetable gardens, and the mansion. Both the larger property and the enclosed asylum are admired by the narrator and his companion for their beauty, order, and fecundity.

Millenium Hall, like the asylum for monsters, is a protected place whose residents can pursue self-sufficient lives that are free from the oppression and violence they suffered in a society dominated by men. However, looked at from the perspective of the society they reject, those women are misfits and outcasts, either willfully or by misfortune. Nina Auerbach reminds us, in *Communities of Women*, that men have always viewed women without men as monstrous and deficient. Going back to the ancient Greeks, she recalls the mythical Graie, three ancient sisters whose single eye was stolen by Perseus, who was then able to bring them helplessly to defeat. She also recalls the legendary Amazons, who despite their vigor and the strength of their will, were continually being vanquished by the solitary hero who used them as material on which to "chisel his heroism." As communities of women without men, the Graie and the Amazons "are seen immediately as mutilated"; consequently, "both groups are outcast" (3–4). From the perspective of the dominant male society, groups of women without men are monstrous, at best to be pitied, at worst to be despised and destroyed. One might well wonder if the parallels between the monsters and the ladies of Millenium Hall suggests that Scott, herself a refugee from the heterosexual world of urban society, saw her characters and, by projection, herself, as monstrous or disabled misfits who were forced to hide in a protective enclosure away from the gaze and the power of men.

It is difficult to avoid getting caught in a maze in search of authorial intent or unconscious subtexts. Nonetheless, I want to take a leap into such a maze by suggesting that one of Sarah Scott's purposes, conscious or not, in *Millenium Hall* was to question and subvert the male assumption that a community of women should be pitied or despised as monstrous and physically deficient. Recognizing that communities of women who have rejected heterosexuality were generally seen as "maimed and outcast," Scott appropriated those qualities, embodied them in the disabled servants and the misfit dwarfs and giants, and created a safe, orderly, and clearly defined space for them. She further subverted the anticipated criticism of her all-woman community by acknowledging the similarities between the monsters and the ladies, establishing a kind of sisterhood based on the mistreatment of a male-dominated society that models its behavior on the cruelty and tyranny of Procrustes. Instead of avoiding or denying the common assumption of the "unthinking multitude" that any group of women without men are inherently defective and monstrous, Scott brought the disabled and the deformed into her vision of an ideal society, and gave them a function, a space, and dignity. She then brought two men, the narrator and Mr. Lamont, emissaries from the exploitative and corrupt male world, into the idealized and cultivated society of Millenium Hall, with its proper gardens and its evening concerts of Handel; indeed, right into the asylum for monsters. The result is that because of the context and the attitudes of the residents of Millenium Hall, the male narrator's perceptions of deviance are radically changed. He is thus led to see the monsters as exemplars of virtue, not creatures of scorn or pity. In his words: "Instead of feeling the pain one might naturally receive from seeing the human form so disgraced, we were filled with admiration of the human mind, when so nobly exalted by virtue" (46). This is an important moment of insight for the male narrator, a former owner of slaves. In Scott's conception of the world, the mind *can* triumph over the body, and virtue is the unquestioned goal of all human beings. By changing his perception of the monsters, the narrator begins his conversion and is prepared to respond properly to the histories of the ladies.

Millenium Hall belongs to the age of enlightenment, and is no glorification of uncontrolled passion over civilized reason. Just as it is a mistake to assume that the monsters are simply an unconscious projection of the author's sense of her own deviance, so it would be a mistake to interpret them as a romantic alternative to the orderly society of eighteenth-century England. The powerful image of the Procrustean bed used by Miss Mancel serves as a metaphor for a destructive form of social organization that is based on forced conformity to artificially established norms. The society criticized in this book is one that fails to value individual differences and attempts to eradicate them by force; it is the external or "actual" society to which the idealized world envisioned at Millenium Hall is an alternative. In contrast, the society that Scott imaginatively created at Millenium Hall is devoted to the nurturing of the individual and the protection of personal freedom—in short, the principles of good mothering. The organization of the entire community, on all of its levels, is designed to promote the abilities of the individual women who inhabit it, just as the ideal family is organized to foster the healthy development of all of its members. This entails, as we have seen, a high level of structure, which is manifested physically in the well-designed landscape, and politically in the rules that govern the behavior of the members of the community. The natural world presented in *Millenium Hall* is controlled, regulated, and domesticated. It is a nature of pastures and gardens, not the wild, stormy, violent nature that would become the metaphor for the feelings in Romantic literature. The idealized society that is proposed in *Millenium Hall* is similarly regulated through a series of rules and understandings regarding proper behavior that are dedicated to the protection of individual rights and the promotion of self-fulfillment. It is a world that demands consideration and order in the study and drawing room so that each woman will have the peace she needs to create and to think. It is a world that also values the supportive company of women who will appreciate and take interest in each other's creations and thoughts. This society has no place for the violent and lonely rebel who would later be manifested in the Romantic hero.

In this world, emotions are as tightly controlled and regulated as nature and social interactions. So is sexuality. As we have seen, *Millenium Hall* offers a social and affectional alternative to heterosexuality and the social necessity of marriage by creating a community of women friends whose relationships are based on the model of mothering. But it is an alternative that, for the most part, relies on the repression of sexuality and of the more violent emotions that accompany it. Heterosexuality is clearly rejected by the six women who have their permanent residence at Millenium Hall, but it is not replaced by homosexuality.[10] The nature of the relationships between women in the novel are not represented in a way that suggests that they allowed for sexual expression. In only one instance, when Miss Mancel was separated from Miss Melvyn, just before the marriage of the latter to Mr. Morgan, are we given a glimpse of the free expression of passion and that expression took the conventional form of uncontrollable tears.

The issue of sexuality in *Millenium Hall* is complex, and we have to guard against imposing assumptions that are more appropriate to our own times than to the eighteenth century. Having demonstrated that the monsters in the enclosure have a symbolic link to the ladies of Millenium Hall, I think we can push this aspect of the text even farther and see the monsters as representing those aspects of the ladies that are most unacceptable, most deviant, most vulnerable, and most oppressed by the dominant male culture. In short, I want to propose that the monsters stand, in some sense, as metaphors for the sexuality of the ladies of the Hall. If this is so, we have to question the nature and status of the sexuality represented by the monsters, given that they are enclosed behind a seven-foot fence that protects them from the gaze of the world. From our present post-Romantic, post-Freudian perspective, the meaning of the enclosure can too easily be interpreted negatively, misread as a prison for the emotions rather than as a sanctuary for them. For most women today, the ability to be wholly and freely sexual is important to the fulfillment of our humanness, and the conscious repression of sexuality seems a high and unnecessary price to pay for intellectual freedom or peace of mind. But I think the histories of the residents of Millenium Hall show us that, in the eighteenth-century world that provides the context of this narrative, liberation for women came through celibacy, not through sexual freedom. Viewed in this light, the enclosure for the dwarfs and giants, who stand in for the residents of Millenium Hall as societal misfits, represents order and protection, not imprisonment. Just as Miss Mancel vigorously insisted when she allowed the two gentlemen travelers to enter the enclosure, it is, indeed, an asylum, not a zoo. And, like the asylum for monsters, Millenium Hall itself provides a safe, orderly, well-defined space in which women can nurture and protect their minds, their souls, and their sexuality.

As the Age of Reason seemed to explode into the age of the Romantic imagination, the figure of the monster appeared in literature with greater frequency and the set of meanings it evoked shifted significantly. A new set of questions emerges as we place the monsters of Millenium Hall up against the host of dwarfs, giants, and other human aberrations that appeared in the gothic novel that developed during the late eighteenth century (Horace Walpole's *Castle of Otranto,* was published only three years after *Millenium Hall.*) More questions come to mind as we place Scott's monsters in the context of other monsters appearing in later works by eighteenth- and nineteenth-century women writers. What is their relationship to the numerous references to monstrous women in Mary Wollstonecraft's *Maria;* or to the gigantic monster in the masterpiece *Frankenstein,* written by her daughter Mary Shelley; or to the ominous hunchbacked dwarf in Charlotte Brontë's *Villette*—to name but a few. Monsters in these later works seem to have served as the manifestations of a complex mix of social persecution, defiant identification, and self-loathing, lurking within the subtext. Do these later monsters serve as tropes for female sexuality in ways that relate to the monsters in *Millenium Hall?* Does the apparent shift from a kind of benevolent protection to horrified loathing suggest a parallel historical shift in the perception of the sexual self, or does its meaning change with individual authors? The significance of the monstrous misfit, especially when depicted as female, is a strand in the tradition of women's writing well worth following.

⌐

Gaskell's Feminist Utopia
The Cranfordians and the Reign of Goodwill
Rae Rosenthal

I n her landmark essay, "Feminist Criticism in the Wilderness," Elaine
Showalter explains that outside of the dominant male culture the
muted women's culture has a space, a "wild zone," that "stands for the
aspects of the female life-style which are outside of and unlike those
of men" (262). According to Showalter, in an attempt to enlarge and
endorse such spaces, "women writers have often imagined Amazon Utopias, cities or countries situated in the wild zone or on its border" (263).
In a subsequent list of examples, Showalter cites first, "Gaskell's gentle
Cranford" (263).[1] And indeed, when read as an exploration of
Showalter's wild zone, Elizabeth Gaskell's *Cranford* suddenly explodes
with resounding power. This text, seemingly so innocent, now presents
the most stirring of visions; it creates the possibility that the muted
culture might accept its marginal space, reject the dominant culture,
and establish itself as an alternate community—a feminist utopia—a
separate and better world in which women live pacifically and where
"good-will reigns among them to a considerable degree" (*Cranford* 40).

The utopian aspect of *Cranford* has not gone unnoticed by Gaskell
scholars. Coral Lansbury, in her 1975 study of Gaskell's novels, entitled
her chapter on *Cranford* "*Cranford*: Old age and Utopia"; Lansbury here
argues that the text offers an alternative to the stereotype of lonely,
embittered spinsterhood and that Gaskell's depiction of "a group of
middle-aged and old women [who] can order a society to their own pleasure" (93) contributes greatly to the success of the novel.[2] In her 1978

study, *Communities of Women: An Idea in Fiction*, Nina Auerbach argues, similarly, that the Cranfordians have developed a notably communal life-style. Auerbach emphasizes too the Cranfordians' collective femininity and their strength, the combination of which earns them the appellation "Amazon."[3] In a more recent article, Rowena Fowler describes *Cranford* as a "specifically female Utopia," adding that it offers "a softening and blurring of categories and hierarchies in place of More's or Plato's clearly-ordered systems" (718). However, only Helen Kuryllo, in her 1989 essay, stresses the highly political nature of the text, maintaining that *Cranford* should be read as "both subversive text and feminist utopia" (102) and that as "an alternative community—one of old women who lead pleasant, full lives without men—[*Cranford*] calls for a redefinition of terms" (102). Ultimately though, Kuryllo's argument, while stimulating, is brief and serves largely to invite additional dialogue.

So while there has been some critical recognition of *Cranford* as a utopia, much remains to be said about the nature of this utopia—its origins, its design, and its future. In particular, I would like to explore the way in which this utopian community becomes increasingly feminine and feminist rather than just female, the way in which the women do battle with and defeat the succeeding invasions of patriarchal forces, and the means by which the Cranfordians ensure the preservation of their utopian society through the education and assimilation of the narrator, Mary Smith.

When establishing a definition of feminist literary utopias, scholars note, repeatedly, three distinguishing traits: emphasis on feminine values and issues, commitment to communalism, and an ability to overcome male intruders through either expulsion or conversion. For example, in their respective defining essays, Carol Pearson, Carol Farley Kessler, and Lee Cullen Khanna each note the regularity with which feminist utopias reject the patriarchal values of the dominant culture and substitute, in their place, the feminine values of the muted or outside culture. Specifically, Pearson states that "feminist utopias are critiques of patriarchal society" (50) that "do away with the division between the inhumane marketplace and the humane hearth, and pattern the entire society on the principles which ideally have governed the home" (52). Kessler points out too that female authors of utopias tend to "make issues of family, sexuality, and marriage more central than do men" (*Daring to Dream* 7). And Khanna adds that when "women artists create societies reflective of a female value system . . . communication, education, and creativity are primary values" (99).[4]

In their attempts to define female values, both Kessler and Khanna cite Carol Gilligan's compelling work, *In a Different Voice*, which examines through a series of case studies the moral and psychological development of women. In terms of feminist utopias, what Gilligan's study offers is a description of female values and an explanation of how women come to embrace a value system so different from that of the dominant culture within which they reside. Gilligan's research reveals that, while at play, young girls tend to participate in small group activities that avoid hierarchies and competition and thus argumentation; as a result, girls develop a large degree of "empathy and sensitivity" (11). Further, because "the primary caretaker in the first three years of life is typically female, . . . for girls and women, issues of femininity or feminine identity do not depend on the achievement of separation from the mother or on the progress of individuation" (7–8). Consequently, "femininity is defined through attachment" and "female gender identity is threatened by separation" (8). Thus, females tend to value egalitarianism, cooperation, connection, tolerance, generosity, and most importantly, harmony, all of which lends itself naturally to the creation of utopias. In fact, Kessler goes so far as to suggest that "feminism itself is a type of Utopianism" (*Daring to Dream* 6). It follows logically, therefore, that feminist utopias tend to privilege precisely those traditionally feminine values that lead to their creation.

The second distinguishing trait of feminist utopias is a commitment to communalism, an ethic that evolves readily from the feminine values of egalitarianism, cooperation, and connection. Pearson explains that, ironically, the patriarchal culture has inadvertently provided the women's culture with this particular strength because the "socialization to serve and to sacrifice one's own needs for those of others makes it possible for women to envision a society in which people cooperate, instead of compete, and nurture instead of dominate one another" (54). As a result of this socialization, feminist utopias tend to arrive at what Khanna sees as the center of their communities—"a politics of consensus" (99)—by a process of discussion and persuasion that enables them to become, in Kessler's phrase, "more responsibly communitarian" (6).[5]

Finally, feminist utopias are characterized by their ability to defend themselves through either expulsion or conversion of the frequent male intruders who so often arrive under the guise of curious visitor. In fact, Pearson suggests that the "most common plot structure of the feminist utopian novel is the conversion story in which a male narrator comes to see a feminist society as superior to a male-dominated one" (59).[6] (See, for example, *The Kin of Ata, The Dispossessed,* and *Herland.*) Even, Pearson continues, "the societies which rid themselves of patriarchal consciousness by slaying the men, usually end by converting men to 'mother consciousness,' when male explorers from another world stumble upon their perfect society" (59). (See, for example, *Mizora, Herland,* and *The Female Man.*) In doing so, the feminist utopian community creates, in addition to a means of self-protection, what Kessler describes as a significant new opportunity for men who now may be forced "to learn to value what our culture has labelled as female, that unknown 'wild zone' whose practices may be crucial to the survival of humankind" (*Daring to Dream* 19).

Clearly, the community of Cranford, as it has evolved by the end of the novel, corresponds closely to this appropriately collective definition of a feminist utopia. In Miss Matty, the most influential of the Cranfordians, we see the blend of the "marketplace and the humane hearth" of which Pearson speaks, and radiating from Miss Matty, we see the way in which the entire society gradually becomes immersed in feminine values, including generosity, connection, and above all, harmony. This desire of the Cranfordians for harmony, combined with their commitment to egalitarianism, leads to a communal system of governance whereby, in moments of crisis, they utilize a "politics of consensus" in order to resolve their difficulties collectively. The development and implementation of such a system proves them to be truly, what Kessler describes as "responsibly communitarian" (*Daring to Dream* 6). Cranford proves adept too at self-defense, in that it manages both to reject those males who cannot be co-opted and to convert to "mother consciousness" those outsiders, both male and female, who can.

When Mary Smith begins her narrative, "Cranford is in possession of the Amazons; all the holders of houses, above a certain rent, are women" (39),[7] and Deborah Jenkyns, the late rector's elder daughter, presides firmly over the small community of women. Although Mrs.

Jamieson, by virtue of her being daughter-in-law to a baron, outranks Miss Jenkyns, Mrs. Jamieson's torpid nature leaves her disinclined to make any of the assertions necessary to social domination; consequently, Miss Jenkyns, who abounds in energy and aspiration, governs the other women without challenge. So at this point, Cranford is both utopian and female, for "whatever does become of the gentlemen, they are not at Cranford" (39).[8] Yet under Deborah's reign, Cranford is neither feminine nor feminist. In truth, the town continues much as it was during Deborah's father's lifetime; it is hierarchical and rigid in its social code, and the governing structure remains distinctly dictatorial. Deborah is in all matters social and political the staunchest of conservatives, as evidenced by her adoration of Samuel Johnson, the great arbiter of eighteenth-century manners. In matters of dress, Deborah favors peculiarly male fashions, as she generally "wore a cravat, and a little bonnet like a jockey-cap" (51), and for Captain Brown's funeral, she makes a mourner's bonnet that immediately reminds Mary of a helmet (57). Deborah's manner often has a corresponding military orientation: she is described as having "stood . . . like a dragoon" (59) and when offended, having aimed to "give a finishing blow or two" (48).

In matters of governance, Deborah strives to imitate her father, who was said to be a "strong man" (98) with a "stiff and stately" (86) demeanor. She endeavors, as Kuryllo points out, "to uphold and embody the stern, inflexible codes of her father" (105), and like her late and adored father, Deborah is both autocratic and patronizing. Deborah insists upon a hierarchical social structure with rigid class distinctions, and she chooses to make all decisions about that structure independently, exacting thereafter strict adherence to her edicts. Such a system is diametrically opposed to that of a feminist utopia, with its emphasis on communalism and consensus. Such a system is, however, typical of patriarchal cultures, which are by definition hierarchical because there can be no patriarch without the presence of what Kuryllo aptly terms "the eternal Other to be excluded and subordinated" (105). Once this two-tiered ladder structure is in place, various substrata naturally evolve, as evidenced by Cranford's "strict code of gentility," which determines who shall and shall not be visited and of which only Deborah has a "clear knowledge" (109). Accordingly, in the event of newcomers to Cranford, it is Miss Jenkyns alone who determines whether they may or may not be visited. And in her youth, it was she who saw to it that her sister, Matty, refused an offer of marriage by a local yeoman whom it appears Matty was inclined to accept. In this way, Deborah dominates her sister and the other Cranfordians thoroughly and proves herself to be, truly, her father's daughter.

In an early (and exceptionally misogynistic) essay, Martin Dodsworth argues that Deborah represents the text's "dangerous elements of . . . feminism" (143), which must be purged before "the community of Cranford is restored to a fuller life" (143).[9] Writing in response, Patricia A. Wolfe claims, similarly, that "Cranford is pictured as a fortress of feminism defended by the indomitable Deborah" (163). However, Deborah neither accepts the feminine role her culture has deemed appropriate for women—consider her masculine dress, her militaristic behavior, and her highly aggressive, competitive nature—nor does she advocate, as did eighteenth- and nineteenth-century feminists (for example, Mary Wollstonecraft, Harriet Taylor, and Margaret Fuller), the redistribution of social and political rights for women.[10] Considering also Deborah's likeness to her father, it may more appropriately be said, as does Kuryllo, that "[b]oth Deborah, the first and favorite child, and her father, the church rector, are associated with the strict codes and institutions of a male-dominated world" (105).

Deborah then neither represents nor exemplifies feminism, but she does instead illustrate the fairly common role of deputy husband which Laurel Thatcher Ulrich defines as a temporary, substitute-male position: "Should fate or circumstance prevent the husband [father] from fulfilling his role, the wife [daughter] could appropriately stand in his place" (36). Ulrich adds too that "almost any task was suitable for a woman as long as it furthered the good of her family and was acceptable to her husband. This approach was both fluid and fixed. It allowed for varied behavior without really challenging the patriarchal order of society" (37–38). This substitute-male system thus allowed for the illusion of female independence and power, even though in reality all that was gained was a temporary stand-in position. Nonetheless, considering the other alternatives—neither power nor independence of even a temporary sort—many women, Deborah included, chose to accept the limited opportunity being offered. So what Deborah does, and perhaps wisely, is to recognize the possibility for the attainment of power through cooperative participation in the very political system that limits her. She chooses to maximize her opportunities and, as a result, gains as much control as a woman might under her circumstances. Yet, and here is the catch, by doing so, she supports the status quo and, in the long run, furthers her own oppression. In addition, her power obviously exists only as long as no appropriate (i.e., middle-class) male appears, which no doubt explains why Deborah adopts so combative a stance with Captain Brown. Deborah, then, despite initial appearances to the contrary, proves to be merely a stand-in for her father; under her reign, Cranford is distinctly female and utopian, but still patriarchal in its values, just as it was during her father's regime.

However, Deborah dies at the end of chapter 2, and so does not constitute the focus of the novel. And the central issue of the novel is not her governance of the community but what happens to that community after her demise. Nina Auerbach notes that even though the "death of Deborah Jenkyns, and with it the waning of Cranford's strict code of gentility, has been seen as the healthy demise of the town's female militancy" (see Dodsworth), Deborah's death more likely signifies, as Auerbach goes on to suggest, "the end of the severe patriarchal code which Deborah inherits from her remote, adored father and enshrines throughout her life" (82). Accordingly, when leadership passes to Matty, who unlike her sister is "meek and undecided to a fault" (67), the utopian town becomes more and more unpatriarchal and nonhierarchical; it is now not just female but feminine and increasingly feminist.

Indeed, of all the Cranfordians, Miss Matty is the gentlest, the kindest, and the least patriarchal. Matty says of herself, "I never was ambitious . . . but I thought I could manage a house" (158) and "I am just as fond of children as ever and have a strange yearning at my heart whenever I see a mother with her baby in her arms" (158). As the text begins to foreground Matty, her femininity is brought into sharper focus by its constant differentiation from that of her late sister Deborah, and it quickly becomes clear that Matty posses in abundance precisely what Deborah lacked most—a feminine soul, one that attaches itself readily and communes well with others. Matty also shows more interest in collectivism than did her sister. For instance, in a strong display of selflessness and loyalty, Matty keeps her shares in the Town and Country Bank because Deborah—the sister whom she admired and still reveres—had originally made the now clearly erroneous decision to invest their small property there.[11] And once the bank fails, Matty's sense of communalism prompts her to feel responsible for others who have lost their money; hence, she insists upon reimbursing a farmer who has come to town to buy his wife a shawl with checks from the now defunct Town and Country Bank. Later, after having been virtually impoverished by the fall of the bank, Matty decides to sell tea, but she generously refuses to open her shop until she has checked with Mr. Johnson, a local merchant who also sells tea, in order "to inquire if it was likely to injure his business" (200). Apparently, Mr. Johnson has been infected too with the feminine values of Cranford; he not only assures Matty that her new shop will not affect his sales, which cannot be entirely true; he frequently sends her business. Furthermore, even though the sale of tea provides Matty with her sole means of support (or so she thinks), she continuously warns her customers against buying green tea because she fears it will damage their health; she persists too in giving away almond-comfits to the children because the " 'little things like it so much' " (204). But in spite of Matty's being clearly ill-equipped for the commercial world, she manages to survive; indeed, one suspects that she survives precisely because she is so ill-equipped. And by doing so, Matty demonstrates the thoroughness with which Cranford has managed to, in Pearson's words, "do away with the division between the inhumane marketplace and the humane hearth, and pattern the entire society on the principles which ideally have governed the home" (52), thus allowing feminine values to pervade the entire society.

Although Matty tries to follow Deborah's rules carefully after she is gone—"Miss Jenkyns's rules were made more stringent than ever, because the framer of them was gone where there could be no appeal" (66–67)—Matty finds that she cannot, except in the daily minutiae of managing the household. As a result, the Cranford community undergoes several changes, each reflective of its new leader. Servants now have followers; ladies dine with bachelors; and most important, the "strict code of gentility" is gradually relaxed. This hierarchical social code to which Deborah had adhered religiously first begins to break down during the Cranfordians' shared debate about the appropriateness of allowing Mrs. Fitz-Adam into their circle. During this debate, Matty, in a characteristic show of empathy and generosity, determines that Mrs. Fitz-Adam will be visited by explaining that she "thought it might have been the hope of being admitted in the society of the place, which would certainly be a very agreeable rise for ci-devant [the former] Miss Hoggins; and if this had been her hope, it would be cruel to disappoint her" (109). Significantly, most of the changes in Cranford are brought about by means of this newly implemented collective decision-making process, whereby Matty and the other Cranfordians consult together regularly and, as a group, make various decisions, as in the instance of Mrs. Fitz-Adam.

The burgeoning sense of collectivism becomes most apparent, however, after Matty loses her small income in the bank failure. The Cranfordians set out together to find a means of sustaining Matty, and they rather quickly arrange matters to their mutual satisfaction. Mary arranges for Matty to sell tea, by which she earns an annual income of more than twenty pounds; Martha provides Matty with a home; and Matty's friends make anonymous provisions for her to receive additional funds. In fact, her friends not only each offer a portion of their own, equally small incomes, they insist that the gift be anonymous because, as Miss Pole explains, " 'in consideration of the feelings of delicate independence existing in the mind of every refined female . . . we wish to contribute our mites in a secret and concealed manner, so as not to hurt the feelings I have referred to' " (191). The women go so far as to write their contributions on sealed pieces of paper, so that even they will not know how much the other has given; in this way, they prove that they are motivated neither by the hope of glory nor gratitude, but rather by sincere generosity, mutual loyalty, and a strong sense of collectivism.

Matty's expressly feminine mode of governance further distinguishes her from her sister Deborah. When Deborah ruled Cranford, she used patriarchal tactics—intimidation, aggression, and open directives—whereas Matty is so well-schooled in indirectness that she seems unaware of the extent to which she leads the other Cranfordians. Yet Matty, through her self-effacing style of governing, influences Cranford as thoroughly as did Deborah, only Matty does so without being dictatorial; in fact, by using the traits that so often have been held against women—timidity, emotionality, delicateness—Matty leads without the appearance of doing so. She guides by example, a quiet self-assurance, and gentleness, yet neither she nor her friends ever make the mistake of confusing her gentleness for feebleness. Matty chooses, rather than to reject all that is feminine, as did her sister, to endorse and enlarge the feminine, thereby converting their otherness into a triumph of femininity.

On several occasions, Matty demonstrates exactly how one's feminine nature can become an invaluable source of strength and influence. Mary tells us, for example, of the episode of the coal man whom Matty leads to honesty simply by trusting him to be so: "I have heard her put a stop to the asservations of the man who brought her coals, by quietly saying, 'I am sure you would be sorry to bring me wrong weight;' and if the coals were short measure that time, I don't believe they ever were again. People would have felt as much ashamed of presuming on her good faith as they would have done on that of a child" (201). Surely too it is because of Matty's example that the town develops a strong sense of communalism, as evidenced by the way in which the women imitate Matty, making financial sacrifices for her in much the same way that Matty does for the unknown farmer in the shop. It appears to be just as Mary says: "her unselfishness and simple sense of justice called out the same good qualities in others" (201). Matty's gentle, trusting nature thus becomes a constant source of regeneration and self-propagation. And as a result, under Matty's rule, Cranford undergoes a revolution. It is no longer merely a utopian community occupied by women, but rather a fully developed feminist utopia that has dedicated itself to the furtherance of feminine values and to communalism, both with a marked measure of success.

Significantly, the characteristics that distinguish Matty from her sister—support of feminine values, commitment to communalism, and the ability to influence others in the adoption of feminine values— are precisely those that scholars associate with feminist utopias in general. Yet Matty shows little evidence of being a feminist if we accept the nineteenth-century definition of feminism, as outlined by Mary Wollstonecraft in *Vindication of the Rights of Woman*: according to Wollstonecraft, feminism is "a REVOLUTION in female manners" that devotes itself to the pursuit of "the rights which women in common with men ought to contend for" and the belief that "the sexual distinction which men have so warmly insisted upon, is arbitrary" (318–19).[12] Matty actually evinces little interest in political issues, choosing rather to concern herself with matters relating directly to her small, homogeneous society. Nonetheless, by so thoroughly exemplifying and advocating feminine values and by contributing to the development of a female community based on those values, Matty does, albeit perhaps unconsciously, lead Cranford into an era of feminist utopianism and does thereby help to further the cause of feminism in general.

In the transition from Deborah to Matty, Cranford proves itself to be highly stable in that it adapts well to internal change yet simultaneously proves invulnerable to external change, as evidenced by the series of male invasions that punctuate the text and the thoroughness with which these invasions are repelled. We are told in the first paragraph of the text that "whatever does become of the gentlemen, they are not at Cranford" (39). But in the course of the novel, there are three attempts at male infiltration, and in each instance, the town proves itself immutable, as it must be in order to maintain its utopian structure. The women of Cranford are amazingly adept at maintaining the status quo and seem to have mastered the art of self-preservation; no sooner does a man arrive in Cranford than he conveniently disappears, much to the satisfaction of the women, who exclaim, " 'A man . . . is so in the way in the house!' " (39). The Cranfordians realize instinctly that their authority would be destroyed if men were allowed to remain in the town, and that thus, a man would, literally, be in their "way."

The first invasion of Cranford is by Captain Brown who immediately upon arrival violates the first rule of Cranford—Elegant Economy—and to the Cranfordians' great dismay actually "openly spoke about his being poor" (42). His newly established residence in town leaves the women "moaning over the invasion of their territories by a man and a gentleman" (42), but gradually, over a period of months, the women develop an appreciation of his "masculine common sense, and his facility in devising expedients to overcome domestic dilemmas" (43). Yet, despite his being handy, Captain Brown brings change, as signified by his preference for "Boz" (i.e., Dickens) and his "connection with the obnoxious railroad" (42), and change of this sort is detrimental to Cranford. So, useful as Captain Brown may be, the Cranfordians come to realize that his presence upsets the balance of power and that, as a result, he poses a very real threat.

Brown's unwanted domination first becomes apparent during the tea parties that constitute the center of Cranford's social life. Here Brown manages, under the guise of chivalry, to usurp the women's beloved self-sufficiency: "He immediately and quietly assumed the man's place in the room; attended to every one's wants, lessened the pretty maid-servant's labour by waiting on empty cups, and bread-and-butterless ladies; and yet did it all in so easy and dignified a manner, and so much as if it were a matter of course for the strong to attend to the weak, that he was a true man throughout" (46).

By assuming that he is "strong" and they are "weak," and that he, therefore, needs to be in charge, Captain Brown threatens the utopian existence the Cranfordians have so enjoyed. He implies too that in the past Cranford was somehow lacking when, in fact, the women had "rejoiced, in former days, that there was no gentleman to be attended to, and to find conversation for, at the card-parties" (45).

Captain Brown's battle with Deborah Jenkyns over the relative merits of Dr. Johnson and Mr. Boz further exemplifies the disturbance his presence is causing. By opposing community standards and by insisting upon deviating from those standards, Brown presents a clear challenge to the static insularity of Cranford and to Deborah's leadership. Deborah, understandably, wants to maintain her power, and by championing Dr. Johnson, she champions the status quo against Captain Brown and Boz, both of whom represent external change and the inherent dangers therein. The Cranfordians, of course, follow Deborah's example, and they too come to recognize that in exchange for Captain Brown's usefulness, they have granted "him an extraordinary place as authority" (43), a costly bargain at best.

But ultimately it is Brown himself who proves, through his highly inappropriate solution to the crisis of Betty Barker's Alderney cow, how ill-suited he is to be an authority in Cranford and how little he understands its residents. When asked his opinion as to how to remedy the cow's baldness, Brown suggests that Miss Barker either "get her a flannel waistcoat and flannel drawers" or "kill the poor creature at once" (43). No doubt, Brown offers the first suggestion as a jest, but the jest fails because he doesn't realize that the Cranfordians do not see themselves as funny; they find nothing amusing in out-of-date clothes, a fifteen-minute visiting rule, or a cow in flannel drawers. And Brown's second suggestion—to kill the cow—is even worse because it is strikingly unfeeling and the women, given the choice of dressing a cow in a man's clothes or needlessly slaughtering it, understandably choose the former. This episode, more than any other, demonstrates Brown's carelessness, his inappropriate sense of humor, and his unsuitability as a Cranfordian.[13]

Still, Captain Brown's fatal accident might at first seem startlingly harsh.[14] Yet, for the women of Cranford and for the future of their utopia, Brown's death is imperative, and the way in which the railroad makes what Nina Auerbach terms "a single obliging appearance to kill off Captain Brown" (81) leads one to believe, as does Auerbach, that Cranford has an "unsettling power to obliterate men" (81). Had Brown been a benign invasion, he would have been allowed to remain (as Peter Jenkyns will later); instead, Brown is eliminated and for good reason—he is dangerous, as Deborah Jenkyns knows instinctively. Accordingly, after his death, Deborah quickly assumes governance over Brown' daughters, conveniently burying one and marrying off another, so that Cranford is as though the Browns never existed. As a result, Cranford is once again "in possession of the Amazons" (39), and Deborah can now leave her sister, Matty, a legacy intact.

The second male invasion occurs in chapters 9, 10, and 11— "Signor Brunoni," "The Panic," and "Samuel Brown"—which describe the appearance of Signor Brunoni, the subsequent alarm caused by rumors of a nearby band of robbers, and the discovery of the Signor as the bedridden Samuel Brown. It has been suggested by Patricia Wolfe that the "panic which follows this invasion manifests the *irrational* fear of masculinity which characterizes the psychological condition of Miss Matty and the other Cranford ladies" (169; emphasis added). The assumption behind this argument—that a male invasion does not present a real threat and that the women's fear of such an invasion is irrational—ignores a fundamental reality of Cranford life and one the women know well: while the Cranfordians may control Cranford, outside of Cranford in the dominant male culture, they have virtually no power. So their "panic" is in reality a highly rational dread of the potential loss of control over their community that would inevitably accompany a successful male invasion. But by yet another strikingly convenient stroke of fate, much like that of the railroad and Captain Brown, Brunoni's spring-cart breaks down, he "sustained some severe internal injury" (152), and Lady Glenmire and Miss Pole find him bedridden at a public house several miles outside of Cranford. The awe-inspiring Brunoni thus becomes the rather ordinary Samuel Brown, the second invasion is defeated, and the women emerge victorious yet again.

Auerbach notes particularly the thoroughness of Brunoni's reversal, observing that "the cynosure who makes them tremble is brought low in an accident which renders him helpless, while the ladies survive to pity and nurse him" (84). In this way, Brunoni/Brown is eliminated, as was Captain Brown before him, and once again, Cranford manages to "obliterate" the intrusive male, leaving behind a utopia intact. Now, Cranford can continue much as it did before Brunoni appeared, although perhaps with a heightened sense of its need for effective defense strategies, as shown by the new approach taken during the next male onslaught.

The third and final invasion of Cranford comes in the form of Matty's long-lost brother, Peter Jenkyns, who unlike Brown and Brunoni will become a full-fledged Cranfordian and a valuable member of the utopian community. A number of critics have viewed Peter as the savior of Cranford. For example, Peter Keating contends, in his introduction to the Penguin edition of *Cranford*, that Peter "returns, wealthy, experienced, and unrepentant, to bring 'peace' to Cranford" (25). And Hazel Mews asserts, in a strange denial of the text, that the women have no problem-solving capabilities and that they must wait for Peter to assist them. "In the end, of course, in spite of the rallying round of her friends and the gesture of selling tea, it is a man, her brother Peter, home from India, who really comes to Miss Matty's rescue. The ladies of Cranford have no adequate knowledge or resources to enable them to cope with any crises that occur in their sheltered lives, and in their time of real trouble it is masculine help that must rescue them" (189).

But despite Keating's and Mews's assertions to the contrary (see also Dodsworth), at the time of Peter's arrival, peace already reigns in Cranford; Matty's financial crisis has been resolved, and it has been resolved collectively by the Cranfordians. Thus, a careful reading of the text suggests rather, as Auerbach notes, that although "Peter seems to enter as a providential savior, Matty does not need him to make of Cranford a holy community, for she has already transmuted it herself" (88).

Peter is then not a savior but another invader from the outside. Still he differs in a number of significant ways from his predecessors. Though born in England and thus part of the dominant culture, Peter has spent the majority of his adult life in India where he lived "right in the midst of the natives" (161). Having experienced life in the "wild zone," he has less of a commitment to the dominant culture than do either Brown or Brunoni. Also, Peter does not invade Cranford uninvited, as do the others, but rather appears as the result of an inquiry from Mary. And because Peter was born in Cranford and is related to Miss Matty, the quintessential Cranfordian, he has a keen understanding of the community and is not completely an outsider. Finally, Peter, though male, is not particularly masculine or patriarchal; in fact, like his sister Deborah, Peter displays a strong sense of gender ambivalence. When young, Peter repeatedly appeared in women's clothes; Auerbach sees this fondness for transvestism as Peter's way of "abdicating his manhood and aligning himself with the tender femininity of Matty and their frail mother" (88). In fact, in many ways, Peter and Matty are two kindred souls, both of them having been especially attached to their mother and both still having "the sweetest temper" (95).

The Cranfordians, with their keen instinct, quickly recognize these differences as well as Peter's corresponding affinity for their feminine way of life. As a result, they elect, rather than to banish Peter as they did Brown and Brunoni, to adopt a new strategy, the very one that Pearson and Kessler see as crucial to the furtherance of feminist utopias: assimilation or male-conversion. And a highly effective strategy this proves to be, for it is, in the end, not Peter who co-opts Cranford, but the Cranfordians who co-opt Peter. And suddenly, as Kuryllo says, he finds himself both "welcomed and absorbed by the community" (107). Accordingly, in the last chapter, we find Peter fully participating in Cranfordian politics and social gatherings. And like the other Cranfordians, Peter chooses to take his lead from Matty, aiming at all times to arrange matters precisely to her liking, as in the instance when, in order to satisfy Matty's "love of peace and kindliness" (218), Peter carefully arranges a reconciliation between Lady Jamieson and her sister-in-law, Mrs. Hoggins. In a number of other instances, too, Peter contributes to the continued harmony of Cranford, and by doing so, he becomes an affirmation of feminine power and an endorsement of the communal life-style he has adopted. Consequently, as in so many feminist utopias, the conversion of a visiting male to a more feminine way of life proves to be highly beneficial to the community's stability and to its future. So while Peter may be, literally, the third male invader and the only successful male infiltrator, he serves largely to demonstrate the effectiveness of the process whereby, in Pearson's words, feminist utopias "rid themselves of patriarchal consciousness by . . . converting men to 'mother consciousness' " (59).

By the end of the novel, though, the Cranfordians have managed to assimilate yet another visitor—Mary Smith— and it is she who provides the clearest evidence of Cranford's strength and its capacity for self-perpetuation. George Griffith claims that Mary is "a self-effacing character of no particular significance" (62), but this is a naïve thing to suggest about any narrator, as they are by definition significant. John Gross contends, more accurately, that the truly crucial element of *Cranford* is "Mary's changing vision of the little town" (225), and indeed, during the course of the novel, Mary does undergo a distinct attitudinal change. In the opening chapters, Mary Smith is an observer; she enters the text as first-person narrator who visits the utopia and who is shown around by her friend and host Matty Jenkyns. Although initially Mary speaks as an outsider, albeit a friendly and admiring one, more and more often in the course of the narrative, Mary speaks from within the group, and by the end of the novel, she has completely abandoned her original stance of observer. Mary is the only character in the novel who moves continuously between Drumble, "the great neighbouring commercial town" (39), and Cranford, and in the beginning, both seem to be battling for her allegiance. Yet by the end, Cranford has won Mary over completely; she is no longer a visitor, but an insider, a full-fledged member of the community she first entered as a guest. Being now a true Cranfordian, Mary ensures the continuance of the feminist utopia that the older Cranfordians have established and have fought so hard to sustain.[15]

Although the first chapter of the novel is titled "Our Society," Mary is at this point clearly an outsider, though a welcome one. She receives instructions about visiting protocol, she laughs at Cranford's disregard for fashion, and she fears, after Deborah's death, that she may lose contact with her friends, thereby indicating just how tenuous she perceives her relations with Cranford to be. But once Miss Pole takes the initiative to invite Mary for another visit, Mary affirms her loyalty to Cranford and to its new leader, Miss Matty, by prolonging her stay in order to "settle her [Matty] with the new maid" (65). Also during this visit, Matty tells Mary of her aborted love affair with Mr. Holbrook, a confidence that further ensures Mary's allegiance to Matty. Thereafter, Mary's friendship with the Cranfordians appears to be firmly established.

By chapter 5, Mary has adopted a more involved narrative stance and significantly begins the chapter with a distinctly Cranfordesque confession of her "foible"; Mary becomes annoyed if people waste string, and India-rubber rings (rubber bands) are to her a deification of string: "To me an India-rubber ring is a precious treasure. I have one which is not new; one that I picked up off the floor, nearly six years ago. I have really tried to use it; but my heart failed me, and I could not commit the extravagance" (83). This emphasis on heart and economy is classically Cranfordian. Noteworthy too, Matty's reading to Mary of the family letters, in the same chapter, has the elements of an initiation; the letters are read in the dark, one by one, and then destroyed in the fire. Next, Mary learns of Peter's shocking prank and his subsequent disappearance, a family secret Matty evidently guards carefully: " 'you are sure you locked the door, my dear, for I should not like any one to hear' " (95), and this in a town where "it was impossible to live a month . . . and not know the daily habits of each resident" (49). But Mary is told the family secret and thus enters Matty's confidence and the inner circle. Still, during "the convocation of ladies, who assembled to decide whether or not Mrs. Fitz-Adam should be called upon by the old blue-blooded inhabitants of Cranford" (108), Mary is not yet permitted to participate in the group's decision-making process; she can only await their verdict and comply with their resolution. And when Peggy, Miss Barker's maid, brings in the scandalous second tray of refreshments—" 'Oh, gentility!' thought I, 'can you endure this last shock?' " (113)—Mary can still laugh at the rigidity of the Cranford social code.

Subsequently, Mary is absent from Cranford for a year due to her father's illness, but when she returns after her lengthy stay in Drumble, she appears to be even more committed to Cranford and all that it signifies. Appropriately, it is at this point in the novel that Mary becomes more actively involved in the affairs of Cranford; for instance, when Matty commissions Mary to purchase a sea-green turban, Mary independently decides that it would be better for Matty to wear a lavender cap. Following this act of Cranfordian decisiveness, Mary begins to take a more active role in the narrative and refers more and more often to the communal "we." Thus, during "The Panic," when—note especially the pronouns—"desirious [sic] of proving *ourselves* superior to men . . . in the article of candour, *we* began to relate *our* individual fears, and the private precautions *we* each of *us* took" (147; emphasis added), Mary too has a confession to make: "I owned that my pet apprehension was eyes—eyes looking at me, and watching me, glittering out from some dull flat wooden surface; and that if I dared to go up to my looking-glass when I was panic-stricken, I should certainly turn it round, with its back towards me, for fear of seeing eyes behind me looking out of the darkness" (147).[16]

By chapter 12, Mary has become a full-fledged Cranfordian, as confirmed by her having now acquired, during the redistribution of Matty's home, a "room of her own," complete with furniture she has purchased from Matty. She now also takes it upon herself to make a decision that will affect, not just Matty as in the case of the cap, but all of Cranford: Mary determines to seek Peter Jenkyns's return. Mary's management of Matty's finances after the failure of the Town and County Bank also indicates the extent of her increased involvement. In her decision to have Matty sell tea, an unprecedented act of female independence and a rejection of rigid class distinction, Mary begins to further resemble Matty, whose disregard for traditional social barriers had earlier led the Cranfordians to accept Mrs. Fitz-Adam. Keeping in mind too that polite Cranford society never speaks directly of money matters, no doubt if Mary had still been regarded as an outsider, Matty would never have involved Mary in her financial affairs. Furthermore, when the other women gather to arrange financial assistance for Matty, they call Mary by name for the first time; previously she had never been addressed directly. And whereas Mary had earlier been amused by Cranford's idiosyncratic social code, she is now critical of her father for not understanding the ways of Cranford; thus, when Mr. Smith insists that Matty's checking with the other tea retailer is " 'great nonsense' " (200), Mary loyally responds that "it would not have done in Drumble, but in Cranford it answered very well" (200); and when Mr. Smith dismisses Matty's confidence in the coal man as "simplicity" (201), Mary points out that her father "in spite of all his many precautions, . . . lost upwards of a thousand pounds by roguery only last year" (201). Mary is now an insider mocking the outsiders, a total reversal of her original position. But it is the last paragraph of the novel that demonstrates with the greatest finality Mary's newfound sense of community (again, note the pronouns): "Ever since that day there has been the old friendly sociability in Cranford society; which I am thankful for, because of my dear Miss Matty's love of peace and kindliness. We all love Miss Matty, and I somehow think we are all of us better when she is near us" (218).

In the process of this transition, Mary Smith receives an education in feminine values; she learns to admire the communality and generosity of Cranford and to deplore the harsh competitiveness of nearby Drumble and all that that town comes to signify. In this way, the newly converted Mary becomes, through her role as narrator—a role that necessarily imparts a great deal of power and control—an example of the strength of the Cranfordians' feminine values, a demonstration of the limitations of the patriarchal values that Cranford must repeatedly battle, and a representative of the future of the utopian community she has joined.

At the time of publication, *Cranford* was an inordinate literary success. In the three years after its well-received serialization, there were three editions published in book form, and in the nearly 150 years since, its popularity has continued unabated; A. B. Hopkins estimates that by 1947, there had been 170 editions and reprints of *Cranford* (102). Gaskell too was especially fond of *Cranford*, and once wrote to Ruskin, that it was "the only one of my books that I can read again;—but whenever I am ailing or ill, I take 'Cranford' and—I was going to say, enjoy it! (but that would not be pretty!) laugh over it afresh!" (*Letters* 747). Perhaps Gaskell preferred *Cranford* because it was one of the few works that did not thrust her into the midst of an unpleasant controversy, as did *Mary Barton, Ruth, North and South,* and even *The Life of Charlotte Brontë.*[17] So when Charles Dickens and John Forster, Dickens's friend and literary critic, both described *Cranford* as "delightful," "tender," and "delicate" (Keating 8), Gaskell must have felt great relief. And it is this perception of the text—*Cranford* as a piece of fine social painting—that has persisted. Interestingly though, this critical perception errs in the same way that critics err when they mistakenly assume the Cranfordians, the Amazons, to be helpless and frail. The misunderstanding stems from a failure to recognize that beneath the veneer of fragility lies a very substantial core. Both the text and its inhabitants possess the unique strength of delicate tenderness. It is indeed as John Gross suggests: "Set against the clanking machinery and the grime and the hard faces of the industrial novels, *Cranford* looks frailer than ever. Exquisite workmanship, yes, but if it is inspected too closely won't the charm evaporate? In fact the reverse is true. *Cranford* is indestructible" (224).

Guided by a tradition of genuinely appreciative scholarship based on fond affection for Gaskell, for *Cranford*, and for the Cranfordians, readers have often overlooked the potentially subversive element of the text. *Cranford* is much less innocuous than it first appears, however, and if read carefully, the text may be seen to have a radical political undercurrent. *Cranford* is in fact "delightful," "tender," and "delicate," yet it is also a novel about female self-governance, a tale of a feminist utopia where in the never-ending conflict between the dominant patriarchal culture and the inevitable resistance of the marginalized Other, the Other emerges victorious.

Ƈ

Subjectivity as Feminist Utopia

Jean Pfaelzer

From the framers of the Constitution on, male political idealists and male utopians have had to be reminded to "remember the ladies." Women framers of utopia, by contrast, have offered a revisionist history, albeit a history of the future, that remembers women's different social and biological realities, and their different psychologies. While most male utopians, such as Edward Bellamy, would claim that utopia neutralizes capitalism and patriarchy in one blow, early feminists— Rebecca Harding Davis and Louisa May Alcott in the nineteenth century, and feminist utopians—Charlotte Perkins Gilman, Ursula Le Guin, Marge Piercy, Joanna Russ and Judy Grahn in the twentieth— expose patriarchal assumptions within utopianism. When women construct the future and when they approach men's constructions of the future, they challenge a simple automatic synthesis of utopianism and feminism, utopianism and romanticism.[1] I shall consider here two early critiques through the context of recent work on the relationship between subjectivity and society.

From its inception in the mid-nineteenth century, American literary utopianism has been shaped and deformed by romanticism. Nina Baym defines romanticism as a myth that narrates "a confrontation of the American individual, the pure American self divorced from specific social circumstances, with the promise offered by the idea of America. This promise is the deeply romantic one that in this new land, untrammeled by history and social accident, a person will be able to achieve complete self-definition. Behind this promise is the assurance that individuals come before society, that they exist in some meaning-ful sense prior to and apart from, societies in which they happen to find themselves. The myth also holds that society, as something artifi-cial and secondary to human nature, exerts an unmitigatedly destruc-tive pressure on individuality" (132). I find that American utopian communities and literary utopias, when defined by men, have sought to realize the ahistorical, antiestablishment and antisocial elements of romanticism. These solipsistic tendencies emerge in the patriarchal shape of utopias erected by men.

"The Harmonists" (1866) by Rebecca Harding Davis and "Tran-scendental Wild Oats" (1872) by Louisa May Alcott, fictionalized stud-ies of real utopian communities, recount women's impressions of male-defined utopian communities. They suggest that nineteenth-century intentional communities perpetuated the romantics' view that society dominates the individual, and in particular, the female individual. Society, whether utopian or real, was a male creation; the future perfect could not hopscotch patriarchy. Feminist utopians criticize utopias or-ganized around romantic views of social change and sentimental views of "separate spheres." They fear for utopia, indeed, they fear utopia, when it projects male political goals and represses subjectivity. Typified in the early social contracts of both Rappite and transcendentalist communi-ties, utopia represents a sexual exchange in which women still lacked political power yet also lost authority over domestic life. In the Ameri-can Owenite communities of the 1820s, conflict arose over women's po-litical rights. In some Owenite communities women were "wives of members" rather than members in their own right; and unmarried women were simply not "members." In others, women could vote only on do-mestic matters; elsewhere women could vote only in the "female depart-ment."[2] And so utopia legitimized separate spheres.

From Edward Bellamy to Ken Kesey, ideal communities that prom-ise security through the benevolent patronage of male authority expose the utopian fallacy; a formula whereby the dreams of a single individual shape society as a whole is patriarchal. In defining utopian politics as gender differences, both Alcott and Davis anticipate the modern equa-tion reached by Le Guin, Piercy and Monique Wittig: the personal is political and the political is social.

Traditionally, the notion of political responsibility hinged on the notion of the self as separate from society. The self (in fiction, the represented self) was seen as bounded and autonomous. In Edward Bellamy's *Looking Backward* (1888), before Julian, the time traveler, may join the utopian club he must first complete a lonely quest for his socialist identity. By contrast, in nineteenth-century women's social visions, political responsibility originates in collective ideals of social growth. The very definition of the utopian good is collective. Davis and Alcott do not just reverse gender roles and call it utopia. They do not just offer a social analogue to romance, a romantic relationship which, in Simone de Beauvoir's view, offers women a vicarious access to transcendence. Rather, Davis's and Alcott's critiques of utopia demystify the Western notion of the self, albeit the utopian self, as separate, bounded, and autonomous. The feminist notion of utopia projects a dialectical relationship between the individual and society.

The feminist utopia is synthetic. As in Charlotte Perkins Gilman's *Herland* (1915), the feminist utopia emerged, in part, from women's materialist conceptions of the family, conceptions that picture the family not only as the site of, among other things, unpaid labor, but also as the site of patriarchal forms of child-rearing. Davis's and Alcott's deconstructions of utopia anticipate the modern feminist utopia because they hinge on a demystification of motherhood and a reevaluation of sentimental fiction. Anticipating Piercy and Grahn, in lieu of utopia, Davis and Alcott offer an alternative vision of idealized female space that incorporates the realities of maternity and domestic labor.

According to recent developments in psychoanalytic theory and object-relations theory, male individuality emerges from a young boy's need to realize his male sexual identity by repudiating his early identification with his mother—the powerful and primary love object who is of the other sex. But whom else can he go to? Ever since work moved outside the home and permanently changed patterns of family life in industrial society, the father has become, for the most part, unavailable. This double loss or double estrangement (from mom and dad) in early childhood leads, as Nancy Chodorow has argued, to an idea of individuality and identity that is based on a denial of connection ("Gender, Relation"). Rather than reflect a balance of separation and intimacy, independence seems to exclude connection, that is, "rapprochement." Davis and Alcott see that male utopian communities, paradoxically, reproduced this idealization of independence. Gilman,

Piercy, Le Guin, and Grahn, by contrast, fantasize utopian communities forged through dependence, conflicted though it may be.

As Jessica Benjamin has explored, boys' denial of dependency often leads to domination. "Since the child continues to need the mother, since man continues to need woman, the absolute assertion of independence requires possessing and controlling the needed object. The intention is not to do without her but to make sure that her alien otherness is either assimilated or controlled, that her own subjectivity nowhere asserts itself in a way that could make his dependency upon her a conscious insult to his sense of freedom" ("Desire" 80).

Drucilla Cornell and Adam Thurschwell observe that this explanation traces social and institutional forms of power to individual psychological motivations (157). However, as Jane Flax reminds us, the family is constituted by three types of social relations: production, reproduction, and psychodynamics (223). By considering intersubjectivity within utopian formations, we can contextualize the process of gender formation and consider its implications in the distribution of power and access to activity. This gendered view of child-rearing implicates the psychodynamics of the postindustrial family in the persistence of patriarchy and positions the inversions in personal life of modern feminist utopias.

Clearly, the segregation of spheres is a paradigm of male dominance. But "genuine difference," as Cornell and Thurschwell suggest, is "inseparable from a notion of relationality" (161). In contrast to the notion of rapprochement, utopias constructed by men tend to reify another view—that genuine difference is inseparable from autonomy and control. Feminist psychoanalysts suggest that the situation of separate-but-unequal arises as the son resolves the conflict with his mother by turning to his father, who appears to the son as the agent, the subject of his own will and desire. Seemingly independent, the father represents the world. In "The Harmonists" (1866), Davis shows how the followers of George Rapp sought purity by defining themselves not just against industrial society but also against women, even their own. In their identification with this rigid father figure, they repudiated the reproductive and sexual capacities of women. In "Transcendental Wild Oats"—a satiric mock-history of the Fruitlands community—Alcott explores the paradox of the small utopian community that her father, Bronson Alcott, designed, purportedly based on transcendental ideals but in fact constituted as a site of male authority and individuality.

In contrast to a son's repudiation of his maternal dependence, a daughter can continue to identify with her mother because of the sameness of their gender. Hence, a daughter's separation is less absolute and her course of individuation more ambivalent. In "Transcendental Wild Oats" Louisa May Alcott describes her empathy for her mother, Abba, who is the object, not the subject or agent of desire, an object who often lacks control over her own destiny, her own sexuality, even her own domestic space. Yet because a girl such as Louisa may continue to identify with her mother, she can incorporate rather than resist Abba's maternal model of affection, nurturance and hence, connectedness. In Alcott's portrait, this promise of maternal connection forms the appropriate basis for a community, which we see in *Little Women* (1868–69), and transcends the men's ambivalent bonding. Davis and Alcott challenge the tendency of utopia, a paradoxical tendency to be sure, to make dominance and separateness the route, the goal or the structure of utopia. For Alcott, Gilman, and Mary E. B. Lane, the author of the all-female utopia *Mizora* (1881), matriarchy replaces utopia as the ideal model of social organization. Lane projects the feminine as idealized "otherness" and reifies difference as utopian.

Davis's and Alcott's repudiation of utopia-as-autonomy supports Benjamin's assertion that the self does not proceed from oneness to separateness, but evolves by simultaneously differentiating and recognizing the other, by alternating between "being with" and "being distinct."[3] The powerful maternal constructs of feminist spaces, which we see in twentieth-century feminist utopias, from *Herland* to *Woman on the Edge of Time*, involve the revaluation and hence, the inscription of the maternal bond.

Utopian fictions that predate *Looking Backward*, at least those written by women, also disprove the assumption that the figure of the mother has been "repressed," written out of nineteenth-century texts. They are thereby quite unlike nineteenth-century novels written by women such as Jane Austen, Mary Shelley, George Sand, the Brontës, George Eliot, and Kate Chopin, in which mothers are absent, trivialized, ineffectual, devalued, silenced or dead.[4] What happened to this powerful lady? Sandra Gilbert and Susan Gubar argue that motherlessness becomes a textual emblem for female powerlessness

(*Madwoman* 174). The maternal absence denies the daughter a role model that can facilitate her passage into womanhood. The maternal absence also ignores the power of matriarchy. In contrast to Gilbert and Gubar, Adrienne Rich argues that motherlessness *frees* the Victorian heroine from a model of female subservience; without her mother she can create and determine her own development (91).

What does the absent mother mean to the woman writer of utopian fictions? Mothers are oppressed. Hence, must they be repressed in feminist political fantasy? Nineteenth-century critiques of utopia anticipate the revisionary analyses of motherhood of Nancy Chodorow, Jessica Benjamin, Luce Irigary, and Marianne Hirsch, and the twentieth-century representations of utopia of Gilman, Piercy, Le Guin, and Grahn. Unlike Victorian novelists, Victorian utopians—Davis and Alcott, and later Mary E. B. Lane, Charlotte Perkins Gilman and still later, Marge Piercy—bestow on mothers subjectivity, agency and initiative.

What Davis and Alcott saw as they surveyed the Rappite and transcendentalist communities, is that when men construct utopian spaces, they monopolize the authority of the father to represent or define power and desire. In contrast to figures such as George Rapp or Bronson Alcott, Rebecca Harding Davis and Louisa May Alcott refuse to portray woman's desire through her object status; that is, her ability to attract or repel. Hence, they reject the dualism of subject/object that hinged on maternal repudiation as the road to identity and power. The reader of Alcott's mock-history of her painful childhood stay at Fruitlands discovers images of female power and activities that transcend motherhood and fertility. Davis and Alcott both assert that unless the utopian woman is a political and sexual *subject* rather than a political and sexual *object* we have dystopia. In the twentieth century, the feminist utopian subject inhabits a new social and political space, one that assumes the paradox of healthy motherhood, that is, of independence and connection.

Davis and Alcott anticipate Le Guin's vision of utopian space as dialectical space. The self and others, the self and society, create political space in which the self evolves through relationships rather than quests, in which the society recognizes that integrity and individuality stimulate community; dependence rather than autonomy nurtures personal integrity. Borrowing the model from psychoanalytic feminism, I would term this relational topos, where subject meets subject, "intersubjective space."

Conventionally, psychoanalysis views the healthy self as autonomous and individuated. The healthy self achieves a strong sense of boundary. The happy healthy adult finds *in himself* the origin of action and intention. And this self-reliant state comes from a successful separation from the mother, that is to say, a successful negotiation of the Oedipus crisis.

What's wrong with this picture?

First, it does not account for female development. Second, it locates the self outside society. Third, symbiosis, bonding, and empathy become mired in the stage of pre-Oedipal fluidity, that is, the stage of an undifferentiated relationship with the mother. Little boys are supposed to give up this symbiotic stage with their mothers out of fear of aggressive retaliation from their fathers. And, apparently, men fear their subjectivity and dependency for the rest of their lives. Because girls do not have to relinquish this dependency, they are free to fantasize about symbiosis, dependency, and bonding. They are free to fantasize utopian subjectivity.

In contrast to traditional or "intrapsychic" psychoanalytic views of development, feminist psychoanalysts refuse to define intimacy and empathy as "regressive." Such theorists include George Klein, D. W. Winnicott, Heinz Kohut, Judith Jordon, Janet Surrey, and Jessica Benjamin. George Klein observes, " 'We identities' are also part of the self. . . . Like any biological organ or part, the organism is . . . and must feel itself to be . . . both separate and part of an entity beyond itself" (178).

Empathy is not merger. Empathy requires an articulated and differentiated image of the other. Feminist utopians, from Alcott to Piercy, invoke a particularized image of the other as the basis for intimacy, and intimacy is essential to their vision of an egalitarian society. In other words, feminist utopians have a common view of radical subjectivity that derives, in part, from mother-daughter relations.

Where does it start? A girl's sense of herself is profoundly anchored in relationship, connection, and identification with her mother. She is, for better or worse (and these days I feel it is for the better) encouraged to listen to feelings, including the feeling states of the parent. As Jordon and Surrey point out, in a culture that perceives its task of child-rearing to wean a helpless male infant toward self-sufficiency and independence, for a girl "being with" is self-enhancing; for a boy, "being with" is seen as invasive and threatening (83, 89–90). Hence, from early on, daughters develop in a context of emotional connectedness, in which mother and daughter respond, empathize, and mirror. While this can and often times does lead to projection and overidentification, particularly if other aspects of the mother's life are impoverished, denied, or abusive, it can lead to differentiation. And differentiation is not the same as disconnection. Both mother and daughter, highly responsive to the feeling states of others, become mobilized to respond to the development of the other.[5] The goal is a sort of "oscillating" reciprocity, rather than overinvolvement. I find this image of oscillating reciprocity at the subjective core of feminist utopias. It is this that may someday undermine the culture of narcissism.

Autonomy, aloneness, then, is a point on the spectrum of human relationships. In utopia, autonomy is not the natural state of individuals. I suggest that feminist utopias are organized around social projections of intersubjectivity: "The intersubjective mode assumes the possibility of a context with others in which desire is constituted for the self. It thus assumes the paradox that in being with the other, I may experience the most profound sense of self" (Benjamin, "Desire" 92). The concept of intersubjectivity does not, in my view, replace the unconscious as a way of understanding the psyche. And indeed, utopia, in my view, has as much to do with fantasy, wish, anxiety, and defensiveness as it has to do with economics and ecologies. Feminist utopias, such as Herland and Mattapoissett, put forth the possibility of a subject who can recognize the existence, intentions, needs, and independence of other subjects.

Jessica Benjamin suggests that intersubjectivity is a concept that assumes the human need for recognition. The subject declares, "I am, I do" and the respondent utters, "You are. You do" (Bonds 21). In other words, intersubjectivity involves doing. It involves praxis. Our being is defined by action within a receptive social context. What this view of the origin of feminist fantasy also suggests is that the mother, as well as the child, is a subject in her own right. The mother is also autonomous. The child learns to see the mother as an independent subject, not an adjunct to his ego, not a mirror of her being, not a dangerous agent to repudiate. Benjamin pictures this ideal relationship like

Escher's birds, which fly in two directions at once, away and toward, independent and connected. In words stunningly like Le Guin's hero Shevek in *The Dispossessed*, Benjamin concedes, "Since it is more difficult to think in terms of simultaneity than in terms of sequence, we begin to conceptualize [development] in terms of a directional trajectory" (*Bonds* 26). Simultaneity, I suggest, is the model for feminist utopian personal relations.

Intimacy, even utopian intimacy, is always dangerous. Intimacy is always fraught with conflict. How to fulfill one's own desire and, at the same time, acknowledge the needs and rights of others? How to prevent the maternal imperative to be attuned to the needs of others from being converted into submission to the other's will? How not to use the other as only a vehicle of self-definition, a path to domination and racism? As Hegel pointed out, if I successfully negate the other and he does not survive, he is not there any more to recognize me.[6] Differentiation is not destruction. And intersubjectivity is clearly not simply internalization, wherein the other is consumed, incorporated, and digested.

What this all finally means is that empathy (feminist utopian subjectivity) is about dependence and eroticism. Benjamin suggests, "mutual recognition can't be achieved through obedience, identification with the other's power or through repression. It requires, finally, contact with the other" (*Bonds* 39). D. W. Winnicott goes further, and calls for a change in the reality principle. Reality he says, is the positive pleasure of connecting with the outside. Reality is not simply a brake on narcissism and aggression. Reality is joy in the other's survival, and the recognition of a shared reality. It must be discovered, not imposed.[7] Many feminists would call this shared reality utopia.

I have found that the concept of "intersubjectivity" emerged in American women's earliest critiques of utopia, and has cultural origins in the contradictory ideology of sentimentality. In the nineteenth century, both intentional communities and women's literary renderings of utopia often took the form of societies organized around the precepts of sentimentality. Sentimentality is a cultural fantasy that organizes social obligations along segregated and idealized gender lines. While the world of politics, business, and labor belong in men's purview, domestic life, circumscribed but highly valued, is in women's. Here femaleness, albeit delineated and contained, offers a socializing moral force in an exclusive place: the home. Salvation through motherly love gives women a central position of power and authority in the culture. Contact with the mother, rather than repudiation of the mother, thereby holds forth the promise that men can free themselves of the status distinctions and attitudes that have organized the old society. Thus, through sentimentality, men realize a new social identity. Davis and Alcott, however, are suspicious of the notion that domestic culture can transcend or restrain political and economic hegemony. On the one hand, they find that by intensifying gender distinctions, sentimentality offers nothing new: an idealized order that still gives men authority over women, even in the domestic sphere. On the other hand, they use the utopian topos to expose the tensions of the larger culture in which men define the future.

Elsewhere, I have argued that for Bellamy, the conventions of sentimental romances offered conservative narrative structures that sheltered and indeed neutralized radical economic and political rearrangements.[8] Ken Roemer has argued persuasively that contemporary readers of *Looking Backward* would have, in Jonathan Culler's sense, "competently" understood the intersection of the sentimental and utopian conventions that Bellamy used to invoke political guilt: in particular, the separated lovers' plot, rearranged domestic locales, a redemptive heroine, and a didactic narrative voice. Roemer agrees that the "happy home" is the political metaphor that ratifies the progress of nationalism ("Literary Domestication" 101–22).

In "The Harmonists," Rebecca Harding Davis invokes, in order to parody, the romantic motif of a man on the run from civilization, still marked as women's space.[9] Dr. Knowles, a single father, briefly joins the Rappite community in Economy, Pennsylvania, with the hopes that his fantasies of sentiment and utopia will merge in "the old patriarchal form for its mode of government, establishing under that, however, a complete community of interest" (531–32). But Davis questions the possibility of a community of interests for men and women in a society that is hierarchical, celibate, and disdains children. The traveler, who vows, "I know no child, no wife, nor any brother, except my brother man" (531) surrenders his son to the community, seeking in his place the promise of Romanticism, "a sphere of infinite freedom . . . a home where a man can stand alone"(533). But as we know, women did not conceive of the home, practically or ideologically, as a sphere of one's own. Assigned to impersonal "families" of seven, the women, with "shrivelled breasts" mourn the children they never bore.

Davis's utopian critique engages her sentimental critique; a discourse of political place challenges a discourse of domestic place. Children are the central image and significant absence of "The Harmonists," both Knowles's child and the absent child of the celibate women. As Knowles, his son, and the narrator come upon the community of Economy, the narrator predicts, "Nature was about to take me to her great mother's bosom" (534). But utopia is a sterile mother. The breast, the visitor's projection of female desire as social teleology, is in fact empty. Rapp cast woman in the role of temptress and then rejected her. Unlike celibacy in the Shaker communities, which apparently stemmed from the founder Ann Lee's traumatic loss of her four children, her ensuing sexual traumas, and her eventual attacks against men's carnal natures, celibacy in the Rappite communities represented the subjugation of personal desire in preparation for the Messiah. Shaker celibacy freed women from the risks of childbirth and the duties of child-rearing, allowing women to assume significant positions of leadership. Hence, celibacy deconstructed biology as a social determinant.[10] By contrast, Dr. Knowles discovers that the Rappites have sublimated their sexual and personal urges toward a work ethic so successful that it competes with the "great property machine" of Pittsburgh (536–37).

In "The Harmonists," Rebecca Harding Davis determines that utopia fails because it has reified gender roles at the expense of the natural self. A healthy society, although not necessarily a utopian society, must acknowledge and reflect the role of subjectivity and sexuality. Knowles is redeemed by "mother love" as he comes to understand the priorities of Economy, Pennsylvania. He reclaims his son, suggesting that maternal behavior should take precedence over male theory in determining social relationships: "growling caresses like a lioness who has recovered her whelp" (533). The story ends not in a marriage but with this androgynous mother/man, crooning old nursery songs to lull his child to sleep. Knowles has rejected autonomy, the telos of the patriarchal utopia.

In "Transcendental Wild Oats," Louisa May Alcott satirizes the history of Fruitlands, a community designed by her father, Bronson Alcott and the English transcendentalist Charles Lane.[11] A parody of utopia, it tells about what happens to women when they let men's schemes for social salvation ignore domesticity and personal relations; that is, when women forget, as Louisa's mother puts it, that they are always "under the yoke" (Douglas, 232). Louisa suggests that when men presume to define domestic relationships, the results are at best absurd, hardly utopian and, in the end, dangerous. Women suffer when men lead them into the wilderness, even to inherit the earth.

In June 1843, the communards of Fruitlands entered "the kingdom of peace . . . through the gates of self-denial" (365) only to abandon their small utopia by the end of the year. In addition to the Alcotts, members included Charles Lane, another man once imprisoned for refusing to shave, yet another who claimed to have lived for one year entirely off crackers and the next off apples, a "nocturnal nudist" who soon left for Florida and other visionaries who believed in cold showers, linen togas, and a diet of fruit. Abba, Louisa's mother, bore the full burden of housework for a commune of up to sixteen people.

The leaders held different views of family roles and dependencies. Lane, recently divorced, believed that the family inhibits the infinite possibilities of human relations. In a letter to Emerson, Lane wrote that the "maternal instinct" and the family are "selfish and oppose the establishment of the community which stands for universal love" (quoted in Sears 143). Bronson Alcott sought "associations of human beings" that would attain the "condition of happiness" through "self-renunciation and retrenchment" (Letters 99). Abba Alcott, however, was committed to reform rather than retreat. In addition to rescuing the family from Bronson's many idealistic ventures, she had survived eight pregnancies in ten years, and was long involved in abolition, charities, and prison reform (Showalter, Alternative Alcott, xi–xii).

Louisa's chronicle of the Fruitlands experiment sardonically exposes the dangers of the romantics' notion that society is artificial, secondary to human nature and, incidentally, female. She mocks the hypocrisy and arrogance of the men who sought to define female work, control domestic life and glorify themselves at the expense of the community: "Here [Lane] intended to found a colony of Latter Day Saints, who, under his patriarchal sway, should regenerate the world and glorify his name forever" (365–66). And so, while Bronson asserts that "every meal should be a sacrament, and the vessels used beautiful and symbolical," Abba observes that the tin plate and Britannia ware he has bought for utopia are impossible to keep bright (367).

Eventually Abba rebels. Even though Bronson says leather "sub-jugates" animals, she refuses to make the children go barefoot. And she continues to read with her oil light in the evenings, rejecting the men's suggestion that she find an "inner light." With great bitterness, Louisa condemns the brethren's neglect of Abba's concerns for food prepara-tion, clothing, the children's education, and their refusal to integrate Abba. When asked, "Are there any beasts of burden on the place?" Abba answered, "Only one woman!" (373).

The rhetoric of noble labor not withstanding, the brethren can-not tell an ox from a cow, they try to plow a hundred acres with a spade, they refuse to "profane the virgin soil" with manure because the "befoulment" might infect the soul, they refuse to milk the cow be-cause it would deprive her of control over the product of her labor, and they refuse to plant vegetables such as carrots because they grow down-ward, that is, away from heaven. Yet what infuriates Louisa most was the brethren's hypocrisy regarding shared labor. About the time the bar-ley, the only surviving crop, was ready to be reaped, "some call of the Oversoul wafted all the men away" and Abba brought in the entire harvest in a raging windstorm with four small children harnessed to laundry baskets. The land, like the women, resists mastery and abandonment.

With the first frosts, and with the Consociate Family cold and starving, the brethren left Fruitlands. Abba, with money left to her ex-clusive use by her father (which Bronson and his creditors had vainly tried to obtain), rented four rooms in a nearby village, an act of self-preservation and independence. Ultimately, the matriarch, not the community, is the source of regeneration. The home is fragile. If women defer to men's claims for domestic authority, the home can perish. In despair and isolation, Bronson takes to his bed to starve himself to death. But through the loss of his political power Bronson discovers the superiority of wifely love over brotherly love; the promise of a se-cure home replaces utopia.

In the end, women's loving authority and genuine commitment restores the nuclear family and the segregation of spheres. The sexual contract, universalized as utopian telos, has disguised the competitive and incompatible natures of men's and women's interests. In contrast to utopianism, sentimentality has neither exalted autonomy, hidden the true nature of women's work, or encouraged the repression of female desire. Instead, it has deconstructed the utopian space between independence and community, self and society, reality and possibility.

In "The Harmonists" and in "Transcendental Wild Oats," Davis and Alcott have transformed political states into psychological conditions. They have recast political distinctions as gender differences. In contrast to the fears of the Rappite or transcendental utopians, Davis and Alcott suggest that the mother figure is neither menacing or engulfing. Utopian space need not involve her repudiation.

The concept of intersubjectivity that I am introducing here as a feminist critique of male utopianism, and hypothetically, as a paradigm of women's utopianism, has its origins in the social theory of Jürgen Habermas, who, in 1970, used the expression, the "intersubjectivity of mutual understanding."[12] This concept designates both an individual capacity and a social space. It resists absolutes and permanence on the one hand, and, most likely, androgyny on the other. Intersubjectivity posits a tension between sameness and difference. Empathy and difference exist simultaneously. Together, they evolve through an active exchange with another person, usually, in the first place, the mother. This concept calls for a social model that resolves the historic split between the father of liberation and the mother of dependence. The early narratives of Davis and Alcott suggest that dependence is not a threat but a prerequisite to independence. Polarities, not dependency, they find, set the stage for domination and submission.

Gender polarity and male rationality, according to Benjamin, have eliminated the maternal aspects of recognition—nurturance and empathy—from our collective values and institutions. They have made social authorship a matter of impersonal control. Early feminists, by contrast, resist the impulse of utopia toward definition and domination. Domination only works when one either identifies with or submits to powerful others.

Utopia, as Alcott suggested a century ago, needs to reflect on the role of the other. She anticipates feminist utopians who picture acts of emancipation that reject the ideal of power as autonomy, the power of the father. But in this resides a paradox—indeed, the paradox of the mother-daughter relationship—that is, the notion of difference as rapprochement. A final maternal paradox to ponder in future work: feminist utopians erase the absence where the other is supposed to be.

7

Texts and Contexts
American Women Envision Utopia, 1890–1920

Carol A. Kolmerten

From 1890 through 1919, more than thirty American women wrote utopian novels depicting their versions of a better world.[1] Few of these women were well-known writers. Many were married, like Alice Ilgenfritz Jones, from Cedar Rapids, who teamed up with a friend to write an outspoken criticism of gender expectations in America in the 1890s. Others were widowed or divorced, like Lillian Jones, a black Fort Worth high school English teacher, whose relatives published her only book at their printing shop. Still others, like Charlotte Perkins Gilman, were activists who were known for their nonfiction. While many male utopian writers such as William Dean Howells or Jack London were famous men of letters, and their utopian novel a diversion from their other writing, few of the women writing utopias during this time would have considered themselves to be professional writers of fiction. A few of them were barely competent at their craft and had trouble unfolding a plot or developing a character. For many of them, their one utopian novel is the only record we have of their thought. For all of them, the mere act of writing and publishing a novel—especially a "utopian" novel that criticized aspects of the culture in which they lived—was a subversive act.

The very act of writing—particularly choosing to write a book critical of the mainstream culture's ideologies and practices—encouraged the women writers to envision utopia differently from the male writers. Women's marginalized existence allowed these writers to see around the ideological blinders that made their culture's gender codes appear "natural." This added vision resulted in novels that differ in content and character development from the male novels in three main ways. First, the women writers criticized what they perceived as destructive "male" values. Second, they created a supportive female-centered community, if not always populated with all women, then usually guided by traditional "female" values such as the importance of motherhood and child-rearing. This group, or community, or sisterhood was more important than any individual in it. Finally, arising from this female worldview came meaningful work for the central female characters who pursued a variety of activities that allowed them to produce what their culture valued.

But the potential conflict for women living and working within a masculinist hegemony is nowhere more illustrative than in these women's novels. Despite these women's marginalized lives, the very act of writing is also an act of participation within a culture. Throughout the nineteenth century, women writers had been guiding readers' moral and spiritual upbringing through guidebooks, didactic poetry, and especially the sentimental romance. As participants of the culture in which they lived, women writing utopian fiction adapted the format of the highly popular sentimental novel, following the practice of male writers of utopian fiction and other successful women "domestic" novelists. The sentimental format was a useful way of familiarizing their readers with an unfamiliar world, and, at the same time, it offered an arena that empowered their female characters.[2] Yet, the sentimental structure caused the women immense problems when they tried to end their books. The proper ending of a sentimental novel reinforced and reified the culture's ideology regarding woman's sacred domestic sphere. "Good" women were rewarded with marriage and perhaps a male child, while "bad" women were killed off. What constituted "good" and "bad" women was, of course, linked directly to codes of gender: good women were the angels who sacrificed themselves for the men and children in their lives; bad women were those who threatened men for a myriad of reasons including their superior intelligence or (especially) their sexuality.

The conflict that the women writers faced appeared unresolvable: how to write about a world that challenged the ideology embedded within the literary conventions they used. The conflict was exacerbated by the fact that most of the women writing utopias were not trained creative writers and certainly not modernists who wanted to experiment with literary form. This essay will first delineate ways that the women's visions of utopia differed from the male writer's visions; it will then analyze how these women dealt with the problems they faced as they tried to end their books.

Given the contexts of the women writers' lives, it is not surprising that their visions of a "good" place include no role for powerful men. Unable to vote, unable to live outside of a masculinist world where men, by and large, controlled a family's money, where men could gamble and drink to excess without criticism, the women writers used their novels to criticize, indirectly, many of the cultural practices they were powerless to confront in their own lives.

The most obvious way these women writers go about criticizing the destructive "male" values within their own world is to establish superior worlds without men. In Charlotte Perkins Gilman's well-known 1915 utopian novel *Herland,* men have been extinct for two-thousand years; the co-mothers set the priorities of the culture, which include great physical beauty coupled with technological advances that allow woman's "traditional" work to be professionalized. We see Herland through the eyes of Vandyck Jennings, one of three male explorers who accidentally discover the existence of this tiny, manless nation. The story of Herland is neatly framed by the unbelieving men who discover a perfect, civilized country but cannot locate the builders of the civilization—whom they assume to be male. The men's skepticism at the notion that women could have created an efficient and technologically advanced culture allows Gilman the room to show (often humorously) just how well women could (and would) build such a civilization if they were unhampered by the ideology of gender that limited their development in the United States of 1915.

The conflict in the novel stems from each man's attempt to solve the culture shock induced by the contrast between Herland and his own America. Van, the first-person narrator, possesses the balanced, rational voice that first questions, then finally accepts Herland's ways; his is the voice that we come to agree with. His colleagues, Terry and Jeff, each represent a different type of male populating the early twentieth century, but both see women as gendered objects. Terry, the macho man, firmly believes in the supremacy of man and in an immutable "feminine nature," despite overwhelming evidence that women in Herland have no such nature. Terry's subsequent marriage to a young Herland woman, doomed from the beginning because Terry believes that "a wife is a woman who belongs to a man," ends abruptly when his attempt to rape her results in his banishment from Herland. Jeff, on the other hand, worships women and only wants to place them on a pedestal. Herland women dislike Jeff's attitude, but his acceptance of the loving tenets of Herland is so genuine that he and his Herland bride appear destined never to leave the paradise. Van, too, we discover in Herland's 1916 sequel, *With Her in Ourland*, returns to live in Herland.

If the women writers do not physically eliminate men, they criticize what they perceive to be destructive societal values most often linked with men. In Gilman's first utopian fragment, *A Woman's Utopia* (1907), for example, women establish the New World Party, create a "peaceful revolution," and remake their city, in part by eliminating the individual kitchens that imprisoned women. Gilman's *Moving the Mountain* (1911), a reworking of *A Women's Utopia*, continued the first book's reforms. The novel centers on John Robertson, who was lost in 1910 in Tibet after falling over a precipice and losing his memory. After miraculously recovering his memory thirty years later, Robertson returns to a vastly changed America. The plot describes John's initial resistance to and final acceptance of the new woman-oriented and woman-run America, which has undergone a revolution during his thirty-year absence.

In *Moving the Mountain*, New York City has been transformed into a feminist utopia because a group of far-thinking women formed the "Home Service Company," which subsequently planned and built an apartment complex suited for women. The women architects and designers mandated that the top floors of each apartment contain nurseries or "child gardens," as Gilman calls them, "which were then to be staffed by the best professionals in "child culture." All housework and cooking are provided by the most efficient of experts for the apartments' residents. The apartments were placed in delightful settings by remaking city blocks and removing concrete and adding gardens, trees, and fountains. These apartments freed the women from being trapped as angels in their houses and provided the impetus for a women's revolution.

The focus in this remade world is not moneymaking but living in comfort and beauty while raising healthy children. Because of these new priorities, men in this new world have had some of their previous individualistic pleasures curtailed for the benefit of the public rights; thus, the cultural practices have changed drastically. Women no longer exist to serve their husbands, because women no longer give up their jobs when they marry. Women, no longer possessions, keep their birth names throughout their lives. If a couple has children, a daughter takes her mother's name, a son his father's. Traditional male comforts—tobacco, alcohol, prostitutes, hunting—have been eliminated.

Other women writers also imagined worlds where women rebelled against the patriarchal world and male "lusts." In Agnes Bond Yourell's aptly named *A Manless World* (1891), only when "animal desire" was eliminated could a married couple have a true "union of souls" (30). "Rapture" for a husband and wife now stems from friendship. In Lois Waisbrooker's *A Sex Revolution* (1894), women revolted against war, against drinking, and finally, against the "causes which create a demand for liquor" (57). Lovella, the main character, implores women listening to her to find a system where "one portion of society is not ground up for the benefit of other portions" (61).

One of the most clever utopian novels criticizing male ideas is *Unveiling a Parallel* (1893) by Alice Ilgenfritz Jones and Ella Merchant. Presented by an unreliable nineteenth-century male narrator, the narrative depicts two worlds on Mars—one where traditional "male" values have proliferated and one where female values dominate. In the first part of the book, we think we see a utopia where women are equal to men. The main female character, Elodia, who is both a banker and the president of the local school board, does appear to be the embodiment of all the virtues one would find in women in a completely egalitarian society. Yet, slowly, as the plot unfolds, we realize that Elodia is not an ideal, utopian woman; she has, in effect, adopted all the appropriate characteristics necessary for a "successful" male in America. First we learn that Elodia drinks, often to excess; then we learn that she "vaporizes," or uses the terrible-smelling valerian root mixed with alcohol, a habit that gives some momentary pleasure, but can be fatal. Then we learn that she meets lovers at "Cupid's Gardens," a place where male prostitutes and other kept men can meet their powerful, important woman lovers. Finally, we learn that Elodia has a six-year-old illegitimate child with whom she does not live. The narrator is, of course, horrified that her "woman's nature" is no finer or holier than man's. But we can see that, although Elodia happens to be female, her sex in no way distracts us from the fact that she has typically "male" lusts; her selfishness and concern for her own pleasures make us realize that sexual equality, when that "equality" is rooted in a patriarchal culture, is not necessarily a utopian virtue. Excess, whether indulged in by men or by women does not permit a perfect society.

Just as most of the women writing utopias in this period criticized "male" priorities, overtly by disparaging male "lusts" or covertly, by creating a superior female-only world, they also established the "female" priorities necessary for a utopia for women. With the elimination of selfish lusts—particularly greed for money and power—comes a new first cultural priority: raising healthy children in a nurturing, sensuous, egalitarian environment.

Instead of ending their book with a woman's corruption when Elodia takes on "male" characteristics, Jones and Merchant offer us an alternative to the nineteenth-century dilemma—to be either a passive, chaste female, or a greedy, lustful "male." The entire last quarter of their novel is a description of a second country on Mars, Caskia, where the people have attained a more advanced state of development. In Caskia, our nameless narrator finds that greed had disappeared; in its place is egalitarianism based on honest labor and cheerful good will. Our narrator's guide in Caskia tells him of their struggle to give up "the lusts of the flesh," and Jones and Merchant imply, like so many of the women writers, that a sexless world may be the most liberating for women, though they never write directly about sex. The Caskians had realized that Mars was rich enough to maintain all its people in comfort, "so they sought out and cultivated within themselves corresponding resources, namely generosity and brotherly love" (208–9). This "brotherly" love is really what we would call a "sisterly" love, as it emphasizes child-rearing, meaningful work for women, and a clustering of generations of families so that the young might be near the old. Caskia believes in "mutual helpfulness" as its reigning principle. Here, a woman who is a leading scientist is also a cook. No one in Caskia has the power that Elodia does; no one smokes the valerian root or has illegitimate children, because neither are in the best interests of the town.

Mothers, biological or not, become the most important members of the women's utopias, taking the place of "fathers" in a patriarchal culture. In Gilman's *Herland*, for example, motherhood is so important that no one person is entrusted with its duties and responsibilities. In Waisbrooker's *A Sex Revolution*, Lovella—a name signifying the "spirit of motherhood"—proclaims that the "power of mother love," guided by wisdom, "shall take the place of brute force" (21). Lovella points out that, hitherto, motherhood has been a "negative, yielding love" (27), but now the "subservient sex" must become the dominant one until "a balance is restored" (33). Though she admits that man has done "grand things," Lovella nonetheless believes that because of the "lack of the mother element in his work" he has also caused much unhappiness (41). Her ideal world would place motherhood at its center.

Concomitant with the importance of mothering in utopia is the importance of child care. In Gilman's *Moving the Mountain*, female architects mandated "child gardens" to be established on the roofs of all apartment buildings where children could grow to their greatest potential. Only women with diplomas as "child-culturists" care for children. In *Herland*, the entire culture revolves around raising children; it is a woman's greatest privilege to have a child and to help raise her. The children's houses are full of soft, child-sized furniture, designed specifically for them. In Lena Jane Fry's *Other Worlds* (1905), the "plan" for human liberation on the planet Hershel includes a nursery for all children, from one month on, where trained nurses who only work six-hour days (and who have the "correct" zodiac sign!) will care for the children. In Eloise O. Richberg's *Reinstern* (1900), all men and women who wish to marry, known as "applicants," must take their turn caring for the children of the community: though the infants under one year old accompany their mothers to the fields, the applicants share the child's care in the afternoon. Two-year-olds are in the care of recently married women; fathers care for three-year olds. Because no one "earns the living in the family," both men and women care for the children—the greatest responsibility in the culture. Because motherhood and raising healthy children take priority, other time-consuming, traditionally women's chores are relegated to automation as in Gilman's novels, or are performed by willing "servants" as in *Unveiling a Parallel*.

In all the novels, the addition of beauty in landscape, in housing, in every functional part of life is an important requisite because raising healthy children means raising children in surroundings where their senses are soothed by such a utopian landscape. In Carra Dupuy Henley's *Man From Mars* (1901), the "flower spangled meadow-lands" dotted the "extended arms of trees, arching and roofing avenues, to other groves and forests, by which people passed from one to another, and everywhere in field, forest and grove, could be heard the voices of children and songs of birds" (61–62). In Fiona Wait Colbern's *Yermah the Dorado* (1897), we see "cherry, laurel, cloves, and lavender plants along the highways because they were known to produce ozone" (38). In Eloise O. Richberg's *Reinstern*, we can smell the pine-woods, see the "velvety sod" and taste the "luscious fruit" (3). In Louise Moore's *Al Modad* (1892), the landscape consists of berries—some green some of "a rich cream hue," with many other fruits, nuts, and flowers proliferating everywhere. In Caskia, in *Unveiling a Parallel*, houses are made of a rough gray stone, with delicate vines and verandas and balconies in order to create a spacious, hospitable air.

In Gilman's *Herland* automobiles, equipped with electric motors, are soundless. Even the cats—the only animal allowed except for singing birds—are quiet because their ability to meow has been bred out of them. Everywhere the visitors look they see pink cities filled with parks and roads lined with perfectly pruned trees. Van's first view of Herland captures its visual delights.

> It was built mostly of a sort of dull rose-colored stone, with here and there some clear white houses; and it lay abroad among the green groves and gardens like a rosary of pink coral. . . . Everything was beauty, order, perfect cleanness, and the pleasantest sense of home all over it. As we neared the town the houses stood thicker, ran together as it were, grew into rambling palaces grouped among parks and open squares something as college buildings stand in their quiet greens. (41–42)

It is a world where the most prominent sensation is one of "absolute physical comfort."

In the utopias written by women, traditional "women's" issues became the heart of the culture; thus, motherhood, venerated as a "sacred" but powerless sphere in men's novels, becomes the focus and the center of all power in many of the novels written by women. The children born of Herland women are the raison d'être in Herland. The notion of "motherliness" influences every art and every industry. The houses and gardens are built with children in mind, with no stairs, no corners—"just a babies' paradise" (243). Only the co-mothers best suited for childbearing are selected to take the main responsibility for the children's education.

One of the most important needs of the individual women who populate the women's books is the need for a life where their work is valued and where they are significant producers of what the culture values. Most of the women writers not only proposed meaningful work for their central female characters, but also showed them at work.[3] In some of the utopias, we do see female characters working in uncharacteristic jobs, as we do in the novels by the male writers. Anna Adolph's protagonist Anna in *Arqtiq* (1899), for example, invents an airship and then takes her husband and father along with her to the North Pole; similarly, M. Louise Moore's women in *Al Modad* (1892) "drive" airplanes, also at the North Pole.

Closer to home, many of the central female characters occupy uncharacteristic jobs. The title character of Helen Winslow's 1893 *Salome Shephard* works hard in the tradition of Robert Owen to reform the conditions of the factory workers at her mills. She provides the workers with new housing, with education for all children, with libraries, and with dancing halls. In Winslow's 1909 novel, *A Woman for Mayor*, Gertrude Van Deusen opposes corrupt city officials, runs for public office, wins, and cleans up the town. Van Deusen quite literally cleans the town, as she plants flowers, prohibits smoking and spitting, removes cuspidors in City Hall, and directs the corridors to be scrubbed.

The pleasures of physical labor are extolled in many of the utopian novels by women. In *Reinstern*, for example, women do farmwork and carry their babies to the fields with them. In Gilman's *A Woman's Utopia*, women who do not work are pitied or disparaged. Though the visitor to this utopia is first horrified because "wifehood and motherhood are more primal and sacred duties than typewriting and millinery," (591) his female guide asks him whether he means wifehood and motherhood or "cook-hood and housekeeper-hood?" As all cleaning now "goes with the rent" and dumbwaiters provide food, women who do not work outside the home are bored or "cross" and are much happier as productive workers. Work is a social experience that gives women a sense of worth.

Similarly, the experience of physical labor changed the life of the title character in Martha Bensley Bruère's *Mildred Carver, USA* (1919). Mildred is, at the opening of the book, a rich, blond, blue-eyed New Yorker, engaged to Nick Van Arsdale, the equally rich boy next door. Mildred (and Nick as well) resent having their one year of National Service come before their forthcoming marriage. Sent first to Minneapolis to sew flour bags, Mildred soon becomes a skilled tractor driver and her love of labor intensifies. When she finally returns home after her year is up, she is absolutely unsuited for the traditional life laid out for her by her mother: engagement, marriage, and a life of leisure. To her credit, she abandons this life and goes to work in her father's steel mill. She is, at the end of the novel, a better person because of her commitment to work.

Utopian work in these novels by women means the doing of good for the entire community—a community that values not the making of money, but providing the best goods and services for its people. When Mildred first returns to New York, she takes a job in a box factory, just to be working. But she soon discovers that plowing fields to provide wheat to feed people is inherently more satisfying than doing rote work where the owners, not the general public, benefit. She begins working at her father's steel mill to help produce and disseminate a stronger steel that will keep tractor blades from breaking. This work, she understands from her previous manual training, will benefit society in unlimited ways. Similarly, women in Caskia, the utopian land in *Unveiling a Parallel*, work not for money, but for the sense of contribution to their world. The cook for one family is also a scientist, but she finds she can think best as she prepares delicious food for a group of appreciative people. The teacher at a public school is an heiress, who does not "need" to work for financial gain, but she cannot imagine a world where she does not give something back to her community.

Concomitant with meaningful work is the autonomy that comes from contributing significantly to the community. Mildred Carver, at the beginning of her story, is an innocently self-centered young woman who does what she is told. By the end of the book, she is willing to give up love in order to work because her newly found self-esteem depends on doing what she believes is best for her life. In *Herland*, the three young women who meet and eventually marry the three visiting men, are always self-assured and confident in their priorities. The men must arrange their lives around the working schedules of the women.

Because their radical content challenged certain aspects of the prevailing gender codes, the women writers came to an impasse when they tried to end their books within the format of the sentimental novels, which had few options for a resolution. It insisted on stereotypical plotlines that invariably ended with death (of "bad" women) or with marriage (of "good" women) and often pitted these two kinds of women against each other. Particularly "good" women were often allowed to produce a male child. The sentimental novel reaffirmed the main character's true place in the world, and a happy ending meant finding that place. The place for the heroine was, inevitably, the private home, where she would remain.

This kind of ending reflects a hegemonic, masculinist view of the world, a view that the women writers had in many ways undermined in their texts. The content of the books had reinforced the main characters' power to control their own lives and to search for (or, to create) a supportive community of women or a community based on "female" values. Yet, according to the dominant literary conventions, a "good" woman's individual triumph, as represented by marriage, provided the happy ending. But, marriage, as the women writers knew from the context of their own lives, ended a heroine's power. The cultural practices that accompany marriage necessitated relinquishing autonomy in a myriad of small and large ways such as giving up their names, subordinating their work to their husband's career, or being responsible for housework and child care to the exclusion of worldly things. Thus, by using a masculinist structure that insisted upon marriage for their main female characters, the women writers were left with either accepting the hegemonic attitudes of the "tradition" or subverting masculine traditions by creating their own.

About half of the women writers solved their dilemma by capitulating to masculinist hegemony, even when doing so appeared to contradict their utopian messages. In *A New Aristocracy*, (1891) by Birch Arnold, for example, the main character, Elsie Murchison, refuses a suitor midway through the book by saying: "My hypersensitive soul has a right to its own distinct existence" (283). But by the end of the book, upon seeing this suitor frail and wan, Elsie capitulates and says: "The old wilful [sic], independent Elsie is dead, and I want to prove to you

hereafter how patient and submissive I can be" (313). Elsie is last described vaguely as "the idol of her home . . . with children clinging to
her skirts"; her distinct existence has vanished. The ending thus
refutes the autonomy Elsie has found, turning the utopian message inside out.

Similarly, the main characters in both of Helen Winslow's novels easily give up their meaningful work for marriage. In *Salome Shepherd*, Salome, who has effected excellent Owenite reforms in her mills,
marries in the last pages of the narrative. Despite her successes, she
says: "I shall leave the management of the mills to their new owner
[her new husband]. It's no part of a married woman's business to manage her husband's office" (255). Her husband is pleased because now
he will have her "all to [him]self." Gertrude Van Deusen, the mayor in
A Woman for Mayor, close to the end of the novel, tells her suitor, in
fitting ways for a woman who had accomplished so much in less than
a year, why she cannot marry him:

> you would soon resent my attitude towards life; you would want
> to restrict my life, to surround me with invisible limitations, such
> as you believe all femininity should be hedged with. I couldn't en-
> dure it. I have never had to, and I couldn't submit to being esti-
> mated every day and in the intimacy of home life—according to
> the old-fashioned standards that narrow a woman' heart and mind
> until they hold nothing but pettiness and smallness and meanness
> of spirit. Because I couldn't, I should make you the most unhappy
> of men. (323)

Yet, within a few pages, Gertrude has decided not to run again for mayor
because it is not "appropriate" or "natural" for a woman to run when
there are acceptable male candidates. Her would-be lover, of course, is
elected. After he is almost killed, Gertrude suddenly decides to marry
him, and the book ends "happily" because "the loving heart of the
woman was to stand alongside the strong desire of the man" (342). Both
Salome and Gertrude leave their communities for an individual life that
is guaranteed to be surrounded with all the invisible limitations that
Gertrude astutely predicted.

Another way a few writers capitulated to the masculinist hegemony inherent within the sentimental structure was to kill off their
strong, female hero by the end of the book. In Mary Agnes Tincker's

San Salvador (1892), Iona, the strong, smart, central character, dies protecting her utopia from three travelers who are about to discover it.
She also dies because there is no place for her in utopia: she has loved
Dylar, the strong male character, who, in turn, loves and marries the
sweet, weak Tacita (Latin for "silent woman"). Tacita, a woman who
once she became a mother "ceased to be anything else" (296), is the
woman who lives and gets her man (and a male child to boot.) The
ideal woman is one, like Tacita, who will "rule the state through the
cradle" (302). The "good" woman has won the man from the "bad"
woman, whose intelligence necessitates that she die.

Another novel that kills off the strongest character in the end is
Angel Island (1914) by Inez Haynes Gillmore, a friend of Charlotte
Perkins Gilman and whose novel may have provided the impetus for
Herland, which appeared a year later. *Angel Island* is an extended metaphor about five winged women who can fly and live carefree lives until they discover five shipwrecked men on an isolated island. Although
the narrative focuses on the men and their successful attempts to cap-
ture the women, the pathos comes from the women, who, once captured, are domesticized by the men, who cut off their wings. Unable
to fly away, all the women marry except Julia, the strongest, smartest
character in the text (and who remains that way simply because she is
not married.) The women live with their wings clipped until the men
propose to clip the wings of their daughters when they turn eighteen.
Rebelling as good, self-sacrificing mothers should, they say, "we have
one kind of happiness—the happiness that comes from being loved and
having a home and children. But there is another kind of happiness of
which when you cut our wings we were no longer capable—the happiness that comes from a sense of absolute freedom. We can bear that
for ourselves, but not for our daughters" (338). The book ends with
Julia's death in childbirth, as she gives birth to a son, who has wings.
It is her "greatest glory" (351). We, as readers, are not all convinced
of this glory. We see that once she marries, the only things of importance in her life are private, family matters, instead of running the community as she has effectively done until her marriage.

Some writers capitulate to the prescribed endings, but do so with
little enthusiasm. Perhaps the best example of writing within the acceptable endings, but, at the same time, expressing ambiguity, is the
example of Lillian B. Jones, whose novel *Five Generations Hence* may

be the first utopian novel by a black American woman.[4] In Jones's book, set in Texas in 1899, the main character is aptly named Grace Noble. Noble is a "high brown" twenty-eight-year-old woman who is full of "high and lofty passions" (5). Though her parents had been slaves, she is a respectable schoolteacher. When the man she loves marries another, she moves in with a female friend and, through this small supportive "community," writes her life's work—convincing Negroes that they should emigrate to Africa where, five generations hence, they can live a utopian existence. Grace publishes her book and, through its dissemination, convinces many people to find their utopia in Africa. Rewarded for her years of sacrifice, she meets a most respectable black physician whom she marries. Ironically, at the end of the novel many of the other main characters have followed Grace's dream and emigrated to Africa, where, although they have not found a land "flow[ing] with milk and money," (115) the emigrants will, through hard work and the "sweat of their brows" (115) store away for the future generations. Grace, though, is still in Texas, where her husband's work is. In a typical sentimental ending, Grace is described as needing only "love" to be happy. "Twas only love and the care of little ones needed to make Mrs. Warner's nature truly superb and when her first little boy . . . came, her face became divinely tender and Dr. Warner . . . called her his "Brown Madonna" (120). Yet, the book does not end with Grace's happiness; it ends with her realizing that her missionary friend, Violet Grey, who *is* in Africa, is the true "angel." Grace vows, in the last line, "to teach my little girls to be like her" (122).

Thus we leave Grace with no personal freedom; the only freedom fiction's conventions allow her is freedom to direct her daughters to be like her single friend. The woman who has envisioned a utopia for blacks cannot participate herself because she is a wife and mother. Her private life negates the public life that she has lived and advocated as utopia. Her final advice, then, haunts the "happy" ending.

Although about half of the works of utopian literature by women during this period succumb to the pressures of a "happy" ending, even though that ending contradicts the spirit of the utopia described, the other writers employ narrative strategies that go beyond the dominant sentimental romantic conventions, or, in the words of Rachel Blau DuPlessis, illustrate women writing "beyond the ending."[5] Primarily the women subvert the traditional death/marriage ending by getting rid of the men, by refusing to have an ending, or by trying to incorporate men and marriage into a female-centered world.

As Charlotte Perkins Gilman creates the landscape for a women's utopia at a single stroke by eliminating men, so several writers escape a requisite marriage at the end of their texts by conveniently killing off or otherwise getting rid of the leading man. This strategy is effective in allowing the main female character to be a utopian woman with a happy beginning, rather than an ending, to her story. In Caroline Mason's *Woman of Yesterday* (1900), Anna Mallison wants to become a missionary and marries Keith, who has similar plans. Though Anna soon learns that marriage "turns her out of her own life," she makes the best of it, and suffers silently when they do not go to India. She eventually meets John Gregory, who appears to be her true soul mate, when she and Keith join Gregory's utopian community, Fraternia. Keith conveniently dies, but instead of marrying John, who would like nothing better, Anna uses her freedom to finally go to India; Keith's death has freed her to do the meaningful work she longs to do, without worrying about whether he approves or not.

Similarly, in Alice Ilgenfritz Jones's second novel, *Beatrice* (1895), the title character is a slave in Louisiana who eventually falls in love with her rich, white cousin, Burgoyne, who loves her, too. The subject of interracial marriage is never broached since Burgoyne dies before he can marry Beatrice. But Beatrice has been advised, by her mentor Mrs. Thompson, to do great things with her life. "There is going to be a New Society made up of liberated spirits . . . —an aristocracy of souls . . . Perhaps you were created, with all your rich gifts, in purpose to show that the time for race conflict and race prejudice has gone by!" At the end of the novel, Beatrice is living on a remote island where the races mingle and is being nurtured by another older woman, Madame Rabino. Beatrice finds her life work on the island painting and helping the "poor gentle natives" (386).

Men disappear in a different way in Jones and Merchant's *Unveiling a Parallel*. In it, the male narrator who has been horrified with the valerian-smoking Elodia and has fallen in love with the beautiful Ariadne on Caskia is simply dismissed at the end. In spite of his love, he must leave Mars to return to Earth and the women's lives continue in their utopian and dystopian fashion without him. Jones and Merchant certainly do appear to be using one of the favorite structures of masculinist literary conventions when they pit the "bad" Elodia against the "good" Ariadne. But Ariadne does not end up with the man as a prize at the end of the book; she simply continues teaching in the community's school. And Elodia, who is full of sin according to the male narrator, is not punished in any way; in fact, Jones and Merchant show understanding for why Elodia behaves as she does. Instead of ending their book with Elodia's corruption and subsequent punishment when she takes on "male" characteristics, Jones and Merchant relate to us just how natural it is for Elodia, being a normal human being, to want the power and the pleasures afforded to her as an educated, clever adult.

Another way the women writers subvert the endings of the sentimental romance is to refuse to write an ending in the conventional sense of the word. The subject matter of utopian fiction lends itself to an actionless description of a new, perfect land. Several of the books, including Eloise Richberg's *Reinstern* (1900), Carra Dupuy Henley's *Man from Mars* (1901), and Bessie Story Rogers's *As It May Be* (1905), focus on conversations about or descriptions of a utopia and simply stop at that. But one of the novels appears to set up a typical conflict and then refuses to resolve it. In Mary A. Fisher's *Among the Immortals* (1916) the first-person protagonist, Eunice, had just died and gone to a utopian heaven where families are reunited and live and work together. As on earth, people may marry. Eunice meets the eligible Alpha at her parent's home, but soon Alpha introduces Eunice to his "friend" Celia. We immediately expect a love triangle with the best woman winning the hand of Alpha, but Fisher surprises us. Instead of a conventional plot with growing conflict and a resolution that rewards the best woman, we instead hear stories of people waiting for their loved ones to come or descriptions of the horrors of World War I, which the immortals watch on their telescopes. Fisher never sets up a conflict between the two women or gives us a resulting resolution. We conclude with neither marriage nor death, which of course would be redundant. The book simply stops.

Finally, a few of the women writers allow their main female characters to marry but insist that they also be able to live in a female-centered world and retain their autonomy. These endings may be the most pleasing to readers of the late twentieth century, accustomed as we are to our own cultural context of trying to "have it all." Few of us living in the final decade of the twentieth century can fully understand the impulse behind the turn-of-the-century women writers' desire to get rid of the men and their "male lusts." Having access to birth control, to our own money, to our children in cases of divorce, we are no longer so dependent in our private lives on the goodness of men. Should our husbands be alcoholics or gamblers, our own destinies are not irrevocably doomed as well.

Mildred Carver, the young woman who was ennobled by work in Martha Bensley Bruère's 1919 novel, is one heroine who is allowed to retain both her new-found autonomy and a love relationship at the end of the novel. Mildred has been changed by her year in the National Service, a requisite of all young adults in a new, utopian America. Through her labor, she has found a community of women, with whom she performs meaningful work. On the final page of the novel she asserts to her longtime lover that "I've got to do my work as a citizen too. I can't give it up" (288). But she adds, ambiguously, as the book's last line, "if you think we could do it together . . . "(289). Bruère carefully avoids mentioning marriage, and the very ambiguity of the ending—teasing us with the possibility they will marry but not telling us outright—allows a potentially happy ending on all counts.

Certainly all of Charlotte Perkins Gilman's utopian novels also fit this category. *Moving the Mountain* ends when the male protagonist marries a country girl, Drusilla, and rescues both of them from the past. In the country, Drusilla is a meek, patient, helpless, uneducated young woman, grown old before her time because of her constant toil. In the city she finds a utopia where technology has freed women from lives of dependence and ceaseless work; there, women have "wide, free lives, [and] absorbing work." The new woman-centered world was "like heaven" to Drusilla and to John, as well, who "grew to find the world like heaven too—if only for what it did to Drusilla."

In *Herland*, although we may wonder why the three Herland women, who have had the sex instinct bred out of them, might want to marry, marry they do, but on their own terms. They make fun of women taking men's names, of women following after men, of women being possessions of men. The one male, Terry, who can only think of a married woman as a possession of her husband, is banished from utopia for trying to rape his wife. The scene where Terry is expelled from utopia because he cannot and will not understand Herland's main te-

nets illustrates how the woman-centered values of Herland have pre-
vailed, allowing heterosexual love, but only on Herland's terms. As he
thinks about Terry's attempted rape and subsequent banishment, Van
recalls that he cannot remember a similar case in all history or fiction:
"Women have killed themselves rather than submit to [rape]; they have
killed the outrager; they have escaped; or they have submitted—sometimes seeming to get on very well with the victor afterward" (142–43).
But Terry's wife, he points out, did not submit, and the outrager was
expelled from the perfect world, a new plot twist validating the utopian message.

For Van too, the values of Herland have meant a change in his
attitude and behavior. As the book ends, Van and Ellador have decided
to travel to America. Because of this trip, Ellador decides they won't
"try again" to have a baby until they return to Herland, because she
does not want to give birth or raise a child outside of her community.
Van agrees, albeit painfully, having discovered that "Ellador's friendship, Ellador's comradeship, Ellador's sisterly affection . . . were enough
to live on very happily" (141).

Gilman's *With Her in Ourland* (1916), her sequel to *Herland*, traces
Van and Ellador as they travel to America. The juxtaposition of what
Ellador expects of the land of plenty and the reality of the poverty and
sexism that she discovers creates the tension in the narrative and leads
them in the final pages back to Herland. They return at Ellador's suggestion because she "would rather die childless than . . . bear a child
in this world of yours" (321). When asked why they can't just retreat
to a remote island, Ellador explains, once again, the lessons Herland
has taught her: how children need the teaching of many women and
the society of many children. Ellador, Van realizes, is not "his." She is
a woman of Herland, and her country and her hope of motherhood
"were more important to her than life in our land with me" (322).

When they return to Herland, Ellador, with passionate enthusiasm, begins touring her country, lecturing and writing about her experiences in America. She stirs up the Herland women to find a new sense
of responsibility to the whole world. Once they understand what the
outside world is like, they begin to make plans to "spread to all the
world their proven gains" (324). In the last line of the novel, Ellador
and Van give birth to Herland's first male child. But instead of implying that Ellador is now somehow "complete" because of this birth,

Gilman gives us a quite different reason Ellador was hoping to have a male child: to begin a new kind of men. Her vision, and thus ours, is still focused on the community and its values instead of on a private victory for self.

The ending of *With Her in Ourland* is straightforwardly utopian without compromise. Ellador returns to her lovely, child-oriented community, where the female center is found in every aspect of the landscape. She has meaningful work, is married to a man who completely accepts Herland's lessons, and has begun an entire new sex of people for Herland. It is, quite literally, a vision of a better world in birth.

ℚ

Consider Her Ways
The Cultural Work of Charlotte Perkins Gilman's Pragmatopian Stories, 1908–1913

Carol Farley Kessler

he utopian fiction of Charlotte Perkins Gilman takes on as its "cultural work" the demonstration that women are not confined to one traditional mode of being—wife/motherhood—but can fill as varied social roles as can male counterparts.[1] Jane Tompkins in her introduction to *Sensational Designs* (1985) suggests that we can speak of the "cultural work" of texts as an "attempt to redefine the social order" (xi). Further, Tompkins argues that we should study novels and stories "because they offer powerful examples of the way culture thinks about itself, articulating and proposing solutions for the problems that shape a particular historical moment" (xi). Like her great-aunt Harriet Beecher Stowe, included in Tompkins's study, Gilman wrote "to win the belief and influence the behavior of the widest possible audience": she had "designs upon her audiences, in the sense of wanting to make people think and act in a particular way" (xi).

In her 1910 study called *Our Androcentric Culture; or, The Man-Made World*, Gilman devoted one chapter to discussing what she labeled "Masculine Literature." Here Gilman explains her understanding that readers would more readily accept heretical views if presented as stories with morals for future action. In her stories, Gilman "represented" her ideas clothed as characters. She explains this view of the social function of literature.

The thought of the world is made and handed out to us in the main. The makers of books are the makers of thoughts and feelings for people in general. Fiction is the most popular form in which this world-food is taken. If it were true, it would teach us life easily, swiftly, truly; teach not by preaching but by truly *representing* [emphasis added]; and we should grow up becoming acquainted with a far wider range of life in books than could ever be ours in person. Then meeting life in reality we should be wise ["Bee Wise" or be utopian, which suggests a pun on one of her story titles]—and not be disappointed. (21)

She thus subscribes to a literature that can be called "cultural work," can enact social changes, can function as social action, can convey alternative versions/visions of human action—a position of clear self-consciousness regarding literary didacticism.

To this end of advocating particular changes, Gilman has situated her utopian fiction on the cultural boundary between genders. The Russian cultural critic Mikhail Mikhailovich Bakhtin reminds us that

> in our enthusiasm for specification we have ignored questions of interconnection and interdependence of various areas of culture; we have frequently forgotten that the boundaries of these areas are not absolute, that in various epochs they have been drawn in various ways; and we have not taken into account that *the most intense and productive life of culture takes place on the boundaries of its individual areas* and not in places where these areas have become enclosed in their own specificity. (2)[2]

This productivity of culture then occurs exactly along such boundaries as gender, and utopia becomes a primary locus for culture-creation, or "cultural work." By refusing to accept definitions of traditional "male" and "female" roles, and instead of offering clear alternatives to such mainstream notions, Gilman forces readers to question boundaries defining behavior assumed acceptable on the basis of gender—her views being still in the 1990s ahead of widespread social practice. Within the context of her utopian novels—*What Diantha Did, Moving the Mountain, Herland, With Her in Ourland,* and the fragmentary "A Woman's Utopia"—this discussion recovers from oblivion nine lesser known short stories, seven from Gilman's magazine *The Forerunner*.[3] These stories taken as a group offer as great a challenge for social transformation as do the novels: three stories suggest transformations specifically for men, complementing those suggested for women.

In contrast to Gilman's utopian fantasies, her utopian short stories could be labelled "pragmatopias," a term Riane Eisler coined in *The Chalice and the Blade: Our History, Our Future* (1988) and defines as a "realizable scenario for a partnership future."[4] Eisler uses the term "partnership" to name a principle of organization that lacks the domination hierarchy of male over female, typical of patriarchal societies (105). To make clearer her hypothesis, she offers "androcracy" (male-rule) to replace "patriarchy" (father-rule) as a more accurate name for a society organized according to the dominator principle. As a name for the partnership principle of social organization that she advocates, she posits "gylany," a term she coined from Greek antecedents meaning "a social system in which women [gy] are linked with or re/solved or set free [l] from men [an]" (105).[5] Now Eisler can precisely contrast "androcracy," a society in which men dominate women and whose social organization occurs through domination hierarchies, through force or the threat thereof, and "gylany," a society in which women and men are partners and whose social organization occurs through actualization hierarchies. "Actualization hierarchies" are systems within systems, such as the hierarchies of molecules, cells, and organs of biological systems—each being "a progression toward a higher, more evolved, and more complex level of function" (106). Eisler notes that because domination hierarchies actually inhibit the actualization of higher functions, gylanic systems pave the way for "greater evolutionary possibilities for our future" than do androcratic systems (106).

The "partnership" society that Eisler defines seems already to have been present in the "pragmatopian" imagination of Charlotte Perkins Gilman as revealed in her turn-of-the-century fiction, especially the short stories: the alternative or partner-oriented gender roles she depicts *could be* realized or attained then or in the present-day society that we know. To convey her view Gilman relies not so much upon fantasy in these *Forerunner* short stories—as one might anticipate in utopian writing—but, in fact, upon realism. But she uses realism subversively, her "design" for effecting the "cultural work" of her utopian fiction. Most often, as Anne Cranny-Francis reminds us in *Feminist Fiction: Feminist Uses of Generic Fiction*, realism is the narrative mode employed to naturalize ideology into the lives of readers (137).[6] These are, of course, her words for naming the "cultural work" of texts, which may (1) encourage the maintenance of a status quo—that is, may make what is ideology appear as if derived from natural order—as well as (2) encourage the social transformation that is the goal of utopian writers. Thus Gilman in a realistic mode[7] seeks to dislodge traditional gender ideology by presenting alternative, "realizable" possibilities for more egalitarian gender roles: critics typically decry "alternative" possibilities by alleging how "unrealistic" they are. (I would suggest that what critics may mean is that they are afraid of the implications of these possibilities: they would lose power, feel too guilty, have to accept responsibility, have to give up comfortable habits, have to learn new roles as nurturers, have to become the servants they wish to be served by, and so forth.) It is this quality of "realizability" that I wish to examine in these nine utopian short stories antedating *Herland*. This examination will include discussions of how the fiction can be construed as "cultural work" and how Gilman imagines "gylanic pragmatopia."

To clarify how Gilman's utopian short stories anticipate, extend, or particularize the programs of her utopian novels, let me begin by first commenting briefly upon these novels. Many readers are familiar with Gilman's utopia, the 1915 *Herland*, but lacking knowledge of three important biographical contexts, some misconstrue the centrality of motherhood as primarily prescriptive and miss both its compensatory solace and its silent subtext. First, Gilman's childhood was defective in maternally expressed affection: Gilman's mother, hoping to spare her children the grief she had experienced over lost affection when her marriage failed, thought that by refraining from showing her children any affection, they would not develop a dependence upon it and would better learn to do without. Second, the short story "The Yellow Wallpaper,"[8] an eventual therapeutic outlet for postpartum depression within a disastrous first marriage, provides a dystopian underside to *Herland*: the narrator, as had the author, experiences as maddening the requirement that she provide maternal care within a patriarchal context. Third, Gilman partially rejected her own motherhood, both because, as a single mother, she could not pursue her work and care adequately for her daughter, and because she wished her daughter to experience life with a father, as she had not: Gilman's daughter, however, felt her mother's action to be primarily rejection, not parental concern. In

Herland, Gilman centralized motherhood not only for reasons of utopian or feminist social principles, but also personally to re-imagine childhood, this time to include the love she believed that she had missed, and to idealize a motherhood she had neither experienced nor been able herself to practice. *Herland* provides an idealized validation of the socially acceptable motherhood Gilman both missed as a child and escaped as an adult, as well as an ideological program. However, this idealized version of motherhood, unlike the social practice both she and we know, receives the support of a whole society's resources: it is central to the society's structure. To the extent that motherhood is a conservative role for women, *Herland* may seem less forward-looking within Gilman's corpus than, say, her 1898 feminist treatise, *Women and Economics: The Economic Factor Between Men and Women as a Factor in Social Evolution.* To the extent that Gilman radically altered conditions for the practice of motherhood, *Herland* remains a utopian goal. Its sequel, the 1916 *With Her in Ourland* surveys the condition of a world engaged in its first global war, as reported by an appalled Herlander.

In contrast to the utopian fantasies, *Herland* and *With Her in Ourland,* both *What Diantha Did* and *Moving the Mountain* could be labeled "pragmatopias" because they define "realizable scenarios," attainable alternatives to the present society that we know. In the 1910 *What Diantha Did,* Gilman focused particularly upon the fit between a woman's professional and personal roles, as well as upon several domestic reforms needed to free women from daily drudgery, steps in the "grand domestic revolution" foreseen by Elizabeth Cady Stanton, the intellect behind the 1848 "Declaration of Sentiments." Gilman's 1911 *Moving the Mountain,* a futuristic romance, offers sundry innovations for urban neighborhood living. It revises and completes Gilman's earliest utopian fiction, the fragmentary 1907 "A Woman's Utopia,"[9] which presents the improved physical, social, and residential environments that the elevation of women would effect, as Gilman laid this out in *Women and Economics.* In particular, in "A Women's Utopia," she imagined such issues as specialization of domestic labor, remunerative work for both parents, and residential blocks incorporating the physical proximity of workplace and child care. Exploring such "cultural work" as pragmatopias can perform is the point of examining Gilman's utopian short stories.

Traditionally these stories might not have been included in bibliographies of utopian fiction: their mode is realistic. They are "thought experiments" that extrapolate possibilities from present day society. They make explicit how Gilman's readers might go about realizing her utopian visions. They locate us in the here and now: the setting is her contemporary United States. The nine stories present re/locations (or is it dis/locations?) of the individual with respect to gender in the structuring of families, neighborhoods, occupations, and societies as a whole. I discuss these stories in an order of increasing social complexity—an ordering that in Eisler's terminology could be conceptualized as an "actualization," instead of as a "domination," hierarchy. Social structure need not encase us in oppression: democratic and socialist structures can be envisioned as liberating or actualizing. In these stories, Gilman focuses not upon the macrostructure of a capitalistic economy (which she ignores here as a social problem), but upon the microstructure of everyday living that Erving Goffman first problematized in *The Presentation of Self in Everyday Life* and Bettina Aptheker discusses in *Tapestries of Life*. As her strategy for effecting "cultural work," Gilman creates subversively realistic fictions that offer us in "pragmatopias," or realizable utopias, erasure and redrawing of gender boundary lines.

At the lowest level of social organization is the family, the usual location in Western and European cultures for the process of child care, examined in two early stories, both of which adjust the male gender role to provide greater autonomy and support to women. The earlier story, "A Garden of Babies," particularizes the role of the female child-nurturer, while at the same time showing that not all women have either the desire or the ability to be good at nurturing. Both men and women work together to establish a baby garden for the health and welfare of mothers and children. Women provide the actual care; men provide medical expertise. Together they make possible mothers' recovery from the physical exhaustion of caring for small children, a necessity Gilman learned from personal experience and fictionalized in "The Yellow Wallpaper."[10] "A Garden of Babies" demonstrates men participating in the changed behavior necessary for women's lives to expand. It also presents child care as a societywide responsibility by including specialized training in the proper nurturing of small infants and children, and thereby contradicts the then-prevailing assumption that every mother naturally knew how to care for her baby. On the other hand, Gilman's fiction demonstrates her agreement, for the most part, with the assumption that primarily women should perform child care. The insight of Nancy Chodorow—that we need to experience as children nurturance from adults of both sexes—was not then current.[11]

Published a half-year later, "Her Housekeeper," however, does anticipate Chodorow. A male realtor and manager of boardinghouses provides the environment in which the woman he loves, also mother of a son not his own, can pursue her career: he finds for her live-in help—a governess to provide child care and a maid to keep house; a cook to her taste; and friends as co-tenants. He provides tea and conversation by a fireside, but no "undesired affection" (3), and for her boy his own listening ears, real artifacts for play, large books for perusal spread out upon a floor. She finds him a "real comfort" because he can "leave off being a man" and "just be a human creature"(4). The "plot" consists of his refutation of her list of six reasons why she won't "remarry." (We eventually learn that she has never married, however, and had borne a son out of wedlock.) Gilman has placed the institution of marriage at the center of this story—an institution requiring radical reform for a woman to flourish. Reform it receives: she may retain her freedom, keep her profession, take lovers—so long as she doesn't love them, and need never keep house (6–8)! Her son would figure as "an added attraction" to this successful suitor (6): if she wanted to take a foreign tour, he would care for her son (7). What appears is a model feminist partner, as caring of a woman as of her child. Dare we call him, by analogy to Joanna Russ's *Female Man* (1975), a "male woman"? The transformative redrawing of male gender boundaries enacted in both these family stories is "realizable," pragamatopian.

At the second level of social organization—the neighborhood—three stories pertain: "Her Memories," "Maidstone Comfort," and "Mrs. Hines' Money." More than two and a half years after "Her Housekeeper," Gilman published "Her Memories," another story with a central male presence, this time as an unnamed narrator, who recounts his female companion's memories of life at Home Court. This utopian community, situated in four high-rise buildings, provided child care and baby culture in covered, connected rooftop playgrounds; its adult amenities included a quiet, central courtyard with fountains, surrounded by cool arcades. Individual families resided in kitchenless apartments, their meals coming up from a common basement kitchen on a service

elevator. Gilman regularly privileges the nuclear family unit in her realistic stories. Again she stresses the varied capacities that different
women have for mothering—some suited to the very young, some to
the school-aged, some utterly out-of-tune with any children, including their own. And Gilman forces us to rethink commonplace daily
activities and recognize their relatedness to social goals. Although not
limited to gender adjustments, "Her Memories" restructures the domestic environment to permit more equitable relations between the sexes.

The next month after "Her Memories," Gilman published
"Maidstone Comfort"; here, utopia was a summer resort community of
the same name, featuring kitchenless cottages. The female narrator is
a friend of the manager-owner Sarah Maidstone Pellett, and Mrs.
Beninga McAvelly,[12] who in connecting the inheritance of Molly Bel-
low with the ideas of Sarah Pellett at Maidstone Comfort located the
funding for this enterprise. The capitalistic basis of this tale may seem
at odds with Gilman's professed socialist beliefs: rather than her earlier more radical innovations, after her 1900 marriage, she appears more
willing to depict bourgeois, middle-class solutions, but she makes
women the primary actors on her stage. The next spring in "Mrs. Hines'
Money," Gilman again depended upon capital, rather than behavioral
and structural change—the basis she credits for social improvements
in the first three stories discussed. In "Mrs. Hines' Money," Eva Hines
independently creates social innovations that improve the quality of
life in her town. Widowed as the result of an accident, she retains her
own legal counsel (rather than depending upon that of her brother)
and obtains additional information from the social service-oriented
magazine *The Survey*,[13] as well as from her own travels. Then with careful planning according to the new ideas she has gained, she uses money
inherited from her husband Jason to build in his memory the Hines
Building—a utopian scheme to raise the consciousness and knowledge
of the town by housing within this building a library, an auditorium or
theater, men's and women's lounges, a swimming pool and a gymna-
sium, a roof tea-garden, and meeting rooms for clubs with memberships
of all ages. Capital to support social services could, of course, accumu-
late from taxes rather than private inheritance, but the egocentricity
of voters makes taxes often appear an unrealizable mode for financing
social change. Although these last two tales may be less convincing to
us today as social change than the first three stories discussed, we must

recall that in Gilman's time, family summer "resorts" were commonplace and a women's club movement was strong and influential. What remains nonetheless transformative about them is the broad social agency attributed to individual, capable neighborhood women.

Occupational structure, especially of gender, is the third locus for utopian concern in an actualization hierarchy of social organization. In addition to the already discussed "Her Housekeeper" are two more stories: "Aunt Mary's Pie Plant" and "Forsythe & Forsythe." An editorial headnote to "Aunt Mary's Pie Plant" proclaims that "Mrs. Gilman's characters show in a convincing way how her beliefs and remedies would work out in practice. [This story] will be found a realistic miniature 'Looking Backward' " (14). The traveler to utopia here is a reporter, Aunt Mary's niece, who has come to describe the sleepy town she expects to find. Instead, encouraged by the town's minister, women of rural New Newton have established businesses offering various household services. A cooked-food service, run by the best cooks, delivers hot fare "better and cheaper" than individual homes earlier provided.[14] Aunt Mary now runs a factory, M. GARDINER, PIES, and has organized a Women's Farm and Garden Club, whose members bolster each other's business projects; their cooperative networking has changed their town. Traditional women's work is more efficiently, profitably, and competently accomplished as businesses run by skilled practitioners. Overall town prosperity has led to the construction in a parklike setting of a New Central School, equipped both to serve luncheon to students and to offer a crèche and kindergarten facilities. This story demonstrates how evolution toward cooperation and community might occur through club activity. It also suggests—though both Aunt Mary, and her niece, the reporter who will marry, reside in New Newton, and mail her articles to journals wherever they may be located—that women can pursue the world's work in a domestic setting, an early version of flex-time.

Treating primarily the mesh between domestic relationships and occupations, "Forsythe & Forsythe" stars husband-and-wife law partners, George Forsythe, and his cousin and wife Georgiana Forsythe, whose firm is located in Seattle, Washington. They resolve the problem of housekeeping by living in a residence hotel. A former best friend from college days, businessman James R. "Jimmy-Jack" Jackson, renews his friendship with George. He finds that his wife Susie, a self-centered pleasure-seeker, pales in contrast to his first love, George's sister, Clare Forsythe, now a sanitary engineer who lives in the same residence hotel. With the arrival of Susie's divorce decree, he proposes marriage to Clare, whose independent competence he admires. Gilman undermines popular wisdom by showing a nondomestic career woman to be more attractive to a suitor than a woman for whom marriage is the "crowning event of her life" (2). She also suggests that men might find female competence not a threat, but a boon. In both these tales, gender adjustments erase the separation of private and public in the occupational structure, and thereby permit the equal participation of both sexes.

Finally, during the summer of 1913, Gilman published two visions of a whole society, the last and most complex level of a social actualization hierarchy included in this discussion—"Bee Wise" and "A Council of War." In "Bee Wise," as in "Mrs. Hines' Money," an inheritance again makes possible the establishment of a utopian experiment: a ten-million-dollar gift permits a group of friends at a women's college to form a "combination" to create "a little Eden" in California (171). Their college Morning Club of some twelve to twenty members—including Mother, Teacher, Nurse, Minister, Doctor, Statesman [sic], Manager, Artist, Architect, Engineer—become the nucleus for this experimental community. A utopian visitor, again in the guise of a reporter as in "Aunt Mary's Pie Plant," arrives to discover that the mayor of Herways is a former college classmate. Reporter Jean finds "a perfectly natural little town, planned, built, and managed— . . . by women—for women—and *children* (171). She learns that the founders aimed "to show what a bunch of women can do successfully": they were willing that men help, but they expected to manage (171). The reporter remains, working in the beach town of Herways (the location of businesses and industries) and living in Beewise (the Residence Club), according to the community's plan. Herways and Beewise take their names from a biblical verse found in Proverbs 6.6: "Go to the ant, thou sluggard; consider her ways and be wise" (173).[15] As the fictional social structure becomes more complex, Gilman correspondingly expands women's social roles: what a woman has done, women can do, she demonstrates.[16]

The next month Gilman published another woman-centered story focused upon the larger society, "A Council of War." Here, in the only story I discuss not set in the United States, London women plan "to re-move this devastating error in relation [namely, male rule, the "war" of the title] and to establish a free and conscious womanhood for the right service of the world" (198). They plan "a government within a govern-ment; an organization of women," or "an Extension committee," "a Co-operative Society" (199). (Recall the Outsiders' Society that Virginia Woolf would imagine in her 1938 *Three Guineas*.) They would employ "women only," or the "right kind" of man (199). At the prospect of a "woman's world, clean and kind and safe and serviceable, . . . the women looked at one another with the light of a new hope in their eyes" (201). This conclusion, however, verges on an essentialism that many feminists today find problematic, nor is it consistent with Gilman's own recogni-tion in "A Garden of Babies" that nurturing skills must be learned, even by mothers. These last two stories strongly prefigure 1915 and 1916 uto-pias to come, namely, the all-female society of *Herland* and the critique of modern society found in *With Her in Ourland*.

In the utopian stories published between 1909 and 1913, Gilman seems to have moved from (1) imagining changes for men that would permit women to achieve the emancipation that she suggests in *Women and Economics*, to (2) deciding that a better persuasive strategy would be to suggest to (especially male) readers that women have abilities important to society as a whole. Perhaps she thought that persuasion including an appeal to male self-interest might be more effective than an appeal based solely upon altruism: needed transformations improve women's lives, and such improvement could make women more sub-stantially contributing members of society—a benefit to men as well. Demonstrating in *Herland* how benefits to women could be benefits to the whole of society is part of Gilman's two-pronged strategy for im-proving women's lot: change minds to change behavior. Gilman's utopian stories exemplify the didactic literary purpose to which she unashamedly subscribed. As her strategy for effecting "cultural work," Gilman created subversively realistic fictions that offer us in "pragmatopias," or realizable utopias, erasure and redrawing of gender boundaries. Gilman's demonstration of various grassroots innovations and reforms suggests the utopian potential of the realistic mode. What we might be tempted to dismiss as UNrealistic—when located in real-izable, gylanic pragmatopia—may subvert our tendency to dismiss and, instead, transform our vision of the possible. Such is the "cultural work" of Charlotte Perkins Gilman.

9

Science Fiction by Women in the Early Pulps, 1926–1930

Jane L. Donawerth

E ven though they are not well represented in science fiction ency-
clopedias and histories, a significant number of women wrote science fiction in the early years for the pulps: Clare Winger Harris
published a short science fiction in *Weird Tales* in 1926, and in 1927
won third prize in a short story contest in *Amazing Stories*. In 1929 and
1930, she was joined by a host of other writers: Sophie Wenzel Ellis,
Minna Irving (Minnie Odell), L. (Louise) Taylor Hansen, Lilith
Lorraine (Mary Maude Wright, née Dunn), Kathleen Ludwick, Louise
Rice, and Leslie F. (Frances) Stone (Mrs. William Silberberg).[1] The
works of these women writers, especially those by Lorraine, show that
the feminist utopia continued in the pulps even though it virtually disappeared in the hardback book trade from the 1920s through the 1950s
(Kessler, *Daring to Dream* 9). Their utopian transformation of domestic spaces and duties through technology, their revision of gender roles,
and their reliance on male narrative voices suggest that these women
writers form a bridge between the nineteenth-century technological
utopias by women and the constraints on women writers in the new
twentieth-century science fiction.

Both traditional historians of science fiction and also feminist ones
have expected women not to appear in the pulps, and have invented
reasons for their absence (see Curtis Smith viii–ix, and Pamela Sargent,
Women of Wonder xvi–xx). The women writers of the 1920s seem, by

the many references in their works, to have found a model and permission for writing in Mary Shelley's Frankenstein, and to have further
acquired confidence to write in college science classes.[2] Like their 1920s
male contemporaries writing for the science fiction pulps, the women
writers of science fiction romanticized science and technology. Clare
Winger Harris, for example, formulated plots out of scientific puzzles,
romanticizing the basic scientific principle that solved the puzzle—mo-
lecular chemistry in "A Runaway World," for example, or evolution
in "The Ape Cycle." L. Taylor Hansen's stories rely on the romanticizing of technological description—of pneumatic rail travel in "The Undersea Tube," for example. And many of these women writers
romanticize alien life forms. In Harris and Breuer's "A Baby on Neptune," the alien that welcomes humans to Neptune resembles a "multicolored chandelier," "scintillating throughout the chromatic scale"
(798), and in Hansen's "What the Sodium Lines Revealed," the aliens
from one of Jupiter's moons "pulsated like the turquoise transplendency
of a nebulous aurora" (130). In the decade in which men writing science fiction invented BEMs (Bug-Eyed Monsters), women writers
showed great empathy for their imagined aliens.[3]

Although the women writers shared with men the romanticizing
of science, they offered one particular application that the male writers rarely offered: the transformation of domestic spaces and duties
through technology. Here the women writers show themselves descendants not of male science fiction writers like Jules Verne and H. G.
Wells but, instead, of women writers of technological utopias like Mary
Griffith, who proposed in 1836 a utopian Philadelphia with cooking
cooperatives and refrigerated produce in the markets; like Mary E. Bradley Lane, who in 1880 pictured a land of women who had made housekeeping and food preparation into chemical sciences; and like Charlotte
Perkins Gilman, who in 1915 had imagined a land of women who had
converted their entire country into a child-proofed home and had made
child-raising into a science.[4]

Like Mary Bradley Lane, all these women science fiction writers
of the 1920s imagine that in the future food will be chemically produced (M. Lane 19–20). In Clare Winger Harris's "A Runaway World,"
everyone stocks up on "meat tablets" in the face of disaster (22). On
Minna Irving's earth of 3014, people imbibe "essences" of "roast beef,
wheat, chicken salad, cheese, potatoes, oranges, coffee and wine" and,

so, "avoid taking waste matter into [their] stomachs," and eliminate "servant trouble and expense" ("Moon Woman" 753). In Stone's *When the Sun Went Out*, future humans are nourished on "liquid food" dispensed at their home faucets (20); the narrator observes that "consequently the pleasure of eating had been lost, but the tripled efficiency of the food overcame the loss" (21). In Lorraine's "Into the 28th Century," food "essence" is inhaled, not eaten or drunk, and a feast consists of "a couple of jewelled food-flakes, a sparkling beverage and some foamy concoctions" (262). In Sophie Wenzel Ellis's "The Creatures of Light," the scientists try "chemical nourishment" (210), while in L. Taylor Hansen's "The Prince of Liars," the space travelers dine on "broth and capsules of nourishment" (594). By doing away with eating, these women writers have also revised women's domestic duties, doing away with shopping for food, gardening, cooking, canning, preserving, cleaning up, and managing servants. And just as the food technology of Mary Bradley Lane coincided with the development in the United States of the new science of home economics, so these utopian visions of efficient chemical diet coincide with the campaign in women's magazines for a scientific homemaker (see Davison 88–105).

Domestic interiors in these stories by women are designed, like food, for efficiency, cleanliness, and psychological well-being. In Leslie Stone's "Out of the Void," published the year after Marie Curie's second visit to the United States, energy from radium powers light, heat, and refrigeration (Part 1:452; Part 2:549), and the alien swimming pool imparts a feeling of well-being to all bathers owing to the radium-treated water (Part 1:452). In Stone's *When the Sun Went Out*, future homemakers have designed interiors with knowledge of the psychological effects of lighting and color on human moods and health, comfort is the primary purpose of furniture (19–20), and clothes are made of a material scientifically designed to retain body heat (11–12). In L. Taylor Hansen's "The Prince of Liars," lighting is accomplished by phosphorescent plants, and in Louise Rice and Tonjoroff-Roberts's "The Astounding Enemy" by phosphorescent insects (96). In Hansen's "What the Sodium Lines Reveal," the houses are complete with sliding doors and elevators, and tables rise already filled with food from hidden recesses in the floor (131–32, 134). Lilith Lorraine's "Into the 28th Century" features glassed-in sleeping porches in roof gardens, with sunken tubs and music psychologically designed for inducing sleep (262). By means of technological devices and a requirement that each citizen serve in rotation as a servant, Lorraine has done away with the servant class (262) (as had Mary Bradley Lane, by professionalizing housekeeping). And in Leslie Stone's "Women With Wings," "mechanized robots" "[h]ad been perfected to such a high degree . . . that the care of the house and the kitchen was left to them" (987). All of these women agree in seeing science in the service of human comfort as a major principle of interior domestic design.

Technology also affects the exterior world of women in these stories. In Leslie Stone's "Letter of the Twenty-Fourth Century," cities have been abolished as unhealthful, and everyone lives a pastoral dream among gardens in the countryside, a dream shared by many later women's utopias (Pearson 53). In Lilith Lorraine's "Into the 28th Century," "There were no signs of . . . smoking factories, . . . ugly office buildings, . . . malodorous warehouses" but "instead . . . airy homes nestling in the midst of cool and verdant parks" (261). On L. Taylor Hansen's Allos, people live in domed cities, where "the air is . . . continually washed chemically so that it will not be disease-laden . . . [with] bacterial life" ("Prince of Liars" 595). And in Stone's "Men With Wings," smoke from kitchens is carried off by fans and "chemically dissolved," while all air in the city is "cleansed and purified before it [is] distributed" (74). The living spaces that these women imagine, then, are beautiful and healthful, because both wild nature and also urban dangers have been abolished.[5] With a healthful, clean environment, women's domestic duties disappear: in these stories, women are neither cleaning or nursing, since dirt and disease are banished.[6]

Just as these women abolish food and urban dirt, and so change the domestic circumstances of women, so they also contemplate the radical revision, even abolishment of childbirth and its dangers. In Leslie Stone's "Letter of the Twenty-Fourth Century," humans "have discovered how to make child-birth a safe and beautiful function" (861), and in her "Out of the Void," aliens have discovered a way "to bring forth a child without a woman's help" (Part 2:549). The utopian from Lilith Lorraine's "Into the 28th Century" tells her time-traveling lover that "birth is entirely different from the horror that it was in your day. The embryo is removed from the womb shortly after conception and brought to perfect maturity in an incubator" (258). In Sophie Wenzel Ellis's "Creatures of the Light," embryos are removed immediately to

Leisurely moving bright-colored passenger vehicles skimmed along, keeping a foot or so above the pavement, as though held in that position by some gravity controlling device. People equipped with artificial wings actually flew through the air.

Illustration by Paul

2. From Lilith Lorraine, "Into the 28th Century," *Science Wonder Quarterly* 1.2 (Winter 1930): 260. Illustration by "Paul." Courtesy of the Azriel Rosenfeld Science Fiction Research Collection, Special Collections, Albin O. Kuhn Library, University of Maryland Baltimore County.

an artificial glass womb—"the Leyden jar mother"—for "the human mother's body does nothing but nourish and protect her unborn child, a job which science can do better" (213). The Leyden jar mother shortens gestation, and special rays shorten growth so that childhood occurs in under a year. In Stone's *When the Sun Went Out*, children are raised in "the City of Children," presumably by professionals (13); and in Stone's "Men With Wings," children from the age of five are raised by "educationalists," not by parents (74), while in "Women With Wings," all women are temporarily sterilized to prevent childbirth while scientists work to produce "our young through mechanical agencies" (989). Thus women writers of science fiction in the 1920s handle the dangers of women's reproductive role in the same way they handle the tiresomeness of women's role as cook: by abolishing the necessity for the role. Their radical alteration or abolishment of birth and child-raising (and in Lorraine's case, of sex) frees women from domestic duties, as the later feminists Shulamith Firestone and Marge Piercy also imagined, for further education and for public responsibilities. In this final use of science to alter domestic duties, these women writers of the 1920s look forward to the writers of feminist utopias in the 1970s, not back to the writers of the earlier utopias, which revolved around child care.

The utopian transformation of domestic spaces and duties is as much a result of the transformation of gender roles as of science and technology. These women writers of the 1920s introduce into science fiction visions of women's roles as socially constructed, changeable and, so, potentially utopian. But the stories vary considerably in the vision of future roles.[7] Almost all of the women writers offer in some story the exceptional woman who enters the man's world of science or public office. In Clare Winger Harris's "Menace of Mars," Vivian Harley prepares herself for a career in science by majoring in chemistry, to assist her father, and by minoring in astronomy, to assist her future husband (582, 584). In Leslie Stone's "Out of the Void," the astronaut for the first trip to Mars is a woman disguised as a man. In Harris and Breuer's "A Baby on Neptune," the decipherer of the first communication from outer space, in 2099, is a kindergarten teacher, Miss Geneva Hollingsworth (791). L. Taylor Hansen's "The Prince of Liars" includes a paeon to the ancient female scholar Thora (591), and women serve as rulers in the alternate universe of Leslie Stone's "Through the Veil" (179). These stories thus provide portraits of strong women, but as ex-

ceptions. And exceptional women may perpetuate rather than challenge existing gender roles.

The women writers of 1920s science fiction go further, however,
to imagine revised roles for women, and these revisions fall roughly into
two categories. The first group—Minna Irving, Kathleen Ludwick, and
Lilith Lorraine—imagine revised gender roles along the lines of Victorian feminism and the theory of women's work. Irving's revision offers women the role of social reformer: her moonwomen bring superior
knowledge to earth, become rulers, and save earthmen from disease,
war and, through marriage, even from decadent genes (753–754).
Ludwick pictures women as equally heroic to men, but contained in
separate careers: her hero, Linnie Chaumelle, is a trained nurse, and
possesses "that unlimited sympathy of that maternal character which
persists . . . [in all] femininity" (568); she dies heroically with many men
when her Red Cross tent is bombed by the Germans. The narrator in
Ludwick's story looks forward to a future when the "Mrs. Sangers of
the day will be heard with respect" (560); just at the time of this story,
Margaret Sanger was in the middle of her campaign to legalize birth
control in all states. Lorraine presents a socialist revision of marriage:
in *The Brain of the Planet* a socialist revolution removes the economic
pressure on women to marry, and so "[t]he relations between the sexes
became perfect, for . . . all marriages were based on real love, on affinity of tastes" (19). Here Lorraine indicates one difference between these
women writers of the 1920s and the earlier women writers of technological utopias: the all-women communities of the earlier writers are
gone, and these writers of the 1920s are unrelentingly heterosexual in
their depiction of women's sexual role and emotional needs. However,
Lorraine's revision still offers women a separate sphere of influence from
men. Iris, a college coed born in the twenty-eighth century, explains,
"the functions of government today . . . concerned . . . with education,
with . . . patronage, . . . with the beautification and spiritualization of
all life . . . finds in woman its ideal director. Man still leads in invention, mechanics, mathematics and the more strenuous sports. Woman
has ceased to imitate man, being content in her own sphere. She has
intensified her femininity, wherever it can be done without a sacrifice
of her health and freedom" (257). Having done away with war, men's
game, Lorraine extends women's sphere of influence to all government.
Her revision suggests the appeal of the doctrine of separate spheres of

influence: one can pretend that the old roles remain intact while a profound shift in power occurs.

Leslie F. Stone, Louise Rice, and Clare Winger Harris, in contrast, envision revised roles for women along strict lines of equality between men and women, influenced perhaps by an early equal rights feminism emphasizing suffrage and education for women. In Stone's "Out of the Void," Dana Gleason, the first astronaut, is a woman, but disguised as a man. When Richard, her best male friend, guesses the truth and jumps on board, calling her "brave, strong, great willed, yet . . . at a disadvantage" (Part 1:453–54), Dana curls her lip and goes to check the gauges of the spaceship. But soon the two are sharing everything equally: they alternate cooking, compete in dishwashing, and read together (454). In Stone's *When the Sun Went Out*, the female astronomer is dressed exactly as the male astronomer, and they both are named for their occupations, not for their marital status (11). They fall in love not with their differences, but with their similarities: "The two of them had much to tell each other. Astronomers both, they spoke the same language, had the same hopes and desires" (15). And they live in a society where men or women have an equal chance of governing, for "sex made no difference" (17). In Stone's "Men With Wings," women and men work side by side, even together in the army in war, for "[h]ere men and women worked alike" (75). In Louise Rice and Tonjoroff-Roberts' "Astounding Enemy," Mildred Sturtevant is a career scientist and also an officer in "The Woman's Party" (83). She works with her fiancé-scientist, and maintains a correspondence with many "young scientists like herself" (91). Women soldiers, in the battles against the invading insects, distinguish themselves for their "considerable courage and strength" (84). And when her friends try to put Mildred in a safe place, she insists on women's equality: "Fancy trying to put me into my place—in the rear! You'd think we were back in the nineteen hundreds. I have a perfect right to go, too, since I have all my money in the venture" (84). In Clare Winger Harris's "The Ape Cycle," Sylvia, airplane mechanic and pilot, offers Wilhoit the tools to check the plane after her work on it. When he taunts her as "a relic of the age when women were not at all mechanically inclined," she defends her work with a view of gender as socially constructed: "It was purely a matter of environment. . . . You know women finally came into professions that had been hitherto considered solely man's field, and they found they could do as well as their brothers" (353). In Dana, disguised as a man, in Ramo, dressed just like a man, in Richard, who cooks just like a woman, in Mildred, who manages her own finances (Rice and Tonjoroff-Roberts 90), and in Sylvia and Wilhoit's sharing of airplane mechanics, Stone, Rice, and Harris offer androgynous visions of future gender roles.

Yet the androgyny threatens at every crisis to disintegrate into the old gendered roles of hero and victim: most of these women eventually need to be rescued by most of these men. In "Out of the Void," when Dana is captured by an evil politician on another planet, her lover becomes a revolutionary who handles her rescue with gusto (Part 2:560–61). When the two astronomers face the dying of our sun together in Stone's novella, it is the man who comforts and the woman who sobs (24). When Mildred is kidnapped by the giant insects, it is a male soldier, not one of the women, who carries her out of the cavern (102). The exception is Sylvia, who rescues herself. But when Sylvia and Wilhoit finish fixing the airplane and save the planet, Wilhoit gets rewarded by the presidency, while Sylvia gets marriage to Wilhoit (365).

Finally, I think, the writers of these stories were limited not by their visions of gender roles, of education for women, or of careers for women but, instead, by their assumptions about literary form. All except one of these stories are narrated by a male first-person narrator, or by a third-person narrator with a male point of view. The brief science fiction tradition that women writers inherited was entirely male in narration, and mostly first-person. They could take as their models the first-person adventure stories of most of Gernsback's 1920s' stable of writers, the elegant voices of H. G. Wells's scientist-explorers encased in a male representative of the audience who stayed behind to tell the story (as in *The Time Machine*), or the multiple male narrators—audience, scientist, monster—of Mary Shelley's *Frankenstein*. In any case, whether one or many, the voices were male.

And the stories by these women writers of science fiction in the 1920s, despite their development of the themes of education for women or equality of careers for women, were stories in men's voices, about men making scientific discoveries and undertaking scientific exploration. Clare Winger Harris's "Miracle of the Lily," for example, is the story of Nathano, a future male historian, who relates humanity's doing away with all other life forms, and their gradual return; as a discoverer of seeds and the grower of the lily, he is the hero. L. Taylor Hansen's "Prince of Liars," the lead story of that issue of Amazing Stories, centers on Gnostes, an ancient Greek who experiences time distortion because of his space travel with aliens, whose story is related to us by a male narrator who becomes his friend. Minna Irving's "Moon Woman" is the story of Professor James Holloway Hicks, who discovers a serum for suspended animation, and who wakes to meet the moon woman. In Lilith Lorraine's "Into the 28th Century," the narrator, Anthony, journeys into the future, hears there the details of the future socialist utopia and falls in love with Iris, accidentally returns to his own time by drinking a potion, and ends the story with hope of his return—with the help of a mad (male) scientist. Rice and Tonjoroff-Roberts imagine a cooperative effort, including women scientists and soldiers, to combat invading insects, but the third person narration is from the point of view of Nicholas Ivanoff, and the protagonist is Colonel Mortimer Fortescue. Even in Leslie Stone's "Out of the Void," Dana Gleason's attempted voyage to Mars is recorded by a man kidnapped from his fishing trip, who collects the story from the alien male Sa Dak, from Professor Rollins and his daughter, and from Dana Gleason's diary; Dana Gleason is the protagonist only until we discover that she is a woman, and thereafter her lover Richard Dorr takes the central role of actor and adventurer. As Sarah Lefanu complains, in early twentieth-century science fiction, "women's participation necessitated becoming one of the boys, joining in on their terms, becoming a Female Man" (Feminism and Science Fiction 2).

But not quite. Judith Fetterley has argued that American literature is a male tradition, and that the best posture for feminist critics is that of a "resisting reader" (xxii). While the women who wrote science fiction in the 1920s did not experiment much with women's voices, they did make a place in their stories for the resisting reader, and they developed several strategies for doing so.

We can best see why they retained the male narrator, I think, by looking at the one experiment with a female narrator, Clare Winger Harris's "Fifth Dimension." From the beginning, pouring her husband's coffee, the narrator is defined as a woman, and so as housebound, serving, careful of her husband's ego: "There was no doubting that John [the husband] was a greater success in life than I, whether he grasped the significance of certain cosmic truths or not!" (824). The plot is a puzzle: what is déjà vu? After the narrator refuses to acknowledge a premonition and her neighbor is killed, she experiences months of depression; she follows up on the next premonition, and keeps her husband off a train that wrecks, killing all its passengers. The husband and wife together advance the causal explanation that resolves the story: time is circular, like space, and so we repeat the events of our lives; change, however, is possible, and so each revolution is an improvement (850). Although a woman in the traditional role of wife can fill the role of scientific thinker that Harris assigns her heroes, she cannot fill the role of actor and persuasive leader. This is the shortest story that Harris wrote, and the woman hero saves only her husband, not the trainload of people, not even the neighbor: her power is defined by the boundaries of her house.[8] Harris seems unable to revise both gender role and, also, narrative structure at the same time. The other writers do not try: like C. L. Moore, who follows them in the 1930s, they retain the male narrator or point of view and make a place for strong women characters and resisting readers within the man's story.

The place that Clare Winger Harris and Kathleen Ludwick make for the resisting reader is not a spacious one, but it is interesting. Harris and Ludwick favor male narrators who are not "normal," who do not share the values as defined by other males of their society. In both Harris's "Fate of the Poseidonia" and "The Diabolical Drug," the male narrators end up in insane asylums ("Fate" 252; "Drug" 180). And in Harris's "Miracle of the Lily," the narrator, Nathano, is a rebel who wants to see the return of plants and even the enemy, insects, to the earth—his empathy for other life forms is viewed as traitorous by other men. Kathleen Ludwick's "Dr. Immortelle" is framed and authorized by a two-page first-person narration from a white, male mining engineer. The body of the story, however, is narrated by Victor de Lyle, a black who has served through hundreds of years as assistant to the evil Dr. Immortelle. Victor was freed from slavery and educated by his master in return for his aid as an assistant and site of experimentation: before Dr. Immortelle tried out his techniques of rejuvenation on himself, he experimented first on orphans, and then on Victor. Victor includes pleas for just treatment of blacks: "There never was the same prejudice on the Continent against colored people that has always existed here in America" (563). But Victor also authorizes many stereotypes of blacks: Victor is lethargic (564), passionately desirous of children (565), and clairvoyant (569)—because these are here presumed to be inherited traits of the Negro race. He rejoices when the transfusions that combat aging also turn him Caucasian (564). Like Leslie Stone's androgynous hero, who stands between genders, Victor stands between races. His identity as a black seems derived not from black experience, but from the sympathetic identification of a white woman writer who accepted an essentialist definition of her own identity but yet resisted discrimination against her sex—and transferred these to her black narrator. In Harris's and Ludwick's stories, male readers may be comfortable with male narration, but women readers are not asked to identify with normative male values, and are offered, instead, narrators who stand outside of their societies.

L. Taylor Hansen also makes a place for the resisting reader, by refusing to mark her first-person narrator as male for a great part of the story. Hansen prefers the technique of H. G. Wells in *The Time Machine*, of assigning the role of audience to the male narrator, who tells the adventures of another male, the protagonist. What makes her strategy accommodating to the woman reader is her reluctance to name her narrator as male. In "The Man from Space," for example, the narrator, unnamed, listens to a lecture in a college classroom, and a third of the story has passed before we learn the names that mark him male: "Bob," then "Mr. Hunt" (1036). In "The Prince of Liars," we are fairly certain that the narrator is male because he walks on a dark street (582) and visits the mysterious Gnostes in his apartments (584), but since this is science fiction, we are not sure; Hansen never tells us his name, and marks him with certainty as male only on the final page, when Gnostes laughingly calls him "Mr. Newtonian" (599). Such a strategy of withholding the gender of the narrator allows the woman reader, or any resisting reader, a sympathetic place within the text, at least temporarily. Hansen's strategy anticipates by nearly sixty years the experiment of Melissa Scott in *The Kindly Ones*, a first-person narration where the gender of the narrator is never revealed.

More spacious are the places offered the resisting reader by Minna Irving, Louise Rice, Lilith Lorraine, and Leslie Stone; they provide multiple narrators, women's voices and stories within men's stories. Although they would not have known her eighteenth-century utopian novel, they are following in the steps of Sarah Scott, whose male narrator records the stories of the women who live in Millenium Hall.

Minna Irving's third-person narrative, "The Moon Woman," offers us male points of view for most of its pages—first Professor James Hicks, then Dr. Blinkman, and then again Professor Hicks. But by the end of the story, the moonwoman, Rosaria, has intruded her point of view, and is so intent on revealing the glories of the reformed earth to the professor awakened from suspended animation that she threatens to turn the narrative into first-person. The story closes by a return to the male point of view through the disclosure that Rosaria and her future were only a dream of the professor. But this containment does not quite contain, since it is the woman's voice that offered the visionary science of the story, the tale of flight, of chemical food, and of freedom from disease and war for all humans.

Rice and Tonjoroff-Roberts's "The Astounding Enemy" combines two techniques for resisting male narration. The story is a third-person narrative from the point of view of a white male, Nicholas Ivanoff. But within this narration are contained, briefly, two others: reports by Gerald Chin, the Scottish-Chinese assistant to the scientists (84–85, 103), and letters from Mildred Sturtevant when she is kidnapped (94–95, 98). The heroes of the story are a coalition of white males, Asians, and women—all scientists—who resist the villain's racism, as well as the invasion of insect enemies. The narration is thus, politically, a compromise: Chin represents Asians but is only half-Chinese, and Mildred assumes a voice only when she becomes a victim separated from male protectors; racial and gender difference is included but also contained.

More intricate yet is Lilith Lorraine's narrative structure of "Into the 28th Century," a structure that mimics that of Mary Shelley's *Frankenstein*, but replaces one of the three male narrators with a woman. The story is a first-person narrative of Anthony who time-travels to a future utopia, and accidentally returns to our time, only long enough to leave his story. But just as Walton in *Frankenstein* sends his story to his sister (who presumably publishes the letters), so Anthony sends his story for publication to his "aunt, . . . somewhere in the Orient . . . [who] had always been a wanderer, writing when the mood swayed her" (251). Within Anthony's story, as within Walton's, we have two other voices: the voice of the scientist Victor Frankenstein is paralleled in Anthony's story by that of the future university teacher Therius, but the voice of the monster is displaced in Anthony's story by the voice of a woman,

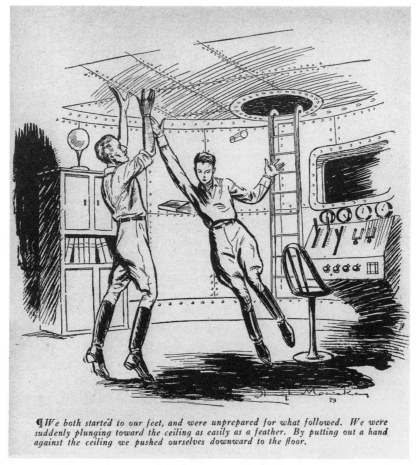

¶ *We both started to our feet, and were unprepared for what followed. We were suddenly plunging toward the ceiling as easily as a feather. By putting out a hand against the ceiling we pushed ourselves downward to the floor.*

3. From Leslie F. Stone, "Out of the Void, Part I," *Amazing Stories* 4.5 (August 1929): 441. © TRS, Inc. Used with permission. Courtesy of the Azriel Rosenfeld Science Fiction Research Collection, Special Collections, Albin O. Kuhn Library, University of Maryland Baltimore County.

Iris. In this utopia, Therius explains the scientific transformations, but Iris is allotted the social transformations. It is from Iris that we hear of the series of socialist revolutions and the accompanying feminist movement (255–57). And, while Anthony's voice telling his adventure story occupies the most pages, Iris speaks more than a third of the story. As in Irving's story, the female narrator is lost at the conclusion, but returning to her future and her voice is Anthony's goal when we leave him. In Lorraine's story several spaces are thus left for the resisting reader: although the narrator is male, the story promises within itself that it will be published under a woman author's name, and the male narrative of loss and desire frames the utopian female narrative of hope and fulfillment.

Even more complicated is the narrative structure of Leslie Stone's "Out of the Void." In this story the unnamed narrator recalls Hemingway's narrators, an American male who begins his story by escaping from his wife on a fishing trip and ends it with a misogynistic joke at his wife's expense. Within the male narrator's story are contained several other narrators. The first is Sa Dak, a silver male alien, who captures the narrator, introducing us to the protagonist, whose message he brings, and offering us a vision of alternative science. Partway through the story, however, Sa Dak's voice is left behind and the narrator's returns, but with information he could not know. We later learn that this record was compiled with the help of Elsie, the professor's daughter, who quietly loved the hero, Dana Gleason (Part 1:447, 454). Elsie "had already passed her twenties; the bloom of her youth was gone, given without thought of self to the service of the old scientist," her father (Part 1:447). Her self-effacement is so complete that her story is told by another's voice, and we have only the barest clue that it is hers: it is a love story of admiration for Dana Gleason, traveler, explorer, wit, woman-hater, with "regular features that were almost girlish except for a masculinity developed by the full life of a globe-trotter" (Part 1:448). Elsie's participation in the adventure story, as Dana prepares for "his" rocket ship exploration of Mars is that of observor and caretaker, who "sat in her corner mending and embroidering" (Part 1:448), and who made sure that the ship was equipped with handkerchiefs intialed "DG" (Part 1:449). Suddenly we come to Dana Gleason's own story, the silver metal manuscript brought back by Sa Dak to the professor and his daughter, and we learn that Dana is a woman. Part 1, then, ends with a first-person narrative by Dana Gleason of her falling in love with Richard Dorr, who guesses her disguise and joins her in the first rocket exploration of Mars. Dana's diary, though, ends very early in Part 2 with the crash of her rocket not on Mars, but on an unknown planet, and her separation from Dick. Even though the rest of the story is ostensibly based on reports from Dana, Dana loses her "I" and becomes a third person in the narrative; at the same time, she also loses her place as hero in the narrative, and becomes the victim—she is kidnapped by the aliens and is eventually rescued by Dick. Gradually we realize that our perspective for the rest of the story is that of the alien villain, and at the end Sa Dak reveals himself as that person. Briefly, then, in the middle of this tale, we have heard from two women. Elsie speaks only through a man, whispering her information to him and letting him do the talking. Dana is allowed a voice only to tell the story of her falling in love; even though as a "female man" she is the hero of Part 1, as soon as she loves she becomes the victim to be rescued and loses her voice. The narration, however, is wonderfully androgynous: this story is related by a man's man on a fishing trip, by a silver alien villain, by a woman who loves a woman, and by a woman disguised as a man who attempts the first trip to Mars. It is significant, I think, that the author's name, Leslie, as well as the hero's, Dana, are names that may be worn by either sex. In a simpler way, Stone varies her androgynous narration in "Through the Veil." There the male narrator in our universe tells the story of his friend who steps through to an alternate universe that is explained by a female narrator. At the end of the tale his friend is missing. For Irving, Lorraine, and Stone, who retain the framework of male narration but resist it, female narration is possible in a dream, in the future, or in an alternate universe.

10

Difference and Sexual Politics in Naomi Mitchison's *Solution Three*

Sarah Lefanu

$\int$ *olution Three* was published in 1975, more than ten years after Naomi Mitchison's first science fiction novel, *Memoirs of a Spacewoman* (1962). *Memoirs* is an extraordinary book, not least because it is a science fiction novel that centralizes a woman's sexual and emotional experiences at a time when female characters barely appeared in science fiction, let alone had autonomous sexuality or experienced anything other than being squashed by the male characters. *Memoirs* is, as the title suggests, the recollections of the life and adventures of a spacefaring woman through a variety of expeditions, experiments, and relationships with other life forms. The two stories described in most detail in *Memoirs* concern a women-only expedition to a planet inhabited by caterpillars and butterflies, and a series of experiments around the reproduction and nurturing of an alien life form in which Mary, the memoirist, herself becomes host to an alien graft (or pregnant with it, although the alien life form is not carried within the womb). Mary is both a scientist and a mother and, far from this being presented as a contradiction, the two roles are shown to complement and enrich each other. It is fitting that her area of expertise is communications.

Naomi Mitchison was certainly not the first woman to write science fiction. But *Memoirs* is remarkable for inviting the reader to identify throughout with a female character, from a female perspective. It also offers an interesting illustration of female science fiction writers' sympathetic identification with the alien: *Memoirs* is packed with

153

species other than human. If there is a difficulty in interspecies relationships, it is that the women love too much, with tragic consequences
in the case of the expedition to the butterfly planet, and with surprising and comic results in other instances. During the graft experiments
Mary becomes increasingly distrustful to the point of paranoia of all
human relationships, while remaining sufficiently dispassionate to grade
the levels of her growing empathy with the other animals involved.
Dogs score high: hyenas and jackals low. And it is unusual, to say the
least, to find in science fiction of the 1960s a relationship with an alien
of the quality of Mary's with the Martian Vly, and its chance result,
her beloved haploid daughter Viola.

While *Memoirs* stands out as remarkably different from other science fiction novels of the time, *Solution Three*, after a gap of twelve
years (during which time Mitchison published a variety of other books,
including most of those on Africa), was published in the same period
in which feminist writers made an energetic entry into science fiction:
Suzy McKee Charnas's *Walk to the End of the World* in 1974 and
Motherlines in 1978, Joanna Russ's *Female Man* in 1975, Marge Piercy's
Woman on the Edge of Time in 1976, and Sally Miller Gearhart's
Wanderground in 1979.[1] Feminist science fiction writers of the 1970s
came, on the whole, from America. In *Solution Three*, however,
Mitchison is similar to those American writers in her foregrounding
of sexual roles and sexual behavior. Because of this, it is tempting to
read *Solution Three* in the context of the American feminist utopian
and dystopian novels of the seventies, with their deconstruction of
sexual roles and sexual identities and their insistence on the fundamental importance of sexual politics.

Alternatively, as the sexuality in *Solution Three* is presented quite
specifically within a role-reversal setting, with homosexuality as the
norm and heterosexuality defined as "deviant," it might perhaps be read
alongside such works as the British writer Esmé Dodderidge's *New
Gulliver* (1979) or Gerd Brantenburg's *Daughters of Egalia* (translated
1985), both of which reverse the power relations between women and
men to satiric effect. But this reading raises problems. My heart often
sinks at a role reversal because, without a satirical intent, the purpose
becomes confused. Feminist role reversals are purposeful, indeed polemical. Both Esmé Dodderidge and Gerd Brantenburg highlight the
gross and subtle forms of injustice and oppression that women suffer at

the hands of men by making their female characters masquerade as men. It is masculine behavior that is being illuminated for the reader through having her sympathy evoked for the underdog, for the women who are, in these books, men.

What is the purpose of the role reversal in *Solution Three*? Is the compulsory homosexuality of the world in the novel meant to be a mirror image of the compulsory heterosexuality of the real world? This difficulty of interpretation springs from a lack of credibility in the sexual behavior of characters in the novel. To be more straightforward: I find Mitchison's strangely unrealistic portrayal of sexual relationships a problem right from the start.

Despite this difficulty of interpretation, *Solution Three* raises a variety of interesting questions. As I hope to show, it is more fruitful to look at the novel in the light of Naomi Mitchison's own background and development than to compare it, despite its obvious thematic similarities, with contemporary feminist science fiction. As much as anything, her three adult science fiction novels, *Memoirs of a Spacewoman*, *Solution Three*, and *Not by Bread Alone*, seem to me to be an exploration of Naomi Mitchison's ambivalent feelings about science, technology, and the nature of progress.

First, let me give some background. Naomi Mitchison was born in Edinburgh in 1897. Her first novel, *The Conquered*, was published in 1923. Since then she has written more than seventy books—historical fiction, science fiction, folklore and mythology, poetry, short stories, diaries, memoirs, and travel books. She spent much of her childhood, as she describes in her memoirs, writing poetry, writing and performing in plays, and making up lengthy stories in her head. At the same time, she was in and out of her father's laboratory, drinking in the feeling of "scientific excitement" that, as she says, "came through most to my brother with a small spill-over to me" (*As It Was* 123).[2]

Her father, John Scott Haldane, was a physiologist and philosopher, an expert on gases and respiration. Before the First World War he was a gas referee and regularly went down mines and sewers to check on their safety. Later, when the war broke out, he and his colleagues produced from their laboratory in Oxford the first effective gas masks to be used at the frontlines. Mitchison's uncle was a physiologist and Regius Professor at Oxford, and her brother Jack—J. B. S. Haldane— was to become a leading scientist.

Naomi Mitchison's assessment of her own scientific capabilities has always been, and remains, modest. Surrounded by scientific experimentation, she felt that she was too imaginative and too irrational to become a scientist. And, of course, she was a girl. In the early years of the century, before the massive social changes brought about by the First World War, a girl with her upper-middle-class background was destined for one thing: to become a lady. The Haldanes, however, were a liberal-progressive family and Naomi's education into ladyhood was fitful. She was sent, like her brother, to the Dragon School at Oxford, where she was the only girl. But while Jack went on to Eton, Naomi was hastily removed from school when her periods started, and then shared, with a few other girls from academic families, a governess at home.

"Did I ever become educated?" she asks. "If so, only accidentally and occasionally, with a few questions filled in during odd times in the lab, or perhaps talking with distinguished guests. I suppose it was in late 1913 or early 1914 that I sat 'Locals' in some Oxford public building. I'm not sure what they corresponded to, and have an idea that there were Junior and Senior, the latter being equivalent to university entrance. The standard, especially perhaps in science, was clearly much lower than today. I don't recollect being worried by these exams or even doing any hard work, in fact all I remember is a very easy Botany paper, with a specimen flower to dissect and label. It had two small green caterpillars inside it, which I made race across my desk" (*All Change Here* 91).

Racing caterpillars or no, from an early age Naomi Mitchison kept diaries that show a close scientific observation of natural phenomena. Here she is at eight years old, in the Kyles of Bute in Scotland, where her father was conducting deep diving experiments for the Admiralty: "we went to the beach and watched the barnacles opening and shutting their shells; a barnacle opens with slits like this" [here a little pencil drawing of a barnacle]. "When it opens it puts out a little brown arm and sweeps the water in and gets food from the water" (*As It Was* 119). For a child who felt she wasn't really cut out to be a scientist, who felt she only got a "small spill-over" of the scientific excitement, she was impressive.

As a teenager, she and her brother did some serious work on genetics on guinea pigs. This necessitated performing postmortems on

females that died during pregnancy, to look at the coloring of the unborn litter. They saw the results were not working out as they should
have along expected Mendelian lines. She says, "We had in fact happened on what was then called linkage and later cross-over, but as nobody had yet got on to the chromosome structure it was very puzzling"
(*All Change Here* 62). She kept up her work on the guinea pigs for some
years (and genetics plays an important part in all her science fiction
novels), taking them to London with her in 1915 when she went to
St. Thomas's Hospital as a VAD nurse, and having to dash out at nurses'
dinner time—"before the pudding, which was no great loss" (*All Change
Here* 125)—to visit them.

In fact, Naomi Mitchison's formal education didn't end with her
hasty removal from the Dragon School. She became a home student
at Oxford, at what was later to become one of the women's colleges,
St. Anne's. But then the war, marriage, babies, writing, and, increasingly, politics intervened. These years, from 1920 to the Second World
War, are documented in her third volume of memoirs, *You May Well
Ask*. She became active in the Labor Party and increasingly interested
in the position of women and in matters of sexuality. In 1918 she read
Marie Stopes's best-selling and enormously influential *Married Love*, and
she became involved in the early birth control movement, helping to
found the North Kensington Birth Control Clinic.

In 1939 she and her family moved to Carradale House in Kintyre,
in the west of Scotland. This was the beginning of her close identification with the aspirations of the Scottish people for self-government.
For twenty years after the Second World War, she was a member of
the Argyll County Council and, for ten years after that, a member of
the Highlands and Islands Advisory Council. Since the early 1960s,
she has had close links with Botswana, through the chief of the Bakgatla
tribe, Linchwe II. She was adopted into the tribe and has spent time
with them every year since.

Perhaps had Naomi Mitchison been born a boy she would have
become, like her brother Jack, a distinguished scientist. But becoming
a scientist was not really an option for English upper-middle-class
women in the early years of the century. Or perhaps it wasn't just her
gender that stopped her following that path: it is just as likely that it
was her unruly imagination and her passion for storytelling and writing that disallowed it. As she said in 1985, in a biographical introduc-

tion to her science fiction short story "Words": "I have always hung around on the edge of science, but could never have made a good scientist because my imagination has always been too wild. Scientists need imagination, but not as something overwhelming as it must be for a writer" (*Despatches from the Frontiers of the Female Mind* 164).

Naomi Mitchison's fusion of a sympathetic imagination with a scientist's capacity for detailed observation has produced some fascinating work, including the diaries she kept for the social research organization "Mass-Observation" during the years of the Second World War. She is perhaps best known for her historical novels, especially *The Corn King and the Spring Queen* (first published in 1931), and her mythological novels, such as *Travel Light* (1952) and *Early in Orcadia*, (1987), novels made memorable by the mixture of detailed research with free-ranging imaginative sympathy. But she has kept coming back to science and scientific research. Her role, as she sees it, is a modest one: "to doodle on the edge of the pages of *Nature*" (*Despatches* 164).

That spillover of excitement remains: scientific endeavor, the reader is made to feel, is exciting. But the human element is all-important, and if scientists fail to recognize that, then science becomes dangerous. In *Solution Three* she explores that area of danger.

The future world of Naomi Mitchison's *Solution Three* is an odd mix of science, religion, and social planning. The world is run by a group of Councillors who see themselves as holding everything in trust for the cloned children of Her and Him, two historical figures around whom Godness has accreted, who set up the first Council and who initiated the solutions to global problems that have led to what is now called "Solution Three."

The Solution Three of the title of the novel is a political and social answer to the problems of human overpopulation and food underproduction. A scientific response, imposed with the backing of heavy ideological and religious conditioning, its purpose is to eliminate chance in the affairs of the world. Crops and plants are genetically manipulated to produce high yields; and, while genetic engineering on humans is banned by the Code initiated by Her and Him, cloning (which, rather oddly, perhaps, is not considered to be genetic engineering) regulates population levels and, as importantly, regulates human "quality" and behavior. The Clone children, being sons and daughters of the two gods, are as perfect as the gods themselves.

There is no place in this perfectly planned world for sexual reproduction, with its cell divisions, reassortments of genes and resultant unpredictable mix of chromosomal material (the crossover that
Naomi Mitchison had spotted in her guinea pigs many years before).
The processes of sexual reproduction are named as sinful and are
labeled in a suitably scientific fashion: sexual reproduction is called
the sin of meiosis.

To combat sinful desires, the authorities use another strategy
alongside the ideology of Clone perfection: homosexual relationships
are not just validated over heterosexual ones but are positively obliga-
tory. This is a world of compulsory homosexuality.

But already, in this world on the brink of a perfect future, there
are contradictions. One group of people, who are resistant to compulsory homosexuality, insist not just on having heterosexual relationships,
but also on getting married and, worst of all, producing children. These
are the Professorials, the scientists on whom the Councillors are dependent for all the genetic engineering done on plants and crops, and
also, although this is not stated, presumably in charge of the cloning
from Her and Him. During the course of the novel, further contradictions are revealed, and doubts about the possibility, and the desirabil-
ity, of perfection through planning begin to flower in the minds of
various characters.

The Professorials whom we meet are a husband-and-wife team,
Miryam and Carlo, both plant geneticists, who have two small children. Being "deviants" (this is how they are referred to by the Councillors) they are socially disprivileged: given poor housing and refused
access to amenities open to 'normal' people. They are resigned to their
low social status, rather than rebellious. In the opening stages of the
novel, Miryam is being called upon to investigate reports of crops being afflicted by previously unknown blights and diseases in different
parts of the world.

During the course of the novel, the diseases afflicting the plants
become more widespread, and the dangers of genetic manipulation begin to be realized. At the same time, new growth appears on what
seemed to be dead plants. The Councillors and Professorials begin to
see that not everything can be planned for, and, as importantly, that
not everything can be explained. Parallel to this ideological opening
up, the characters, too, begin to shake off their fetters. All sorts of new

personal discoveries are made. Miryam and Carlo remain a devoted couple, but Miryam realizes that she can feel sexually attracted to women as well as to men. Mutumba, the convenor of the Council, begins to question the very basis of Solution Three, wondering whether "a kind of excellence which exactly fitted a certain epoch might, soon or late, need certain alterations" (153). The authoritarian Jussie, who has been in charge of the Clone Mums, learns tolerance for others. A Clone girl and boy, Anni and Kid, fall in love and even hesitantly speculate about having children, who would be, of course, "kind of jumbled" (124).

Cracks appear in the Councillors' utopian vision right from the beginning: the stubborn deviancy of the Professorials, inexplicable crop failure, outbreaks of violence in "underdeveloped" parts of the world. By the end of the novel these cracks have begun to be accepted as the material signs of time, change, and chance that preclude the possibility of a perfect, static society. The Councillors' concept of utopia is shown to be antievolutionary: an impossibility.

I think it is worth looking in some detail at Mitchison's portrayal of sexuality in this novel. It is primarily through their sexual behavior that we see the characters in the novel as individuals (more so, indeed, than is the case with the work of the feminist writers of the 1970s mentioned earlier). The changes that take place during the course of the novel, especially the reassessment of the value of Solution Three, have marked effects on the sexual self-evaluation of most of the characters. Homosexuality and cloning are an integral part of Solution Three; but is the novel suggesting that homosexuality is unworkable, or that any official imposition of sexual orientation and practice is a danger?

In the very first scene (the novel moves from scene to scene; the characters appear in short sequences and there is little sustained psychological internalizing or development) the Council has been convened to discuss how the population policy and the Code, as set out by Him and Her, are working in various parts of the world. After the main business of the meeting is over, the conversation drifts to the question of the Professorials and their deviancy. Jussie admits to her colleague Ric, a historian, that she finds them difficult to understand.

> "You mean their hetero-sexuality?" Ric said it bravely, for it was really rather an unpleasant word.

Jussie nodded. "You see, it means—oh dear, not so much the men, perhaps, but a woman actually admiring, touching, being touched by—so disordered."

"It happened in history," said Ric soberly, "and not so far back either, before Solution Three, the great step in human self-knowledge and control." But why be so pompous! "You must have read about it."

"I hate reading about it—these dreadful external sex organs!" said Jussie, and then, "Oh Ric, I do apologize, I never think of you as a male, but I suppose you're bound to have them."

"I know, I know," said Ric soothingly, "but there are bits of you that flop, Jussie, if you don't mind my saying so." (14)

Bits that flop. Unpleasant words that have to be said bravely. This is preadolescent, yet these people are Councillors, rulers of the world. They are terrified of the flesh, of bodies, but they can hardly think about anything else, it seems. Just after this conversation, Elissa comes over to them to show off a new spray-on costume she is wearing. Ric finds her "just a little repulsive, as after all, women normally were," while Jussie pulls her down onto the chair she is sitting on. "Elissa responded with a quick hand between Jussie's legs, but just as a greeting" (15). I find this jarring, and am not sure how to interpret it. Is it meant to satirize conventional heterosexual behavior? Or are the Councillors simply oversexed?

The Councillors, the Clone Mums and the Clones themselves have all been conditioned into homosexuality. And they're at it the whole time. But the deviants, represented by Miryam and her husband Carl, seem to have no sex life at all, except that their two children prove that they do (or, at least, that they did). One might read this lack of sex as a reflection on the invisibility of homosexuality in contemporary culture. But in the novel the sexuality of the "deviants" is not invisible; rather, it is not addressed.

Other issues around heterosexuality are raised, but not necessarily followed through. For instance, a link between heterosexual behavior and aggression is suggested, and this is offered as a further reason for stamping out heterosexuality, for the Code preaches nonaggression and nonviolence. In some out-of-the-way places around the world, the Code has not been fully implemented. The peoples there indulge in both heterosexuality and aggression. Indeed, Elissa is caught up in an outbreak of violence and is killed, as was, we discover, the Clone daughter of Mutumba. But the link is not explored in depth, and the question is left unanswered at the end of the novel when heterosexuality appears to be vindicated.

All relationships (except those of the "deviants") are sexualized: not just the Councillors, but the Clone Mums and the Clones as well. The Clone Mums live in a garden of Eden, proudly pregnant and indulging in playful sex under the flowering bushes. The sex here, I find, is not very convincing. But then I was never convinced by the children playing happy sexual games in the garden in Marge Piercy's *Woman on the Edge of Time*.

But, as with the Councillors, and with the Clones, who are so clean-living that you really can't imagine they have bodily juices at all, the expression of sexuality between the Clone Mums is not really the issue at all. Instead, at issue is the conflict between self and society, or individual and authority, or even human nature and social planning. There are rebels everywhere, and it is the rebels who are in touch with unpalatable truths.

We see two Clone Mums in the gardens: Gisela, who is not very bright (but very pretty) and her lover Lilac, who is a questioner and a rebel. The Clone Mums are all mothers of God, with babies who are "lent" to them rather than belonging to them. Surrogate mothers, brood mares, and they are, as might be expected, viewed with condescension both by the Councillors and by the Professorials. Lilac asserts her individuality right from the start by arranging her little boy's hair in a different style from all the other little boys. Since she has become a Clone Mum, she has had dreams of aggression, of killing, and finds that, horrible and disturbing though they are, she isn't sure that she would rather not have them. Of all the characters in the novel she is the one who seems most closely in touch with her unconscious. Naomi Mitchison writes well about women and children, with passion and subtlety. Lilac's attempts to hide her boy's development from the prying eyes of Jussie, to delay his separation from her, are very moving. But he is taken from her. "He was mine," said Lilac. "Fed on my milk. My little mammal, my own" (95). Lilac defines the world she lives in as a police state, with the Clones and Clone Mums as victims of the oppressive watchers and carers. Lilac dreams of a different life for her baby boy.

Thus a well-intentioned utopia becomes a dystopia through the denial of difference. If you wish to progress, if you wish to avoid the mistakes of the past, do you have to revise the past? Do you have to rearrange the evidence, which is what Ric admits he is doing with his historical researches? Like Miryam and Carlo, rearranging the genes of crops and plants and flowers, so that the yield will be the same the world over? Like the Councillors, with their perfect boys and girls, all exactly the same?

Rather than satirizing the social construction of heterosexuality, Naomi Mitchison is asking the larger question of whether it is possible for human society to progress toward a utopian state. She is questioning the very possibility of the existence of utopia and asking at what cost such a progress is achieved. The answer is metaphysical: at the cost of truth.

While Lilac is open to what her dreams, her body, and her intellect tell her, the Professorials are involved in and recognize the consequences of the denial of difference. They are the first to see what is going wrong with the carefully cultivated fruit trees and wheats. They experience the difficulties of heterosexual relations. Heterosexuality is validated here, not because it is disprivileged (one of the reasons why it would be in a role-reversal novel), but because it is shown as embracing difference.

What, then, does this say about homosexual relationships? Is the general attitude of the novel homophobic? I think not. But it is confusing because, while the novel is not actually about sexual orientation or sexual identity, all the sexual activity is foregrounded. Mitchison is not making value judgments about sexuality. This might be the reason that she doesn't attempt to write about heterosexual sex: she doesn't want to celebrate it at the expense of other modes of sexuality, although she is, in a general sense, celebrating diversity.[3]

When, finally, the Councillors see the error of their ways, it is the heterosexual Miryam (who has discovered that she is also sexually attracted to the Clone girl Jean) and the lesbian Lilac, who are rewarded: Miryam, rather sweetly, with a decent flat that has always been denied to her before, overlooking a rose garden, and with the hope that her children—non-Clone though they are—will not be outcasts; and the questioning Lilac with the opportunity to research the influence of maternal cytoplasm on the developing embryo (and *there's* a wild card) and a loving relationship with Jussie, her erstwhile warder.

Consequently, I think Mitchison is using sexual orientation as a metaphor for the scientific and metaphysical issues that interest her. Homosexuality is an offshoot of the cloning policy, and the cloning policy is an attempt to create gods, to achieve infallibility and immutability in human form. If the scientific sin in this society is meiosis, then the human sin is knowledge of self, and its corollary, knowledge of difference. As Gisela thinks about being a Clone Mum: "You wouldn't want to mix your own poor little self up with it" (38). But Lilac does. Not everyone wants to be the mother of God.

The depiction of sexual organization in *Solution Three* raises more questions than it attempts to answer. Why, for example, does conditioning work on some people and not on others? Why are the Professorials deviants? What is the link, if any, between aggression and sexual orientation? How do the Councillors, or for that matter anyone apart from the Clones, deal with their own personal histories, the fact that they are products of heterosexual parents? One must assume this last, although there is no mention at all of anyone's parents, no personal or social history. The same could be said of Sally Miller Gearhart's *The Wanderground*, or even of Joanna Russ's *The Female Man* (although not of Marge Piercy's *Woman on the Edge of Time*, where both are richly detailed, as is the same with Suzy McKee Charnas's work). But in all those the implications of a different sexual organization are explored in depth: what if women were free from the authority of men? How might people live outside the conventional sexual hierarchy? How might relationships between women, and between women and men, be different? But in *Solution Three* these are not the points at issue. The sexual organization is symbolic of other matters. It is not, finally, of fundamental interest in itself.

The interest lies in the hard science, the work on plant cells and genetic engineering, and it is this that gives the novel its structure. As reports come in from various parts of the world about diseases that are afflicting the trees and crops, questions are raised about playing god with nature. What do you lose by planning for the best? Do you lose protection against previously unseen viruses? If there is no mixed gene pool to fall back on, might this not be a course heading for destruction? Can nature, human or vegetable, be planned and constrained?

And at what cost? In *Not By Bread Alone* Naomi Mitchison concentrates on these questions. Here, they are extrapolated into questions about human behavior. And the problem with extrapolating from scientific issues to human behavior is surely that the latter is too wild, too complicated by consciousness and knowledge for parallels to be drawn. This, I think, is why it is unsatisfactory to read *Solution Three* alongside the other feminist novels of the 1970s. There, the nature of sexuality and sexual identities is seen as absolutely fundamental to the ordering of society. Here, it is not. To try to read *Solution Three* as a sexual-identity role-reversal novel is to put mistaken emphasis on the sexual elements. This novel finally offers no solution, neither one, nor two, nor three. *Solution Three* is not a polemical novel, but a gentle novel that encourages questioning, that ends with the realization that, as Jussie says, "there are many kinds of happiness" (160), a rose garden being one of them.

11

"There Goes the Neighborhood"
Octavia Butler's Demand for Diversity in Utopias

Michelle Erica Green

O ctavia E. Butler's *Dawn*, the first novel in the trilogy *Xenogenesis*, is an angry utopian novel, a scathing condemnation of the tendency of human beings to hate, repress, and attack differences they do not understand. It pleads for an end to fear and prejudice, insisting that aggressive social intervention must counteract the ancient hierarchical structures of thought that humans share with their closest animal relatives. The illustration on the jacket sleeve of *Dawn* ironically emphasizes Butler's cause for anger. Though the novel clearly identifies its heroine, Lilith Iyapo, as a muscular black woman in her late twenties (*Xenogenesis* 11, 13), the cover depicts a slender white girl apprehensively unwrapping what looks like a blanket from the body of a naked white woman. The girl is Lilith, here young, fair-skinned and delicate, peering shyly at the first potential friend she has had in years because she cannot look with eagerness at naked woman. Following Audre Lorde's description of the role of difference within a capitalist economy, the mass-market paperback industry thus puts its desire to reap profits from off-the-shelf sales of *Dawn* over the demands of the novel itself. In redrawing Lilith as a modest white girl rather than the powerful black heroine her creator described, the publishing industry allows forms of sexism, racism, ageism, and homophobia to be perpetuated on the cover of a novel that demands an end to prejudices and acceptance of differences.

I want to look closely at Butler's fiction and the criticism it directs at popular discourse, particularly at science fiction utopias created by recent feminist writers. I also want to consider the transformation of the utopian form when a writer such as Butler, who challenges various forms of cultural hegemony, adapts it for the purposes of social critique. Several of Butler's critics label her work "essentialist"—a term often used pejoratively by poststructuralist feminists to attack biologically based models of human behavior—because of her insistence that humans will behave inhumanely without a series of checks upon them.[1] But Butler's "essentialism" is tricky; her novels focus on the exceptions to the rules she posits as human norms rather than on those who exemplify them.

Many recent women's utopias deal with contemporary problems by defusing the differences that cause conflicts to develop among people. Joanna Russ and Ursula Le Guin experiment with biological androgyny as a means for ending the battle of the sexes. Marge Piercy and Melissa Scott explore futures in which skin color and racial identity are unrelated. Sheri Tepper unites all people under one religion, while Suzy McKee Charnas erases political struggles under a classless anarchy. Feminist utopias of the past twenty years have launched a powerful attack on the ideologies, practices, and textual strategies of the patriarchy, which their authors posit as the principal source of the rejection of differences. Some texts, like Le Guin's *Left Hand of Darkness* and Scott's *Kindly Ones*, have done so by rejecting the binary construction of sexuality, insisting that the gender-defining characteristics of males and females are socially rather than biologically based. Others, like Cynthia Felice's *Double Nocturne* and Pamela Sargent's *Shore of Women*, have rescripted gender relations with the assumption that, even if men and women are fundamentally different, those differences need not lead to the oppression of women under patriarchy. By refusing to allow women to be posited as Other in a binary social and conceptual system, these and many additional novels defamiliarize patriarchy, calling for a world in which men and women can benefit rather than suffer from one another's differences.[2]

Yet many of the texts that challenge the gender status quo ignore, erase, and repress other differences among people. Though Mattapoisett—the utopia in Piercy's *Woman on the Edge of Time*—

nurtures people of many different ages, races, ethnic groups, sexual orientations, and interests, the differences among them seem only skin-deep. Some people have Southeast Asian features without any sense of Southeast Asian heritage, while others participate in Jewish religious services without any connection to the thousands of years of Jewish culture that preceded the founding of Mattapoisett. Again, in Charnas's *Motherlines*, because of the emphasis on the vast gulf between the genders, little attention is paid to the material differences between the women protagonists, who at times seem interchangeable. In *The Left Hand of Darkness*, neither race nor sexual preference operate as conceptual categories; if they exist at all, they pass unnoticed. Thus, despite their insistence that patriarchy can be overcome, relatively few utopian feminists seem able or willing to tackle even their own tendency to ignore, erase, and oppress human difference.

This tendency is the focus of Butler's critique of both human society and recent utopian fiction. Difference, disagreement, and diversity provide the life force of her utopias. Though the need to rethink women's roles in human society is a central concern, it is by no means the only problem attacked by Butler. Racism, class oppression, nationalism, religious intolerance, homophobia, and mistreatment of animals and handicapped people are all touched upon in Butler's critique of humanism—itself a form of prejudice here, for "humanism" accepts that human beings should be at the center of their own universes. Butler refuses to categorize people through biology, behavior or even species, demanding new solutions cultivated through a community based on differences. And just as Butler insists upon differences among people, she insists upon differences among utopias. Her work implicitly criticizes utopias by women that avoid conflicts stemming from difference and reject challenges and change from within. Her social critique resembles that of another feminist African-American, Audre Lorde, who writes, "In a society where good is defined in terms of profit rather than in terms of human need, there must always be some group of people who, through systematized oppression, can be made to feel surplus, to occupy the place of the dehumanized inferior. . . . Institutionalized rejection of difference is an absolute necessity in a profit economy which needs outsiders as surplus people. As members of such an economy, we have *all* been programmed to respond to the human differences between us with fear and loathing. The future of our earth may depend upon the ability . . . to identify and develop new definitions of power and new patterns of relating across difference. The old definitions have not served us, nor the earth that supports us. The old patterns, no matter how cleverly rearranged to imitate progress, still condemn us to cosmetically altered repetitions of the same old exchanges, the same old guilt, hatred, recrimination, lamentation, and suspicion" (*Sister Outsider* 115, 123). Expanding on Lorde's critique of capitalist society, Butler blames not only human greed for the creation of prejudice, but also the deep-rooted human compulsion to structure societies and thoughts hierarchically. Butler's fictions contain an oft-repeating warning that the human race has long been in the process of destroying itself—a warning that leads several critics to label her work dystopian rather than utopian. Butler's characters often do seem to be living in a nightmare rather than an ideal society; they find themselves trapped among aliens, powerless, angry, and frightened. All of them face the same dilemma: they must force themselves to evolve, accepting differences and rejecting a world view that centers upon their lives and values, or become extinct. In the Patternist books, the *Xenogenesis* trilogy, and "Bloodchild," such evolution requires pan-human acceptance of alien ideas and values, leading to a merger with the aliens to create a new form of life. In *Kindred*, "Speech Sounds" and "The Evening and the Morning and the Night," evolution involves one group of humans accepting "alien" ideas and values from another group of humans, taking personal responsibility for transforming themselves and the species.

Miscegenation: Bloodchild and Patternist Series

Octavia Butler once told an interviewer that she did not write utopian fiction: "I don't believe that imperfect humans can form a perfect society" (Beal 14). But, as any number of texts from Thomas More's prototype onward have indicated, a utopia does not have to be a "perfect" society. "Utopia" is a Greek pun that can be read as "nowhere" (*utopia*) or "good place" (*eutopia*); literary utopias engage the paradox between these two meanings, straddling issues of locality, textuality, and ideology in an attempt to bridge the gap between fictional discourse and everyday life. Thus the utopian form is already a miscegenation of sorts, a blending of pragmatic local concerns with transcendent idealism. For women, utopian fiction permits reimaginings of worlds without patriarchy, without biology-based notions of gender, even without men—all within the context of a critique of contemporary politics. As critic Jean Pfaelzer notes, the question "What if the world were perfect?" is not the same as "What if the world were feminist?" ("The Changing" 291).

The latter question seems to interest Butler more than the former, for her utopias are certainly far from perfect. "The Evening and the Morning and the Night" relates the events that follow a "cure" for cancer that turns lethal; *Clay's Ark*, the last of the Patternist books, tells of the catastrophic spread of an extraterrestrial virus that transforms human genetics; *Dawn*, the first book of *Xenogenesis*, begins shortly after the earth has been rendered uninhabitable by a nuclear war. Butler's worlds often seem far from feminist as well: few possess egalitarian social structures or communities of women; none has eradicated rape, incest, or compulsory heterosexuality; and the females who inhabit those worlds often rely on threats, coercion, and violence to achieve their own ends. As Dorothy Allison observes, Butler's female characters must "heroically adjust to family life and through example, largeness of spirit, and resistance to domination make the lives of their children better—even though this means sacrificing personal freedom" (472).

Both the utopianism and the feminism of Butler's work are slippery because neither emerges in isolation from a variety of other interests. Butler is not interested in creating a utopia of human beings who seem too gentle to be believed, like those who inhabit Piercy's Mattapoisett and never get into fistfights; nor is she interested in glorifying either women or some abstract notion of the feminine. In fact, despite her insistence that human beings can transform themselves and their world, Butler often seems not to like people—men *or* women—at all. Her works border on the dystopian because she insists on confronting problems that have occurred so often in human communities that they seem almost an unavoidable part of human nature, such as greed, prejudices based on appearances, oppression of women, and might-makes-right ideologies. Rather than create utopias in which these problems have simply ceased to exist, Butler demonstrates time and again in her fiction that they must be worked through—even if that process involves the use of dangerous human tendencies like aggression and coercion to counter similar dangerous human tendencies like violence.

Both "Bloodchild" and the *Xenogenesis* books have one explicitly feminist project: to make male characters experience sex and reproduction from the position of females in male-dominated culture.

"Bloodchild," which offers a very short glimpse at a fascinating world, reflects on the extent to which patriarchal cultures find it necessary to use ideology, violence, and oppression to force women to participate in "natural" reproduction.[3] In "Bloodchild," men get pregnant, an ironic twist on a slogan made popular by supporters of abortion rights: "If men could get pregnant, abortion would be a sacrament." In "Bloodchild," an alien race called Tlic require the bodies of healthy young men in which to incubate their eggs. When the eggs hatch inside the men's bodies, the aliens cut the men open to remove the alien grubs.

Although the Tlic attempt to make the process bearable for the men by incorporating them into nuclear families and creating an ideology of spousal love to persuade the men that their participation is voluntary and beneficial, the human male narrator stresses that the men—or, as in his own case, boys—may be "raped," impregnated against their wills, and forced to carry to term fetuses that have never been a part of themselves if they do not submit.

Tlic society is hierarchical, with fertile females possessing the most power—which they use to compete, sometimes violently, for human males. The Tlic who will mate with the narrator is particularly important; she is in charge of the Preserve, the human dwelling on the Tlic planet (an animal farm, ghetto, Native American resettlement, and Nazi concentration camp all at once). As such, she is both protector and pimp. "Only she and her political faction stood between us and the horded who did not understand why there was a Preserve—why any Terran could not be courted, paid, drafted, in some way made available to them. She parceled us out to the desperate and sold us to the rich and powerful for their political support" (195). Despite the fact that they are all female, the adult Tlic employ many of the ideologies and practices of patriarchalism: compulsory heterosexuality, reproductive colonization, marital rape, and oppression of the childbearing sex, to name the most deadly. For, like childbirth, Tlic deliveries can be lethal to humans; if the grubs are not removed at the right moment, by the right Tlic, the infants devour their hosts from the inside out.

Though the interference of the aliens has brought about an end to the struggle between the sexes, human women are as subject to Tlic oppression as men; they are not used as Tlic breeders only because bearing Tlic young leaves them too weak to bear the next generation of humans to carry a subsequent generation of Tlic. Familial relationships are quasi-incestuous. The narrator, Gan, and the Tlic whose children he will carry, T'Gatoi, are both children of the same father, whose sperm produced Gan and whose belly carried T'Gatoi. Gan's mother, who is many years younger than his father, grew up with T'Gatoi as a sort of sister; T'Gatoi has thus served as sister and aunt to her future spouse, and has been a second mother to him as well. Gan's relationship to her is laden with Oedipal conflict—he is grateful that he can stroke her as he cannot caress his mother, but feels revulsion and horror at the thought of their eventual mating—and T'Gatoi's desire for him, expressed alternately through parental and romantic clichés, smacks of pederasty. Under Tlic ideology, biology is destiny; none of the beings involved in a human-Tlic mating perceives an alternative.

"Bloodchild" hardly seems a feminist fantasy. It is impossible to perceive the planet of the Tlic as a radical utopia that empowers women, like Joanna Russ's Whileaway in *The Female Man*; Butler's human women are as oppressed as her men, and her female Tlic begin to act like human male oppressors. But "Bloodchild" is neither dystopian nor essentialistic.[4] The circumstances that oppress the narrator do not stem from any metaphysical imperative; they are not historically inevitable, and therefore can be altered. The "biology" that complicates human-Tlic relationships is neither transparent nor predictable. The traits of human and Tlic nature that have placed Gan and T'Gatoi in the perverse relationship they negotiate are not "essential"; they are constructed out of social and material conditions that result in the appalling crisis at the start of the story—the Tlic have changed themselves and the humans before, and can do so again.

More important, Gan's human agency begins a process of reform that may lead to Tlic recognition of the subjectivity of all humans. Gan does not believe or expect that an ideal space of perfect equality can be created, given the material difficulties of life on the Tlic world for humans and Tlic; he does, however, insist on new social structures with the potential for ongoing evolution. Butler's insistence on maintaining a closed family structure, which Haraway and Zaki criticize as a sign of her "conservatism" in sexual matters (Haraway 378; Zaki 244), serves as her means of emphasizing the vital need for collaboration underlying both the Tlic-human and the male-female relationships of the story; the future of both depends on a joint solution, with mutual extinction the only alternative.

Butler might have chosen to transform reader expectations about "normal" gender behavior by demonstrating how natural giving birth seems to human men, rather than how unnatural. Yet if Butler truly believed that human biology makes rape, compulsory heterosexuality, and enforced childbirth inevitable, she would have no motivation for writing "Bloodchild" in the first place. Like the circumstances of Gan's oppression, the production of the story must be situated within a historical framework. Butler published "Bloodchild" during a year when controversies over abortion, in-vitro fertilization, and the prevalence of unnecessary caesarean sections—topics cloaked in the metaphors of the story—reached a peak. 1984 also witnessed a political campaign characterized by the polarization of complex constitutional issues into monolithic positions: school prayer versus religious freedom, welfare abuse versus urban poverty, "pro-life" versus "pro-choice," apartheid versus sanctions. Rather than accepting such binaries, which lead neither to productive debate nor to a synthesized answer, Butler insists that individuals consider what is left out of such formulations. The social problems of "Bloodchild" cannot be broken down into anything so simple as "Tlic versus humans" or "female versus male." The fundamental problem stems from the need for cooperation rather than binarism—and accompanying hierarchialism—to structure an imperfect but just society.[5]

This problem creates the crux of the Patternmaster novels as well. The last book of the series, *Clay's Ark*, constitutes the beginning of a history played out in the earlier volumes. A man returns to earth from a distant galaxy, inadvertently carrying a disease organism that begins the transformation of the human race. "The organisms were not intelligent. They could not tell him how to keep himself alive, free, and able to find new hosts. But they became intensely uncomfortable if he did not, and their discomfort was his discomfort" (*Clay's Ark* 29). The organisms invade and recode human DNA, threatening the lives of their hosts if they are not transmitted to other humans. Because transmission requires the breaking of the skin of the uninfected person, the organisms trigger violent behavior and overwhelming lust. The children of the inevitable sexual couplings between infected individuals are not human; they look like catlike, graceful "animals" (60) and mature rapidly into highly intelligent quadrupeds with superhuman senses of smell and hearing. Resistance to the organism's need to spread, which is impossible except in the case of isolated individuals, ensures physical and mental anguish culminating in death.

Clay's Ark—the least utopian of the Patternist books—presents three recently infected individuals attempting to maintain their "humanity," which in this context signifies their control over biological drives. Blake Maslin, a doctor, believes physical strength and medical technology can prevent the disease's spread; his beautiful and brilliant daughter Rane relies instead on mental willpower and morality. Both try to escape the consequences of the disease, refusing to adapt to the physical and psychological changes it demands, and both ultimately lose their lives in the struggle. Only the younger daughter, Keira, who was wasting away with leukemia before surrendering to the new disease, survives. In progressing toward death, she has already begun to transform into something "ethereal not quite of this world," with a vastly different physiology and psychology from her father and sister. Keira survives because she takes the step neither her father nor sister is willing to take: she bonds with the disease and its carriers, willingly accepting the inevitability of the changes necessitated by the organism. Such evolution represents the only possibility for saving Keira's life, for the recently invented epigenetic therapy, a process that has all but eradicated leukemia by reprogramming faulty genes, has failed to correct her cells. Keira may have less of a stake in "protecting" human biology because her own biology has never been normatively human; she has less of a stake in protecting human morality because, unlike her sister Rane, she understands it as a utilitarian construct that can be discarded when its social value ceases to function.[6]

The humans "lose" to the organism and to another group of humans carrying a different mutation. The species divides into three competing groups. The self-destructive, telepathic "Patternists," bred by the ancient patriarch Doro for their psychic skills, develop from victims to oppressors in their struggle against nontelepathic humans and "Clayarks" (the descendants of the characters in Clay's Ark). Telepaths treat the nonpsychic humans as an inferior race, referring to them by the denigrating label "mute."[7] The nomadic Clayarks, considered nonhuman by the others, are despised and shunned as carriers of the terrifying disease. The Patternist novels share the interest in "Bloodchild" in the prevalence of patriarchy, tyranny, and slavery across many different human cultures. None offers a universal utopia, though several characters create utopian spaces within a primarily hostile world. In *Survivor*, Alanna resists deep prejudices to join an alien tribe; in *Mind of My Mind*, Mary becomes a tyrant with the hopes of singlehandedly achieving the peace and group survival her father Doro made impossible. In these books human nature again proves more flexible than some of the characters would like to admit. They cannot preserve an "essential humanity" in the face of mutation and disease; instead, they learn to recognize the extent to which human morality and even human biology are constructed through careful breeding and teaching, and can be changed a good deal.

Ex-communication: "Speech Sounds" and "The Evening and the Morning and the Night"

Donna Haraway writes: "[Competing stories of human evolution] have been bound together in a contentious discourse on technology, often staged in the high-technology media that embody the dream of communication promised by international science and global organization" (186). Having argued against claims for Butler's essentialism, I would like to turn to her two most "essentialistic" worlds, found in the acclaimed short stories "Speech Sounds" and "The Evening and the Morning and the Night." Both involve the destruction of "the dream of perfect communication promised by international science," to quote Haraway (186). Each of these fictions is set on earth and begins with a devastating disease that challenges human myths of control over their physical selves and destroys the capacity for traditional verbal expression among victims. Though the diseases are very different—the illness in "Speech Sounds" affects all people, while that in "The Evening and the Morning and the Night" afflicts only children of drug-damaged parents—both trigger acts of violence capable of destroying entire societies. Butler never explains whether the violence stems from the diseases themselves, or from the rage and terror felt by the diseased individuals whose bodies no longer respond to their commands, although the latter seems more likely. The stories thus concern methods for interpersonal contact when verbal communication fails, and when the possibility of life-threatening violence is just under the surface of all relationships. Although grounded in the biology of individual bodies, the problems that arise are primarily social in nature.

"Speech Sounds," set in California, follows a devastating world-wide epidemic that, though initially blamed on the Soviets, has no traceable cause or cure. The illness is "highly specific . . . language was always lost or severely impaired. . . . Often there was also paralysis, intellectual impairment, death" (203–4). Some victims abruptly lose the capacity to read and write; others can still read, but no longer speak; some can do neither, while others can do both but cannot remember what words mean. Of course, one immediate result is the breakdown of late capitalist civilization. The mass communications gone, the vast social apparatus rendered useless, people become like children cut off from parental discipline and love. They are forced instead to struggle for survival against armed criminals, suicidal thoughts, and jealous individuals who will kill for spite those who can speak, read, or write. The protagonist, Valerie Rye, has lost her husband and children to the disease; she can no longer read, write, or remember many things, and her ability to speak can put her life in danger if she demonstrates it in public. Maddened with illness, loneliness, and envy, she is overwhelmed at times with the desire to murder those who can still read; at other times she is overcome by the need for any nonviolent contact with any human being, willing to make love with a man she can never converse with.

Set in Los Angeles—a city where in the 1990s rival gangs fight territorial battles over who has the right to speak which language in which section—"Speech Sounds" reflects and explores the relationship between modes of communication and social structures. Like the biblical story of the Tower of Babel, Butler indicates that, deprived of the ability to share a primary language, individuals will leave off building their cities and wander into isolation. Certainly everyone in the story leaves off constructing skyscrapers and focuses on basic survival issues: scavenging for and growing food, finding shelter, establishing defenses against the robbers and rapists who patrol the streets. Although a large series of gestures to represent curses have sprung up, no real sign system has been developed. Violence is a universal language: people take what they can, keep what they defend, and destroy what they resent, without the need for debate or defensiveness.

The loss of speech is less the cause of social breakdown than the loss of literacy. The necessities for remaining alive have continued—food and fuels still circulate, transportation still runs between cities, and apparently firearms are still manufactured—but without the electronic media, capitalist society cannot function. It is in the process of reverting to feudalism when the story begins. "Speech Sounds" thus tells the tale of an extremely public society forced to "go private" without any warning. Without the printing press and descendant machines, the public sphere falls apart. Everything from government and law enforcement to scientific research and social aid ceases to function, leaving people to an anarchistic state where, although some of the machinery still functions, the superstructure that controls it does not. Society is at best vestigial. Soon the gas will run out, the cars will break down, groups sharing food and protection will begin to disintegrate, men will forget that rape was ever a crime.

Rye, the protagonist, thinks she is lonely because she is not a "private" person; she tells herself she needs people out of a biological need for communication, nurturing, and sex. But she is not a "private" person in a far more important sense: she depends upon a public sphere to satisfy her as a consumer. Not coincidentally, the man she links up with still wears the uniform of the Los Angeles Police Department. Rye finds this anachronism amusing because it reminds her of a little boy playing cop. But it also reminds her of the public life she had before the disease, and she longs for her lover—whom she calls Obsidian, having no way to ask his real name—to protect her, to take her places, to help her get to Pasadena where she may have relatives.

But Rye and Obsidian cannot go back; the world of instantaneous communication, across a room or across the globe, has been destroyed. Obsidian is shot for attempting to interfere in what would once have been called a "domestic disturbance." The police have minimal power because "domestic violence" is still considered a private matter in some areas, but Obsidian is still trapped in a code of ethics from the world before. Rye is as well. Despite her longing for her own lost nuclear family, she feels little sense of social obligation to the two children orphaned in the fight that killed Obsidian, as though she expects a social welfare agency to step in. "She did not need a stranger's children who would grow up to be hairless chimps" (210). But finally the desperateness of their situation reaches her; she realizes that if she does not take them with her, they will die, and she wants no more death on her hands. Then comes the greatest shock: the children can speak normally. Whether the disease has run its course or these two have a rare immunity, they can talk to her.

"Speech Sounds" are not the same thing as "speech"; they are less determinate. To those accustomed to a delimited sign system, speech sounds are crude and incoherent; in eighteenth- and nineteenth-century books on American slave and subaltern cultures, for example, the dialects spoken by the oppressed were assumed to be "speech sounds," not language. Butler's "Speech Sounds" ends with Rye contemplating what it will mean to be a teacher to the children—to educate them in the use of a skill that may no longer be of any use, that others will envy enough to murder them. What will she teach them? The value of the old language, or the need for a new mode of communication? The hierarchical difference between "speech" and "speech sounds," or the need for a common language between the verbal and the mute? The story ends before such questions can be resolved, but it ends on a hopeful note. Rye knows that, speech or no speech, the next generation will never bring back the world as it was. They will have to create instead a new public order, more diffuse in form and more accepting of difference than the old. They will have to be different.

The disease in "The Evening and the Morning and the Night" also leaves different children as the hope of the future. A late twentieth-century "wonder drug," which cures cancer and most viral diseases, causes a genetic disorder in all the descendants of every individual who uses it. The disorder, called DGD (Duryea-Gode disease), initially causes an inability to concentrate, then a psychotic retreat into fantasy; finally, it spurs horrific self-destructive and species-destructive behavior. The father of Lynn, the narrator, killed and skinned her mother completely before dying in an attempt to skin himself alive. This rending of the flesh—"digging out"—is common to all end-stage DGD victims; when they reach this point, they are locked away in exploitative DGD wards, usually chained up, but sometimes allowed to kill themselves if they prove too inventive in attacking their jailers. Although maintaining a medically supervised diet can put off the worst symptoms for several years, eventually the "digging" becomes inevitable. The only alternative to a horrible death in a DGD ward is an innovative private hospital called Dilg, which has a long waiting list. Dilg—named for the Dilg family, which made capital profits from the drug that caused DGD, and then funded research to cure it—also funds scholarships for DGD victims. Lynn is the recipient of such a scholarship. When she visits Dilg, she discovers that the reason has more to do with her biology than her scholarly ability: Lynn is the daughter of two parents with DGD, and as such carries pheremones that enable her to control violent DGD victims.

The Dilg retreat is Butler's strangest utopia, though in some ways her most successful. Under the guidance of "double-DGD" females, patients who would otherwise destroy themselves invent life-saving technology, produce brilliant artwork, and lead otherwise productive lives. Although most of the patients work in isolation because the illness makes collaboration impossible—particularly among members of the same sex—the Dilg community provides a space for education, productivity, and care while protecting DGD victims and their families from exploitation at the hands of high-priced private wards or mismanaged government institutions. The pheremones are both a blessing and a curse. Two females of double-DGD parentage cannot abide contact with one another; Lynn has to fight overpowering urges to inflict violence on Beatrice, the woman who explains Lynn's rare privilege to her. As Lynn acknowledges, she has little choice but to join Dilg, although the thought of spending the rest of her life "in something that was basically a refined DGD ward" does not appeal to her (301). She shares her lover's suspicion that Dilg's complete control over its patients could lead to exploitation, even though the supervisors are DGDs, too—people who have not yet developed end-stage symptoms. However, she sees little alternative for herself or for the violent victims men like her lover will inevitably become. "If the pheremone were something only men had, you would do it," she tells him.

Like the patients aboard *Clay's Ark*, the DGD sufferers subtly resemble AIDS victims. Butler portrays them as heroic, attempting to commit suicide or quarantine themselves to avoid injuring the healthy. As in the case of AIDS, some people angrily blame irresponsible sexuality for the spread of DGD: "The damned disease could be wiped out in one generation, but people are still animals when it comes to breeding. Still following mindless urges, like dogs and cats" (286). Although this sounds like essentialist rhetoric—"People are at the mercy of their biological urges"—it is important to note that the speaker has undergone voluntary sterilization, proving that biology does not have to be destiny. Lynn's response to his urging that she do the same is to insist on maintaining control of the one part of her biology functioning normally. "I don't want kids, but I don't want someone else telling me I can't have any. . . . [Would] you want someone else telling you what to do with your body?" she asks (285). The DGD victims also share some parallels with babies born addicted to crack. They suffer from specific motor and speech dysfunctions; some have never met their fathers for their own safety, while others have met only the brain-damaged ruin of their mothers; the "crimes" that cause prejudice against them are not their own.

Butler's appeal for victims' rights, however, shifts dramatically in light of her insistence that the disease may actually benefit society in the long run. Just as AIDS research has led to new discoveries about the immune system and provided valuable information in treating cancer, leukemia, and chronic viral infections, DGD produces highly intelligent individuals who devote their lives to improving life for others; the special value of double-DGD females was discovered by DGD victims, and their own laboratories represent the best hope for a cure. "The Evening and the Morning and the Night" would thus seem to offer the most essentialistic position yet in a Butler story, dividing humanity into the haves and the have-nots. But even here Butler demands diversity. The first half of the story focuses on the prejudice still-healthy DGD carriers suffer; although many of them have spectacular careers as scientists (ironically, DGD victims cure many forms of cancer), they are ignored or abused by uninformed and frightened associates. Lynn rooms at college with a DGD victim who becomes a special education major, hoping "the handicapped would accept her more readily than the able-bodied." They share a house with other DGD victims because they have "all had enough of being lepers twenty-four hours a day"(283).

As always, Butler subtly points out the multiethnicism of her character—Lynn is the child of two American fundamentalist Christians, while her lover Alan is half-American Catholic, half-Nigerian polytheistic. Butler also indicates that many of the scientists and doctors are female, black, or another minority. The disease itself trivializes most other forms of prejudice in a transformation similar to that caused by the presence of aliens in the Xenogenesis books.

Dilg is feminist by necessity; females simply handle certain aspects of the disease better than males. But never does Butler consider the possibility of having the females shun male society to protect their assets. In what appears to be a calculated attack on Russ's The Female Man and Charnas's Motherlines, Butler insists that sexual cooperation is absolutely vital; the segregation of the genders would be deadly for both. Women take on the roles of leader and nurturer not because they are innately more equipped to do so than men, but because the DGD pheremone coincidentally attaches itself to double-DGD females; as Lynn says, if men had the pheremone, they would take on the guidance positions. Women are certainly no less prone to violence than men. Next to Lynn's father, Alan's mother is the most violent character in "The Evening and the Morning and the Night."

Similar ideas about gender permeate "Speech Sounds," though the roles are reversed. Left-handed men suffer less brain damage than any other group. Rye kills people more easily than Obsidian. Biology thus is never destiny, even when it seems to be so. Even without the ability to read, Rye has a choice: she can work with people, attempting to create a new society, or become destructive like some of the people she witnesses. And Lynn has a similar choice: she can commit suicide, or live for the moment until the illness takes her, or she can work with Dilg to develop a haven and a cure. The characters in these two stories share some basic similarities, but their best chances for survival come from putting their differences to work.

Re-creation: Kindred

In an essay on fiction set in the antebellum South, Deborah E. McDowell writes: "Contemporary novels of slavery [witness] slavery after freedom in order to engrave that past on the memory of the present but, more importantly, on future generations that might otherwise succumb to the cultural amnesia that has begun to re-enslave us all in social and literary texts that impoverish our imaginations" (160–61).

Kindred, Butler's fantasy of time-travel into the past of her race and gender, engraves that past into the flesh of her heroine as well as her memory. *Kindred* is Butler's most troubling novel—yet also, in many ways, her most optimistic. The mechanism for the temporal shifts is never explained; this novel is not interested in alien sciences, and can scarcely be described as "science fiction." Rather, the "aliens" in *Kindred* are all too human. They are white Americans from the antebellum South, and they are more frightening than the Tlic. Dana, the black contemporary protagonist, unexpectedly finds herself transported to Maryland before the Civil War. Her great-great-grandfather Rufus calls her there to save his life, which she does several times. Rufus, much to Dana's shock, is not black; her grandmother never told her that not all of her ancestors were slaves.

Dana finds herself faced with a dilemma similar to those of Butler's other heroines: she must decide whether to collaborate with an oppressive agent that threatens her identity as a human being, or whether to cause her own extinction. *Kindred*'s particular situation requires that Dana cooperate with her white ancestors as they beat, rape, and murder her black ancestors; if she does not, her great-grandmother may never be born, and she may cease to exist. Rufus, who fathered this great-grandmother, closely resembles Dana's white husband. As he grows from a confused child to a murderous patriarch, Dana finds herself forced to suppress every moral, value, and desire she has ever held dear.

Dorothy Allison's criticism of Butler stems from what Allison perceives as Butler's assumption that children and family always come first. Though Butler's black female characters are aggressive, independent, and in control, they often sacrifice personal freedom and autonomy in order to make the lives of their children better—a tendency that makes Allison "want to scream with frustration" (471). Since utopian thought is optimistic, holding out hope for a better future, Butler does insist time and again on the need for people—especially for women—to make sacrifices for their children. But she indicates that such a demand compromises the present, forcing characters to submit to situations they find unbearable. Women make such sacrifices more often than men not because they are genetically more prone to do so, but because they been socially driven to do so. They refuse the consequences of *not* being the ones to take action: the deaths of their children and their future.

If "Speech Sounds" and "The Evening and the Morning and the Night" may be interpreted as theorizing a biological view of human nature to a greater degree than Butler's other texts, then *Kindred* is their opposite; it insists absolutely that personality and behavior are constructed within a social frame. Rufus beats, rapes, and kills not because white men are inherently more prone to do so than black men or white women, but because white men happen to hold the power in his society and he has been taught from a young age that he *can* beat, rape, and kill. Even Dana insists that the differences between herself and Rufus stem from culture rather than birth.

Could I make him see why I thought his blackmail was worse than my own? It was. He threatened to keep me from my husband if I did not submit to his whim. . . . I acted out of desperation. He acted out of whimsy or anger. Or so it seemed. "Rufe, there are things we just can't bargain on. This is one of them."

"You're going to tell me what we can't bargain on?" He sounded more surprised than indignant.

"You're damn right I am. . . . I won't bargain away my husband or my freedom!"

"You don't have either to bargain."

"Neither do you." (142)

Rufus is both more reasonable and more impossible than Dana expects: more reasonable because he will listen to her debate, more impossible because he refuses to change even when he understands her. But Rufus shares this flaw with the other men in the novel—including the sympathetic men. On one of her journeys back through time, Dana's husband accompanies her, and she is horrified to discover the extent to which Kevin acts like a patriarchal white man when people treat him as one. In his own time, he is another person. Kevin becomes horrified as well, although he strongly resists acknowledging that the new conditions have altered his behavior; he wants to believe that his personality cannot be changed by circumstance.

Dana is even more horrified to learn that, treated as an enslaved black woman, she will act like one. Her personality, which she always thought of as her fundamental self, modifies in response to Rufus's and Kevin's betrayals until she is no longer sure who she is in her own time or in the past. Dana helps Rufus against her every instinct, not because her nurturing instincts prove stronger than her need for autonomy, freedom, and self-pride, but because she recognizes the strategic importance of doing so. When she does not assist Rufus, she risks not merely her biological ancestry, but the lives of other slaves. Only when he threatens her autonomy by trying to seduce her—only when she realizes "how easy it would be for me to continue to be still and forgive him even this"—does she strike at him: "I could accept him as my ancestor, my younger brother, my friend, but not as my master" (260).

People in *Kindred* do not change because of humanist impulses or moral imperatives. They respond to the agency of others, either immediately or over time. Readers are meant to feel real horror at Dana's periods of complacency as a slave; like her, we respond with a kind of gratitude to the worst excesses of Rufus's behavior because they remind us of the need for action and challenge, no matter how painful. *Kindred* offers a challenge to utopian fictions that value ideals over survival—like *Women on the Edge of Time*, in which the protagonist sacrifices herself (and kills several other people) in order to defend her values, or like the cultures described in *Dawn*, which decide en masse to commit suicide once it becomes clear they will never achieve perfect stasis. Butler instead acknowledges all that has been and remains unbearable in human society, but insists that human agency can change even the most dystopian world over time. It demands patience; Dana must be willing to work, but she must also be willing to wait for substantial change, not to force it in the past at the expense of the future. The work and the waiting pays off. Although Dana is dispossessed of her era, her nation, her family, her belongings, her values, and her beliefs, she gains the understanding that she can make a difference in history. The novel is unfailingly optimistic in this regard. At the conclusion, Dana and her husband return to Maryland in 1976, to mourn those who suffered and to reassure themselves that they have escaped. Utopia in *Kindred* is thus in Dana's own era, when diversity is celebrated in marriage rather than conquered through rape and domination. Not that the scars go away: Dana loses an arm to Rufus's grip, and her knees and skin are marked by the tortures of slavery—just as all descendants of slaves are scarred from America's racist past. But she is still alive and capable of further change. Butler literally engraves the past onto the present by engraving Dana's body as a readable text.[8] As Deborah McDowell predicts, she also engraves the past onto the memory of the future through the act of writing. The text warns people like Dana and like us of the dangers of complacency; it demands utopian thinking.

Contradiction: *Xenogenesis*

Donna Haraway tells us: "Conventions within the narrative field of SF seem to require readers radically to rewrite stories in the act of reading them. . . . I want the readers to find an 'elsewhere' from which to envision a different and less hostile order or relationships among people, animals, technologies, and land" (15). This statement could easily describe the project of *Xenogenesis*. *Xenogenesis* mobilizes human adaptability to reform a species that arrives on earth to reform human-ity. The Oankali, whose name means "gene traders," arrive in the Terran system at the end of a nuclear holocaust that has decimated the planet. They bring the remaining humans onto their world-ship with a plan to return them to earth equipped to survive there; the "equipment" will consist of Oankali genes, provided by forcing humans to mate with Oankali partners and evolve into a new species. This crossbreeding is necessary for two reasons. The main one, according to the Oankali, stems from a flaw in human biology: ancient hierarchical tendencies drive humans to violence and self-destruction, and human intelligence only exacerbates the dangers.

But the Oankali have another purpose. They desperately desire to mate with the humans not only to trade genes, but because they find humans extremely attractive. Like the humans with the disease of *Clay's Ark*, the Oankali are driven to spread their organelles or become extinct. Humans particularly attract them because they are susceptible to cancers. If they can understand the cancers and adapt the renegade cells to their purposes, the Oankali feel certain they can make them-selves attractive as mates to many new species.

Genetic exchanges occur with the help of ooloi, an Oankali third sex who "mix" the DNA of parents to form genetically desirable chil-dren. The ooloi also give enormous sexual pleasure to human and Oankali partners—so much pleasure, in fact, that humans shun all physical contact with humans of the opposite sex without ooloi inter-vention once they have participated in mating with an ooloi. The ooloi discover what they label the "Human Contradiction":

> You are hierarchical. That's the older and more entrenched char-acteristic. We saw it in your closest animal relatives and in your most distant ones. It's a terrestrial characteristic. When human intelligence served it instead of guiding it, when human intelli-gence did not even acknowledge it as a problem, but took pride in it or did not notice it at all . . . that was like ignoring cancer. I think your people did not realize what a dangerous thing they were doing. . . . Your denial doesn't matter. A cancer growing in someone's body will go on growing despite denial. And a complex combination of genes that work together to make you intelligent as well as hierarchical will still handicap you whether you acknowl-edge it or not. (42)

This incompatible "conflict in their genes—the new intelligence put at the service of ancient hierarchical tendencies" (371), according to many of the Oankali, doom the human race to eventual destruction. Because of the Contradiction, the Oankali never feel remorse about their complete colonization of an independent species; it is for the salvation of the human race as well as for their own purposes that they interfere. The Oankali, who can communicate empathically and work communally, are certain of their superiority. It is never clear that they want anything from the humans other than their cancers and their cooperation, for there is little the Oankali seem to value in human beings except the potential for making them adaptable.

But even the Oankali cannot predict everything. Their "test" group of humans, experimented on while the majority of survivors remain in suspended animation, reveal several surprises: for example, that humans can perform a variety of different identities, that they become uncooperative when information is withheld, that making one human more powerful than others may lead to that person's persecution rather than domination. They also discover that the Contradiction is not equally strong in all people; women, for example, seem to display less of it than men, a fact that the Oankali attribute to male biology, but that the women attribute to conditioning that trains women to demonstrate their skills through nurture rather than force. Most of the Oankali expect Lilith, the strong black heroine of *Dawn*, to choose for a human mate "one of the big dark ones because they're like you" (161); only her best Oankali friend, Nikanj, is not surprised when she chooses instead a short, soft-spoken Chinese-Canadian man. But the humans shock the Oankali most with the force of their drive to survive. When the humans learn of the plan to breed them, they kill the ooloi who have become their mentors and sexual partners to escape.

For relatively few humans, anti-Oankali feelings arise from racial or sexual prejudices—the Oankali have "ugly" tentacles (383), and "take men as though they were women" (581)—but for the majority, the desire to survive as a species is the tantamount issue in the conflict with the Oankali takeover of earth. After bonding chemically with humans—only to have the humans flee—several ooloi are forced to admit that their understanding of genetics cannot prevent them from making errors. Many Oankali agree that intelligence might eventually allow humans to conquer their hierarchical tendencies, particularly if they have a new world to conquer, a distraction that would require co-operation and ingenuity. Eventually, after "resister" humans attempt to kidnap and alter "construct" children (half-human, half-ooloi) in order to maintain their species identity, the Oankali are convinced by a construct child that not all humans should be forced to mate with the Oankali. Those who choose not to can be sent to Mars, made habitable by Oankali technology, to continue as an independent race. Of course the Oankali—and some humans—hope that most of the humans stay. But the Oankali, who have always planned to retain a group of "pure" Oankali in case the Human Contradiction destroys them as well, finally recognize the need for "Humans who don't change or die—Humans to go on if the . . . unions fail" (371).

It is a mistake to interpret *Xenogenesis* as a serious discussion of essential flaws in human genetics. The novels scarcely seem interested in proving whether or not humans actually suffer from the Contradiction; rather, they illustrate how human agency can triumph over prejudice, violence, and essentialism. The humans in *Xenogenesis* express absolutely no racial prejudice; the only subset of individuals other than the Oankali who receive any real group hostility are "faggots," for in the postwar world compulsory heterosexuality becomes an important component of the dream of reproducing the species. In *Dawn*, the group of humans who have been dominant—white Christian men—act exactly as the Oankali expect all humans to behave; having lost the most power and prestige, they fight the most strongly against the dominant alien presence. There is also a large, highly xenophobic German resister village. Among the "non-Aryan" groups of humans, there is less violence; Hispanic and Chinese people may choose to go to Mars, but rarely become gun-toting resisters. It is not surprising that a black woman first joins an Oankali family; after years of oppression by other humans, Lilith has less prejudice toward the aliens and a stronger appreciation of the need for change. While she resents the unequal power relationships between Oankali and humans, she resents as well the unequal relationships among the humans she supervises.

Lilith is willing to work with the Oankali to create change. Her son Akin, the hero of *Adulthood Rites* and the first male human-Oankali construct child, is expected by his elders to be nomadic and prone to violence; instead, he bonds strongly with two separate communities and devotes his life to finding a workable solution to the increasing human-

Oankali conflict. Jodahs, the human-Oankali construct ooloi protagonist of *Imago*, proves to the Oankali that the aspects of humanity they
most fear can be used fruitfully for the benefit of both humans and
Oankali. There may be a biological flaw—or there may not—but Butler implies time and again that culture has the power either to reassert
the old hierarchies or to triumph over them.

Hoda Zaki has argued that in the *Xenogenesis* books Butler demonstrates "a pervasive human need to alienate from oneself those who
appear to be different—i.e., to create Others" (241). Zaki cites the way
humans of different races band together only to oppress the Oankali
in the series as proof of this assertion. In fact, I would like to argue
that Butler indicates exactly the opposite. The *humans* have been constituted as the colonized Other *by* the Oankali; as Donna Haraway
points out, their reeducation on the Oankali ship resembles the Middle
Passage of slaves on their way to America (379). At this point, the
humans are like animals to the Oankali, more interesting for their cancers than their thoughts; their identities have been stripped away, and
they are "reduced to flesh" (Spillers 68)—texts to be inscribed by their
oppressors, who identify them as nothing but a package of genes. The
human resistance to the Oankali parallels the resistance of a slave to
rape by a master who will later claim her child as his property. The
agency required to transform this situation into a relationship of equality and trust is staggering, but the transformation occurs. By the end
of *Imago*, a group of fertile humans enter an Oankali community of their
own free will, after a consensus formed through argument and communication. They can do so because, for the first time, they are not an
oppressed minority victimized by the Oankali.

It is interesting that Butler's sympathy for the oppressor leads so
many readers to interpret *Xenogenesis* as a condemnation of humanity.
Although she points out that in many ways the Oankali are superior
to human beings, Butler insists—through the mouths of many different characters, human and Oankali—that the enforced crossbreeding
of an unwilling species is a terrible crime. The Oankali (like the Tlic)
commit miscegenation not in their attempt to create a new species,
but in an attempt to dominate the old—the humans, who have value
in and of themselves. *Xenogenesis* represents a breakthrough in Butler's
fiction in that, for the first time, the protagonists do not have to work
alone to achieve their ends. Although Lilith initially resembles Dana,

Mary, and other Butler female heroes who take on entire worlds isolated from community support or input, she becomes a member of a large "family" that includes not only humans and Oankali, but animals, plants, and sentient spaceships as well. The world at the end of *Imago* is truly utopian, a society in which all have an equal chance to work together on the construction of a new world. It fulfills Donna Haraway's dream of "an 'elsewhere' from which to envision a different and less hostile order of relationships among people, animals, technologies, and land," and Butler's dream of a world in which differences can be recognized without prejudice and celebrated.[9] "'Human beings fear difference,' Lilith had told him once. 'Oankali crave difference. Humans persecute their different ones, yet they need them to give themselves definition and status. Oankali seek difference and collect it. They need it to keep themselves from stagnation and overspecialization. . . . When you feel a conflict, try to go the Oankali way. Embrace difference'" (*Xenogenesis* 321).

12

The Frozen Landscape
in Women's Utopian and Science Fiction

Naomi Jacobs

Our strongest images of women's utopias are places of warmth and abundance—tropical islands, temperate valleys, green and fruitful places exhibiting organicism and a balanced relationship between nature and culture.[1] But with surprising frequency, a different landscape also recurs: a frozen land, located at the snowbound heights or polar reaches of the planet. The landscape of ice takes on a particular significance in works by women, related to women's sense that the world of generation—of sexuality and reproduction—can be entangling, a hindrance to intellectual or emotional growth. The frozen landscape is one in which physical growth and decay are stilled; it is also free of those institutions and mores that restrict women in the social world. Because untouched by birth, death, politics, or power, the seemingly sterile fields of ice can become fertile ground for the female imagination and a place where radical confrontations and reconceptualizations become possible.

Though the implications of the frozen landscape in women's utopias vary a great deal, its thematic association with questions of sexuality, reproduction, and childbearing is strikingly constant. Some writers imagine the regions of ice as a womblike realm in which they can be the receivers rather than the givers of protection and nourishment, a place in which intellectual freedom and social power are possible precisely because the burdens of passion and of fertility have been deferred. Others foreground the dystopian potential of any such split between woman's warm-blooded body and a cold rationality or scientism. But for all of these writers, a frozen landscape in which natural processes are stilled serves as a locus for examination of conflicts between natural female functions and the individual woman's search for the good place.

The linking of woman's bondage with fertility and of woman's power and freedom with a frozen landscape is clear in the work of one of the first women to write utopian fiction in English. Margaret Cavendish, the duchess of Newcastle, was known as "Mad Madge" for her eccentricities—not least of which, in the eyes of her seventeenth-century contemporaries, was her desire to write and publish. Much of her life was itself utopia as performance art, from designing her own clothing to acting out an elaborate fantasy of herself as scientist and scholar. Cavendish was fascinated with natural philosophy and scientific experimentation, but her gender barred her from participation in scientific societies. So she created her own scientific society by imagining a utopia in which such barriers would not exist: *The Description of a New World, Called the Blazing-World* (1666). A young lady, gathering shells on the shore, is kidnapped by a merchant who has fallen in love with her. When a storm blows their ship to the North Pole, the lady is the only survivor of the extreme cold; she is then carried into another world, parallel to our own, where she rules as Empress over the world inhabited by hybrid creatures including ape-men, bear-men, fish-men, worm-men, spider-men, lice-men, and magpie-men, each representing a particular branch of science. Though Cavendish gives little description of the arctic landscape that delivers her heroine from her insistent admirer, the Pole clearly represents a place from which a woman could find her way to freedom and power, where her bondage to biology—to the "animal" side of her nature—was loosened, and where woman might become the human standard and man the dehumanized "Other."

This implicit linkage of woman's intellectual achievement with an escape from biology—particularly reproduction—is made explicit elsewhere in Cavendish's work. Though she struggled to overcome her own childlessness, she also understood that the absence of children facilitated her writing; when deflecting possible criticisms of her publishing, she argued that since she had no children to care for, she could legitimately spend her leisure in writing. Marriage is at best "but the womb of trouble," according to a Cavendish heroine who resolves to stay single, to marry "my self to my own Contemplations, which I hope to conceive and bring forth a Child of Fame" (in Mendelson 32, 33). Here the metaphoric language explicitly substitutes an abstract and solitary "marriage" to one's own thoughts for marriage to a man, and substitutes a cold "child of fame"—an intellectual work—for flesh-and-blood children. The implication is that a woman may have either a physical life or an intellectual one, but not both; and the intellectual life is clearly preferred.[2]

Mary Shelley's *Frankenstein* (1818), perhaps the single most influential work of science fiction by a woman, explores in a far more complex and ambiguous way this conflict between woman's intellectual or creative achievement and the responsibilities associated with woman's biological role. Here again the frozen landscape is imagined as a place of freedom, power, and achievement, a place clearly set apart from the entangling world of domesticity and fertility. Walton's first letter to his sister, as he prepares to leave on a voyage of arctic discovery, describes the "cold northern breeze" as a "wind of promise" and imagines the pole as "the region of beauty and delight . . . a country of eternal light" (269). He dreams particularly of exploring "a land never before imprinted by the foot of man" (270)—a land of solitude and complete liberty. But from Frankenstein, he will learn that this world of accomplishment and adventure—the world of discovery that lured Frankenstein into creating his monster—is also a world of horror. Far from valorizing an intellectual escape into that abstract realm and denigrating the role of parent or spouse, Shelley demonstrates the destructiveness of freedom and power when untempered by the warmth of human kindness.

In this, her approach to the frozen landscape differs significantly from the less ambivalent one taken by her husband in his famous "Mont Blanc" (1816). Percy Shelley had figured the landscape of ice as a place of fearful confrontation with a massive and impersonal natural power, indifferent not only to the human presence but to all of organic life. For that Shelleyan speaker, the mountain's vast emptiness and brutal power call into question the very significance of human life. To this point, the two Shelleys are congruent. But the destruction wrought by avalanche and glacier, through which "So much of life and joy is lost" (l. 117), suggested to Percy Shelley an image of inspiring power, of the "secret Strength of things / Which governs thought" (ll. 139–40). The mountain offers, to the "wise, and great, and good," a serene transcendence of materiality and mutability:

> All things that move and breathe with toil and sound
> Are born and die; revolve, subside, and swell.
> Power dwells apart in its tranquility,
> Remote, serene, and inaccessible . . . (ll. 82, 95–98).

Mary Shelley, by contrast, finds little inspiration in the glacial emptinesses sought by one who wishes to "dwell apart" from Nature in the form of human entanglements and responsibilities. Frankenstein's attempt to create life, motivated by frigid intellectual abstractions and unwarmed by human contact, is understood as a crime against nature, compounded by his flight from responsibility to the creature he has made. The plot suggests that such an escape from biology into an icy realm of the intellect is neither possible nor ultimately desirable.

Though Mary Shelley associates the frozen landscape with Frankenstein's astonishing scientific achievement, she sees it as offering only a temporary asylum from the fierce pressures of the natural world. It is on a glacier, explicitly compared to the northern sea on which the explorer Walton travels, that Frankenstein first encounters his creature-child and is forced to understand his responsibilities to it. The creature chooses this "sea of ice" as the location for his confrontation with the father-creator who has abandoned him; he almost seems to arise from the glacier, and it is into the frozen Arctic landscape that he will lead his creator at the end, and where both will perish. The ice is the setting for the bitter recriminations of child against father, perhaps reflecting Shelley's own conflicted feelings about both a child she had lost and the baby who, during the time she was writing the novel, restricted her participation in her husband's life of the mind. Like her protagonist, Shelley may have expressed in her creative act a rejection of or flight from the world of domesticity to which she was confined. She associates the cold fascinations of science and thought with alienation from the warmth of human affections and the lush beauty of the natural world, both of which have long been tied to femininity. Her ambivalence is certainly comprehensible in the context of her time: a woman's participation in intellectual life through the creation of a book would have been regarded by many of Shelley's contemporaries as unnatural and irresponsible—analogous to Frankenstein's creation of his monstrous progeny in the sense that, as Frankenstein usurps divine power, the woman writer usurps male power. That Frankenstein's monster-child pursues him even into those realms of freedom suggests Shelley's sense of the inescapability of her biological role. Critiquing her scientist-narrator, she obliquely critiques her own desire to enter the frozen world of freedom and power that ultimately destroys both parent and child.[3]

Seventy years after *Frankenstein*, another utopian writer would seek to resolve the conflicts delineated by Shelley, through the simple expedients of eliminating men and purifying women of the hindrance of their physical natures. Mary E. Bradley Lane's *Mizora: A Prophecy* (1880–81) describes an all-female, parthenogenetic society, entered at the North Pole; it is female supremacist, white supremacist, and vigorously chaste.[4] Once again, the frozen landscape frames a linkage of female utopia with the stilling (or at least slowing) of natural processes of growth and decay. The story is narrated by Princess Vera Zarovitch, a political prisoner in the Siberian mines who escapes on a whaling vessel heading for the North Sea. When the ship, "caught between ice floes" (10), is abandoned, the captainless crew then deserts Vera, who lives for a time with the "Esquimaux." Vera initially emphasizes the isolation and emptiness of the arctic landscape, repeatedly describing it as "destitute," "desolate," and "dreary" (11). After leaving her Esquimaux hosts, she is overcome by "uncontrollable lonesomeness" in this world where "Silence reigned supreme" (13). But her responses will change when her boat is swept through the aurora borealis to the all-female society of Mizora. In this "womblike" (Pfaelzer, *Utopian Novel* 149) world inside the earth, the arctic stillness and sterility will appear as virtues. It is a world, Vera comes to see, free of the "grossness and imperfections of our material existence" (7).

This sense that materiality is gross and low informs the Mizoran concern for purity of every sort. Implicit in Lane's utopia is a desire to undo the familiar Western link between woman and nature, particularly the association of femininity with the natural processes of birth and death, but also the perceived similarities between women and savage or "natural" peoples. At the very foundation of Mizoran perfection is the racial purity of its inhabitants, who are all blond-haired and fair-skinned—emphatically the "cool" type of beauty. Dark-haired Vera objects only silently to the Preceptress's argument that "the highest excellence of moral and mental character is alone attainable by a fair race. The elements of evil belong to the dark race." For these reasons, dark complexions have been "eliminated" (92). Gender is also considered a racial category by the Mizorans (93), and Vera eventually learns that the first step in the eugenic campaign to purify the race had been the elimination of men some 3000 years earlier. All men were gone within a hundred years after the women scientists learned to "control Nature's processes of development," but "It was long years—I should say centuries—before the influence of the coarser nature of men was eliminated from the present race" (104). Reversing the classic equation of men with culture and women with nature, Lane's Mizorans associate masculinity with the natural "grossness" and animality that they seek to remove from every aspect of their culture.

Particularly striking is the Mizoran concern with purity of food. Though the land is lush and fruitful, much of the food is synthetic—bread, for instance, is produced from limestone. The land's chemists hope to learn to synthesize fruits and vegetables as well, even though these have already attained perfection in the natural state through "permanent protections from all kinds of blight or decay" (49). The Mizorans aim to "eliminate from [their] food the deleterious earthy matter. . . . The human body is like a lamp-wick, which filters oil while it furnishes light. . . . If the oil could be made perfectly pure, the wick would not fill up" (45). Their diet, which confers the bloom and suppleness of "eternal youth" (19), is vegetarian, of course. All animals have been "long extinct" (54), not only because animal food is considered deleterious and animals make inefficient use of agricultural resources, but because association with animals is considered "degrading" (113). This is the reason for the stillness of the land: "No hum of life . . . over all a silence, as of death, reigned unbroken" (15, 17). Without even birds to sing in the trees, this utopia is very distant indeed from more recent feminist utopias in which women talk to cats and mate with horses.

Though the temperate Mizoran climate, warmed by a confluence of electrical fields, is hardly a frozen one, the visual effect of the world is that of a glacial landscape, expressive again of the emphasis on purity. Pale granite and white marble are the favored stones for buildings;

icelike crystal and spun glass are common elements in domestic decor. Electrical lighting adds to the glacial effect, providing "a soft and pleasing brilliancy that lent a charm to everything it revealed . . . a dreamy daylight" (75) like that of a snowy day. Nonpolluting fuels make possible a world that is spotlessly clean—a "frozen landscape" reference that will be articulated in another context, when Vera describes the "soft snows of winter" as a "veil of purity" (86). The smooth whiteness of new snow is certainly an appropriate emblem for the uniform purity of the Mizoran world and mind. The fair young women often dress in white, and one particularly striking tableau occurs at the funeral of a girl who has drowned: all the young girls wear white, and the body rests on a "litter composed entirely of white rosebuds" (126). Like snow covering the earth, white rosebuds line the grave and cover the body before dirt is thrown upon it. Thus, even in death, the Mizorans attempt to separate the body from the impure earth to which it must return.

This distaste for physicality is evident as well in the Mizoran attitude to bodily processes. Though the women are physically strong and athletic, theirs is a kind of android strength and control. Despite their rosy cheeks, it is difficult to imagine these women sweating, breathing hard, or even breathing at all. To the Mizorans, the body and its needs are an embarrassment; one never eats in the presence of others, for example. As for the act of human sexuality and the passion of sexual love, the Mizorans regard these as primitive manifestations of a primitive stage of human development. Upon learning that Vera has a husband and a child, the shocked Preceptress pities her: "we have got rid of the offspring of Lust. Our children come to us as welcome guests through portals of the holiest and purest affection. That love which you speak of, I know nothing about. I would not know. It is a degradation which mars young life and embitters the memories of age. We have advanced beyond it" (130). It is not clear whether Mizoran children are gestated in the womb and born naturally, or are fully the products of laboratories. But like the prize cherry tree that is propagated asexually, by slips (49), the Mizorans seem to reproduce without recourse to the messiness of love. Charlotte Perkins Gilman's *Herland* (1915) would envision a similarly purified form of heterosexual love and of reproduction, an ideal understandable in a time when uncontrolled childbearing, along with high infant and maternal mortality rates, was such a horrifying part of many women's lives.

To control and purify nature is the Mizorans' central goal. They often cite Nature as authority, say that "Nature is God, and God is Nature" (120), and claim never to "thwart" (80) or "supercede" (81) Nature. Yet despite their professed reverence for the "great Mother" Nature, it is in fact a nature-controlling Science that they worship. They are "mistresses of Nature's peculiar processes. We influence or control them at will" (91). The result is a largely disembodied ideal of health and of feeling. Vera is told that the Mizorans' capacity for pleasure and pain is as highly evolved as are their intellectual and moral capacities; the touch of a mother's hand brings a "thrill of rapture" (82) unimaginable to the less evolved. Yet that such emotions are hidden behind a "stoical reserve" suggests that the Mizorans find passion itself obscene. Says Vera's guide Wauna at the funeral mentioned above, "True refinement is unobtrusive in everything, and while we do not desire to repress a natural and inevitable feeling of sorrow, we do desire to conceal and conquer it" (128). Like the physical processes of Nature, the natural, physical expression of emotion has been controlled. The characteristic Mizoran face is distinguished by a "fair, calm brow, where not a wrinkle marred the serene expression of intellect" (87); it is unmarked by pleasure or pain, for emotion, purified of "earthy" coarseness, has become a wholly intellectual experience.[5] It was through intellect that the foremothers of Mizora took control of reproduction, thus escaping subservience both to men and to their reproductive role. The arctic setting provides a fitting metaphor for this ideal of a womanly freedom and power made possible by a cooling of the heat of generation.

Though few more recent utopias by women share Lane's open distaste for sexuality, the association of power and/or freedom with a frozen setting has persisted.[6] In Doris Lessing's *The Marriages Between Zones Three, Four, and Five* (1980), for example, the heroine leaves behind her children and her queendom in the fertile Zone Three for the isolated, ethereal heights of Zone Two, which shines with the "piled snows of a thousand years." Joan Vinge's *The Snow Queen* (1980) depicts a world divided into two cultures: the Summer people are spiritual, rural, natural, and open, while Winters are urban, technologically sophisticated, and materialistic. Though this division would seem to reproduce traditional female/male oppositions, Winter is in fact ruled by a Queen. Powerful, ruthless, and greedy, she is as youthful and beautiful after 150 years as she was at twenty. But the "water of Life" that perpetuates her

youth and power has also made her sterile. Here again, female power—
at least of a particular sort—seems attainable only at the cost of
woman's reproductive and nurturing capacities, and is thus figured as
icy and barren.[7]

Ursula K. Le Guin, one of our most distinguished writers of utopian fiction, has repeatedly represented cold, desolate landscapes as
places of great joy, and the remainder of this essay will explore her eloquent variations on the theme of the frozen landscape. In *The Left Hand
of Darkness* (1969), the planet "Gethen" or "Winter" is home to several contrasting societies, none of which is straightforwardly utopian
or dystopian. But as a thought-experiment observing and analyzing life
without fixed gender, the novel maps and explores that "other" place
or no-place implicit in the liberal feminist dream of a world without
our culture's socially created gender differences and hyperawareness of
sexuality.

By comparison with our own culture, Gethen is a place of gender freedom where the female roles as object of desire and as giver of
life are shared by all, as is political power. This is possible because the
inhabitants are hermaphrodites, sexually neuter and inactive for most
of every month; anatomical maleness or femaleness emerges only when
an individual is actually prepared to engage in sexual activity. Every
twenty-eight days, an individual enters the estrus state of "kemmer,"
in which the heightened sexual urge produces male or female sex characteristics for the duration of kemmer. An individual who becomes
pregnant retains female characteristics during the pregnancy, but may
go on to sire children as well as to bear them. Thus, gender inequality
and psychological masculinity or femininity are unknown. The king's
pregnancy is a perfectly natural phenomenon to the Gethenians, while
the exaggerated maleness or "permanent kemmer" of the Terran en-
voy, Genly Ai, is regarded as a perversion. Though kemmer is a state
of powerful arousal that is never to be denied, Le Guin emphasizes the
Gethenians' freedom from sexual tension in daily life. The story itself
is free of sexual tension due to its focus on a character who seems not
to respond sexually to the Gethenians; also, Le Guin's consistent use
of the male pronoun to refer to Ai's intimate friend Estraven largely
removes sexual possibilities from their friendship, given the heterosexist
assumptions of the text. Ai's experience of this degendered and largely
desexualized existence on the planet "Winter," his encounter with

human faces and souls neither male nor female, is both profoundly shocking and profoundly liberating.

In her essay "Is Gender Necessary?" Le Guin has said that *The Left Hand of Darkness* is a "book about betrayal and fidelity. That is why one of its two dominant sets of symbols is an extended metaphor of winter, of ice, snow, cold: the winter journey" (161). The painful trek of Genly Ai and Estraven across a frozen wasteland tests their loyalty as well as their endurance, creating a bond of brotherhood between her hero and his alien counterpart. But for Le Guin the importance of the Ice goes beyond the physical and psychological challenges it poses. The place of extremity, "that magnificent and unspeakable desolation . . . that silent vastness of fire and ice that said in enormous letters of black and white DEATH, DEATH, written right across a continent" (*Left Hand* 220), is also a place of "joy" (*Left Hand* 241) and rebirth.

The deathly emptiness of the ice, where "nothing grows and no beasts run" (24), is described as the antithesis and the refutation of the civilized world of cities, governments, rivalries, hierarchies. Writes the first Terran Investigator, "I really don't see how anyone could put much stock in victory or glory after he had spent a winter on Winter, and seen the face of the Ice" (97). Le Guin imagines that a truly authentic meeting of individuals could be possible in the center of this great Absence; "up here on the Ice," says Ai, "each of us is singular, isolate . . . equals at last" (232). Attempting to understand the joy he found in this winter journey, Ai remembers nights in the tent after days of grueling struggle: "We are inside, the two of us, in shelter, at rest, at the center of all things. Outside, as always, lies the great darkness, the cold, death's solitude" (240). Cut off from social supports and restraints, struggling for survival against inimical nature, Ai and Estraven create and inhabit a womb of security and simplicity—a joy they lose when they leave the Ice (277). For Ai, this is a place of refuge not only from sex roles but from sexuality itself; though Estraven enters kemmer while they are alone together, Ai never seriously considers playing the male to Estraven's female. Sexuality, it seems, would endanger their equality, the delicately balanced reserve of their intimacy.

The Left Hand of Darkness and its successor *The Dispossessed* (1974) have been criticized for androcentrism and bourgeois individualism, because their questing heroes are men who leave behind the domestic and social spheres in order to pursue their lonely goals.[8] As Shelley had done in *Frankenstein*, the early Le Guin addresses feminist issues through male characters; woman is the suppressed term in both narratives. But Le Guin's later work, such as the remarkable *Always Coming Home* (1985), has become more explicitly feminist and gynocentric. And the 1982 short story "Sur: A Summary Report of the Yelcho Expedition to the Antarctic, 1909–10" reconceptualizes and domesticates the frozen landscape. Narrated by an anonymous Peruvian woman, it is the story of a secret exploration by nine South American women, who reach the South Pole before Amundsen but prefer to conceal their achievements, lest "embarrassment or unpleasant notoriety . . . be brought upon unsuspecting husbands, sons, etc." (38). Without denying the dangers and hardships they undergo, Le Guin re-creates and feminizes heroism through her contrast of male and female styles of exploration. The women are motivated not by the desire to be first at the Pole, but simply by the desire "to go, to see—no more, no less" (38). Their expedition is delayed by the difficulty of finding women who could leave their domestic responsibilities to parents, spouses, and children: "these are not responsibilities lightly to be set aside. And those who wished to evade such claims were not the companions we wanted in hard work, risk, and privation" (39). Here, though domestic responsibilities restrict women's participation in adventure, domesticity itself—the traditionally female role of self-denying nurturance—is seen as valuable training for members of an expeditionary force. To this group, a woman who would leave her family as freely as have done the great male explorers is potentially unreliable, lacking in the qualities needed for their common survival and success.

What these explorers seek is not glory, but rather an experience of openness and possibility unknown in the daily lives of such comfortable upper-class women, who will explain their six-month absences by ladylike excuses such as a retreat to a convent or a trip to Paris for the winter season. After returning to conventional family life, the narrator will think with regret of "those friends who wished to come with us but could not, by any contrivance, get free—those we had to leave behind to a life without danger, without uncertainty, without hope"(39). And yet, the differences between domesticity and heroism are smaller than they seem. With her first step on the ice, the narrator feels "that [she] was home at last" (40); and the women quickly create a homelike utopian encampment, "a marvel of comfort and convenience" (42), by carving cubicles into the ice—in contrast to the exposed, above-ground structures left by earlier explorers. The horrified sailors refer to the women's burrows and narrow sleeping tubes as "coffins and wormholes," but to the women the ice itself is "living" (42) and beautiful, the stuff of architecture and sculpture rather than a hostile substance to be conquered.

An absence of combativeness, power-seeking or self-seriousness is evident in these explorers, with their nest-building activities, their consensual decision-making, their birthday parties, their celebrations with cases of Veuve Clicquot, and their playful renaming of the landscape (one peak is dubbed "Bolivar's Big Nose," and the "Beardmore" glacier becomes the "Florence Nightingale" glacier). The group has no leader, leaves "no footprints" (49), and the women feel no need to make their accomplishment known. "I was glad even then that we had left no sign there [at the Pole]," says the narrator, "for some man longing to be first might come some day, and find it, and know then what a fool he had been, and break his heart" (45). Her implication is not that such a man would have been a fool to arrive second, but rather that he would have to face the insignificance of rankings or primacy in the "awful place" where "anything we could do, anything we were, was insignificant" (44). This narrator learns that "achievement is smaller than men think. What is large is the sky, the earth, the sea, the soul" (41).

Like Genly Ai and Estraven, these ice-trekkers find joy in the center of hardship and emptiness; at "that white place on the map, that void," they "flew and sang like sparrows" (43). The revivifying possibilities of the place of danger and adventure are signified by the birth of a child at the base camp. A kind of virgin mother, a convent-educated woman so naive that she hadn't even known she was pregnant, bears a child who is named "Rosa," evoking the winter rose of the Christmas carol and the ancient festivals of light and rebirth at the darkest, coldest times of the year. That this complete integration of domesticity and adventure, of traditional and nontraditional women's roles, can be only a utopian interlude is perhaps indicated by the brief life of the child, who dies at the age of five. All other evidence of the expedition is likewise lost or hidden, though the adventures are recounted to the women's children in the form of "fairy tales." Yet the expedition clearly remains the one transcendent and shaping experience of this narrator's life: an affirmation of the female potential for endurance and achievement.

Over three centuries, women imagining utopia have often imagined shrugging off the burdens of femaleness in a landscape of magnificent barrenness. Their intuitions are confirmed by Davida Kellogg, a geologist who has traveled and worked extensively in the Antarctic. Her first reaction to the place, she says, was a powerful feeling of having come home. In her experience, Antarctica is seen as female by both the men and the women who work there. But the women, who are "not offended by its unattainability," are more likely to feel its womanly presence as a motherly one, to feel a sense of "enormous love and tenderness" in this cruel and beautiful place. Perhaps this is because it is also a place where gender roles can drop away. In addition to the simple release from child-rearing and housekeeping duties, the team's focus on a project, intensified by the difficulties of working and surviving in the cold, gives value to a "woman's adrenalin rush or intellectual engagement," which is "simply a bother everywhere but there." Though many women's utopias prefer to emphasize a lush garden-world in which both woman's biological nature and Mother Nature are loved and supported, the regions of ice remain a powerful symbol of a realm of freedom in which woman's ties to the world of generation need not become the ties that bind.[9]

Notes
Works Cited
Index

Notes

1. Introduction

1. Besides the many definitions and descriptions of utopia, science fiction, and literatures of estrangement that follow, we are also indebted to the pioneering work of Darko Suvin and Lyman Tower Sargent (see Works Cited), who use sets of formal characteristics to distinguish utopian and science fiction work, and to Sargent's taxonomy of kinds of utopias ("Political Dimensions" 4–5). We also found extremely helpful Ruth Levitas's proposal that, while the larger field of utopian studies is defined by "utopia [as] the expression of the desire for a better way of living" (9 and 189), "distinctions . . . between kinds of utopias [can be made] on the basis of form, function, location and content" (199).

2. For mainstream fiction, comprehensive critical works such as Ellen Moers, *Literary Women* (1976); Elaine Showalter, *A Literature of Their Own* (1977); Susan Gubar and Sandra Gilbert, *The Madwoman in the Attic* (1979) and *No Man's Land* (1989); Mary Helen Washington, *Black-Eyed Susans: Classic Stories by and about Black Women*; Jane Tompkins, *Sensational Designs* (1985); and Patricia Waugh, *Feminine Fictions* (1989), have radically altered our understanding of women's writing and the cultural and literary context in which it occurs.

3. On utopias, see Lyman Tower Sargent, "Women in Utopia"; Daphne Patai, "Utopia for Whom"; Sylvia Strauss, "Women in Utopia"; Carol Pearson, "Women's Fantasies and Feminist Utopias"; Anne K. Mellor, "On Feminist Utopias"; *Women and Utopia: Critical Interpretations*, ed. Marleen Barr and Nicholas D. Smith; Patrocinio Schweikart, "What If"; Carol Farley Kessler, *Daring to Dream*; Lee Cullen Khanna, "Frontiers of Imagination," *Women in Search of Utopia*, ed. Ruby Rohrlich and Elaine Hoffman Baruch; Jean Pfaelzer, *The Utopian Novel in America* (141–58); Frances Bartkowski, *Feminist Utopias*; and Angelika Bammer, *Partial Visions*. On apologues, see Rachel Blau Du Plessis, "The Feminist Apologues of Lessing, Piercy, and Russ". On science fiction, see Joanna Russ, "The Image of Women in Science Fiction"; Beverly Friend, "Virgin Territory"; Pamela Sargent's introduction to *Women of Wonder* (xiii–lxiv); Ursula K. Le Guin, *The Language of the Night*; *Future Females*, ed. Marleen Barr; and *The Feminine Eye*, ed. Tom Staicar; Joanna Russ, *Magic Mommas, Trembling Sis-*

ters, *Puritans & Perverts*; Tom Moylan, *Demand the Impossible*; Sarah Lefanu, *In the Chinks of the World Machine* or *Feminism and Science Fiction*; Ursula K. Le Guin, *Dancing at the Edge of the World*; and Jane Donawerth, "Teaching Science Fiction by Women" and "Utopian Science." On speculative fiction, see Natalie M. Rosinsky, *Feminist Futures*; Rachel Blau Du Plessis, *Writing Beyond the Ending* (178–97); and Marlene Barr, *Alien to Femininity*. On feminist fabulation, see "Feminism Faces the Fantastic," Special Issue of *Women's Studies*, ed. Marlene Barr and Patrick Murphy (esp. 187–91); Marlene Barr, "Food for Postmodern Thought" and *Feminist Fabulation*.

4. See Suvin on utopia as the "sociopolitical subgenre of science fiction" ("Defining" 144); Sargent on utopias as currently a subtype of science fiction (but separate before 1940) ("Utopia" 142–44); Sargent on science fiction, utopia, and the fantasy of the Blessed Isles as separate but related ("Political Dimensions" 7–8); and Levitas on the overlapping of fantasy and utopia as expressions of impossible or possible desire (190).

5. Utopian or science fiction by women in the early modern era is very close to fantasy because the fantasies of a better place are based on an education for women that the societies are only beginning to allow, and because the writers enclose their visions of educated women in far-off islands or fairy stories, thereby defusing the threat that such visions posed to male dominance.

6. This is the great discovery of English and French feminism in the seventeenth century, as Hilda Smith has pointed out in *Reason's Disciples*, that women's "inferiority" is socially constructed by denial of education.

7. Catherine Belsey's essay on "Constructing the Subject" is especially helpful in defining "subject position" or subjectivity of women and its ramifications for literature: "The subject is constructed in language and discourses and . . . in ideology" (49); "Women as a group in our society are both produced and inhibited by contradictory discourses. Very broadly, we participate both in the liberal-humanist discourse of freedom, self-determination and rationality and at the same time in the specifically feminine discourse offered by society of submission, relative inadequacy and irrational intuition. The attempt to locate a single and coherent subject-position within these contradictory discourses, and in consequence to find a non-contradictory pattern of behaviour, can create intolerable pressure" (50).

8. For the tradition that Scott's mother was educated at Makin's academy, see Ferguson, *First Feminists*, 311. I am indebted for the information on Scott's borrowing her title from Astell's *Some Reflections upon Marriage* (1700) to a conversation with Vincent Carretta.

2. The Subject of Utopia:
Margaret Cavendish and Her *Blazing-World*

1. *The Description of a New World Called the Blazing-World* first appeared in 1666, appended to Margaret Cavendish, duchess of Newcastle's lengthy scientific treatise, *Observations upon Experimental Philosophy*. A second edition of *Observations* and *Blazing-World* appeared in 1668, and my references to the text are from this edition. A separate edition of *Blazing-World* also appeared in 1668. Since I completed this es-

say, a modern edition of *Blazing-World* has been published. See Margaret Cavendish, *New Blazing World and Other Writing*, ed. Kate Lilley (London: Pickering and Chatto, 1992). This edition is an invaluable resource for the study of Cavendish, including not only *The Description of a New World, Called the Blazing World* in modern spelling, but also two additional works of prose fiction of considerable interest, "The Contract," and "Assaulted and Pursued Chastity." Lilley's prefatory essay is excellent and provides an insightful introduction to Cavendish's life and work.

In his excellent bibliography, *British and American Utopian Literature, 1516–1985*, Lyman Tower Sargent identifies *Blazing-World* as the first utopian fiction in English by a woman. In addition to "The Inventory of Judgments Commonwealth" in *The Worlds Olio* (1655), which Sargent notes as utopian in intent, there are several other works by Cavendish that might well be useful to utopian studies. They include the appendix to *Grounds of Natural Philosophy* (1668), in which Cavendish creates and analyzes good and bad "worlds" at some length. Additionally, her picaresque fiction, "Assaulted and Pursued Chastity" in *Nature's Pictures Drawn by Fancy's Pencil to the Life* (1671) (see Lilley above), includes descriptions of alternate societies encountered by the protagonist, and her plays, notably *The Female Academy* (1662) and *The Convent of Pleasure* (1668), present single-sex utopias with humor and imaginative daring.

2. In a 1990 address to the Society of Utopian Studies, Lyman Tower Sargent suggested that utopian speculation might be defined as "social dreaming" and divided into two traditions: the primitive (hedonistic, natural settings) and the artificial or constructed (urban and rational). Feminist utopias, on the other hand, avoid such oppositions by depicting a full spectrum of desire and the integration of constructed cultures within natural settings.

Because the second, "constructed" tradition, usually seen as originating with Plato's *Republic* and including More's *Utopia* and such nineteenth-century works as Edward Bellamy's *Looking Backward*, centers on the issue of justice, commentary on utopian speculation, particularly in the realm of political theory, has been concerned with problems revolving around the theorization of justice and its practical consequences. However, recent utopian fiction by women has highlighted the issues of gender, race, and class, and critical commentary has begun to center on ideas of difference and desire. For example, Levitas says in *The Concept of Utopia*, "The essential element in utopia is . . . desire—the desire for a better way of being" (191). Her book argues for a more eclectic approach to utopian thought and definition and greater contextualization in the analysis of particular works or movements. See also Moylan's important study of four recent utopian novels, *Demand the Impossible: Science Fiction and the Utopian Imagination*, in which Moylan argues that recent utopias perform a "critical" function in contrast to earlier utopias and analyzes four novels (three of them feminist utopias) to demonstrate the subtle and varied ways this function is performed. In her recent book, *Feminist Utopias*, Frances Bartkowski suggests the distance traversed in utopian thought when women's writing is foregrounded. Rather than notions of justice, utopian thought, she says, can be "read as a feminist eros, speaking the language of female desire" (9). These changes in scholarly commentary on utopia, as well as the production of feminist utopian fictions, indicate the wide-ranging effects of altered subjectivity. The study of a writer like Cavendish demonstrates that a broader perspective on utopian desire need not be seen as only a recent phenomenon.

3. See, for example, Ursula Le Guin's short story "Sur," where nine women journey to the South Pole in 1909 and set up, on the ice, a striking feminist utopia. See also Jacobs, chap. 12 in this volume.

4. See: Sally Gearhart, *The Wanderground*; Judy Grahn, *Mundane's World*; Ursula Le Guin, *Always Coming Home*; Doris Lessing, *The Marriages between Zones Three, Four, and Five*; and Marge Piercy, *Woman on the Edge of Time*. These are just a few of the many utopian novels published from 1969 to the present. For a fuller list of American works, see Carol Kessler's invaluable "Bibliography of Utopian Fiction by United States Women, 1836–1988." This outpouring of utopian fiction has attracted significant critical attention in addition to the essays in this volume and the references cited in n. 2. See, particularly, Goodwin and Jones; Baruch and Rohrlich; Albinski; Barr, *Alien to Femininity: Speculative Fiction and Feminist Theory*; and Cranny-Francis.

5. Margaret Cavendish published biography, autobiography, poems, plays, orations, scientific studies, and prose fiction, as well as work that transgresses generic boundaries. Her writings, sometimes revised and reissued, run to nearly twenty folio volumes. The only one of these works significantly reprinted is her biography of her husband, William Cavendish, the duke of Newcastle. The biography of the duchess by Grant remains richly informative. See also the study by Kathleen Jones. For additional valuable historical information about the Cavendish family, see Turberville and Perry. For an interesting brief biographical summary and thoughtful perspective on Cavendish see Ferguson, *First Feminists*, 305–18. The Wilson and Warnke, Ferguson, and Greer et al. anthologies contain brief selections of Cavendish's work.

6. For an excellent assessment of Cavendish's relation to the "new science" of the seventeenth century, see Sarasohn. Particularly interesting is Sarasohn's discussion of seventeenth-century skepticism and its value in creating a climate favorable to women's intellectual participation. See also Bowerbank's useful assessment of Cavendish's distinctiveness in "modern" scientific thought. Bowerbank says that Cavendish's "work represents, in a whimsical way, a groping towards and alternative vision to Salomon's House with its pretence to finding certain and objective knowledge. . . . And she does attempt a relationship with nature that runs counter to the exploitive mastery proposed by Bacon; her approach is sensitive and reverent as well as subjective" (406). Yet Bowerbank seems to object to Cavendish's "subjective expression" and finds her work "undisciplined." Of course, Cavendish's play with "subjectivity" is one of the aspects of her utopian work I find most interesting. But Bowerbank is not alone among modern readers in expressing ambivalence about Cavendish. Virginia Woolf was one of the first to both admire and disparage the duchess of Newcastle. In *A Room of One's Own* she expresses, in her memorable prose, the views of several recent critics, when she cites Cavendish's prodigious and generous intellect but says her work conveys a "vision of loneliness and riot . . . as if some giant cucumber had spread itself over all the roses and carnations in the garden and choked them to death" (65). Not only might Woolf's striking imagery repay some interpretation, but the unease of recent feminists might reflect the limits of our own interpretive approaches as much as Cavendish's failings.

7. Although Lady Mary Wroth had published a prose romance, *Urania*, in 1621, no other Englishwoman had published a substantial body of secular work before Cavendish. Despite some religious writing and translation, most Englishwomen strictly maintained, in terms of public discourse, the ideal of silence. Mary Wroth's daring roman à clef earned her nearly universal castigation. The full extent of the barriers Cavendish had to overcome, not only to write, but to publish extensively under her own name, can only be imagined by a modern reader. Yet Dorothy Osborne's oft-quoted allusion to the duchess in a letter to her fiancé, William Temple, certainly suggests what Cavendish was up against. Osborne says, "let mee aske you if you have seen a book of Poems newly come out, made by my Lady NewCastle. For God's sake if you meet with it send it mee. . . . Sure the poore woman is a litle distracted, she could never bee soe rediculous else as to venture at writeing books and in verse too, If I should not sleep this fortnight I should not come to that" (37).

A contemporary family allusion to the duchess of Newcastle was brought to my attention by Betty Travitsky, who discovered it in her research into Elizabeth Egerton's "Loose Papers" (Egerton MS. 607). It is a little poem written by Margaret Cavendish's stepgranddaughter to her mother, Elizabeth Egerton, countess of Bridgewater, daughter of William Cavendish by his first marriage. It reads: "Madam, I Dedicate these Lines to you / To whom, I doe confesse, Volumes are due; / Hoping your wonted Godnes will excuse / The errours of an Infant Muse. / Mongst Ladyes let Newcastle weare the Bayes, / I onely sue for Pardon, not for Praise." It seems as though the Duchess's pursuit of literary renown may have been the subject of family bantering. Of course, her extensive literary production may also have been an inspiration to young Elizabeth, but here she had to distinguish her motives for versifying from those of her well published grandmother. This poem is also cited in the introduction to a selection of Margaret Cavendish's work in Greer (165). For an interesting exploration of the Egerton manuscripts and the Cavendish and Egerton connection, see Travitsky.

Margaret Cavendish's success in defining a "female self" in the face of the powerful restrictions on women's roles and speech during the Early Modern period is addressed in an excellent article by Paloma who speculates that "perhaps more than she wanted to be a writer Margaret Cavendish really wanted to be a Hero (not, God forbid, a heroine), but literature was the only "Heroick Action" not totally forbidden her" (56). Certainly Cavendish's protagonist in *Blazing-World* is not only adventurer and then ruler, but heroic general, rescuing her people's threatened kingdom in the second part of the work. Paloma is one of the few scholars writing on Cavendish to appreciate her range of literary accomplishments and public daring, without lapsing into the oft quoted condemnations of her eccentricities (e.g., Pepys's famous parody of her singular visit, in 1667, to the Royal Society). Even recent feminist scholars seem uncomfortable with Cavendish's determined, insistent, flamboyant exploration of her own subjective power; for example, see my discussion in n. 11. In a 1990 article Fitzmaurice suggests that Newcastle may have deliberately cultivated an image of eccentricity and melancholia in order to protect herself from the scandal that Mary Wroth's venture into print provoked.

8. Cavendish's allusion to the Cabala links her work to an important tradition of mysticism, philosophy, and magic originating with Hebrew scholars in medi-

eval Spain. Cabala was eclectic even in its Iberian development and greatly complicated after the Jewish expulsion from Spain in 1492 as European scholars, such as
Giovanni Pico, assimilated its ideas into the Christian tradition. For excellent studies
of the importance of Cabala during the sixteenth and seventeenth centuries, see the
work of Yates. In both Hebraic and Christian versions, cabalistic studies figured spiritual intermediaries, evoked through scriptural names of divinity and mystical numer-
ology, leading to special knowledge and power. In Elizabethan England John Dee was
an influential expounder and practitioner of Cabala; interestingly, in *Blazing-World*,
the Empress and Duchess allude to Dee in their conversation. Indeed, Cavendish's familiarity with the Cabala is a fascinating topic, requiring much more study. For the
purposes of this essay, however, what seems most important is Newcastle's appropriation of a special form of knowledge, a form associated with great power and yet never
before, despite its complexity and eclecticism, taken up by a woman. In other words,
in her quest for her own Cabala, repudiation of earlier male authorities, and decision
to use a female scribe, the Empress signals Cavendish's determination to include gender as a crucial category in the advancement of learning.

Another reason the Cabala may have appealed to Cavendish was its association with the solitary contemplative, inspired to powerful visions by his own thoughts.
Since Cavendish, like most women of the Early Modern period, lacked any formal education, she relied self-consciously on the power of original ideas. For example, see the
following inscription, which appeared below an engraving of Cavendish in her study,
used as a frontispiece to one of her works, *The Worlds Olio* (2d ed. [1671]):

> Studious She is and all Alone
> Most visitants when She has none,
> Her Library on which She looks
> It is her Head, her Thoughts her Books
> Scorninge dead Ashes without fire
> For her owne Flames doe her Inspire.

Finally, a still further significance of the Cabala (and the extended discussion
of natural philosophy and metaphysics so important to Cavendish's utopian world) was
suggested to me by Ellayne Fowler, a graduate student in my seminar on Early Modern
women's writing. Ellayne noticed that the Empress's pursuit of knowledge in the city
named Paradise might constitute a revision of the Hebraic/Christian myth of Eve. In
this early utopia by a woman, then, knowledge is not forbidden, nor does the desire
for it disclose female frailty. On the contrary, in Cavendish's version of Paradise, a new
"Eve" acquires knowledge that leads, not to damnation or exile, but to social improvement and expanded communities. The Empress, of course, is not seen as in complicity
with Satan, but with good Spirits—as, indeed, were Renaissance Cabalists.

9. The hint of erotic intimacy in these words is much more fully realized in
some of Cavendish's other works, notably her play, *The Convent of Pleasure*. In that
all-female retreat, sensual delights abound, as women exclude men in order to more
fully enjoy aesthetic and material comforts—and each other. Most of the play is devoted to a romance between two women, although Cavendish's daring here is recu-

perated at the very end when one of the young women turns out to be a prince in disguise, and the couple marries. For interesting excerpts from this play, see Ferguson, *First Feminists* (84–101).

10. Because in women's fiction the utopian ideal itself is dynamic, the journey motif often becomes central to the transformation of both the characters and the societies depicted. A good example of this is Lessing's *Marriages* where the multiple journeys of the protagonist, Al.Ith, result in successive personal and social changes.

11. In addition to the comments by Woolf and Bowerbank cited in n. 6, other critiques of Cavendish may be seen in two excellent articles by Mary Beth Rose and Catherine Gallagher. Rose compares four Early Modern autobiographies by women and finds that Cavendish's "True Relation" is "an interesting and most illustrative failure" (250). Although the entire essay is both informative and illuminating, her reasons for seeing Cavendish's work as unsuccessful may be questioned. In using Gussdorf's model of autobiography, Rose superimposes the notion of a coherent and consistent persona on Cavendish's text and then finds it wanting. As she says, "The Duchess's disjointed narrative makes clear that she cannot bear to formulate a distinctive identity: she simply cannot decide how she 'wishes to have been' " (254). Yet it may be that Cavendish's depiction of varied subjective stances, both conventional and daringly assertive, convey more accurate images of women's conflicts, and speak more fruitfully to the intersection of private and public in women's experience, than would the projection of a more consistent "self."

Gallagher also does a comparative study. Her argument speaks to the development of women's subjectivity in the Early Modern period by assessing the different historic and personal circumstances of Cavendish and Mary Astell. Gallagher postulates an equation between the political and the personal as she argues, most persuasively, that Cavendish's sense of self is based on her royalism and her gender. As she says, "Cavendish's Toryism largely consists of her commitment to absolute monarchy, but most of her defenses of this form of government turn into defenses of singularity itself. The monarch becomes the figure for the self-enclosed, autonomous nature of any person. . . . Hence, what at first appears to be an absolutism that would merely lead to the subjection of all individuals except the monarch was actually for Cavendish the foundation for a subjectivity that would make its own absolute claims" (26–27). Gallagher responds to the multiplicity of subjectivities in Cavendish's work most astutely, but, finally, interprets them somewhat differently than I do. Although she notes that "Cavendish's texts show the infinitude of selfhood accompanies the birth of the subject" (32), she sees such self-fragmentation as dangerous, bespeaking "utter solitude," and tending toward a "regressive" self-pursuit. In contrast, Mary Astell, according to Gallagher, makes "a more socially engaged use of absolutist politics" (33). Yet, as Gallagher also notes, Astell's urgent call for an institution of women's education was hedged with the dualist hierarchy pervasive in Western patriarchal thought, and was founded on absolute allegiance to a superior (male) God and a monarch, Queen Anne. In other words, Astell's project, appealing and practical as it seems, founders on its hierarchical assumptions. I would argue that, on the other hand, Cavendish's literary production, most notably *Blazing-World,* is radically and effectively utopian. Despite its gestures toward royalist politics, *Blazing-World* depicts multiplicity, diversity, and a generative subjectivity that is relational rather than hierarchical. One might wonder if readers, men and women alike, are made uneasy by a woman writer's determined use of self as referent, even if she succeeds in representing collaborative models of creativity.

12. Within the text, as well as in her epilogue, Cavendish seems to blur the distinction between herself as author and the narrator and character, Margaret Newcastle. For example, when the Empress tells the Spirits she had seen Ben Jonson's play, the *Alchymist*, she undercuts the distinction between her native land and the author's (B-W 65–66). Interestingly, the most recent utopian work of a sophisticated contemporary writer, Ursula Le Guin, pursues a similar breakdown of conventional distinctions between art and life (see *Always Coming Home*).

13. An important study in political theory seeks to delineate the necessary social commitments needed to sustain a viable community; see Almond and Verba.

14. In a recent radio discussion about democracy, moderated by Barbara Goodwin, Stepan said that the ability to sustain multiple identities is necessary for social cohesion in our contemporary world. He gives a successful example of such multiple identity in the ability of Catalonians to see themselves not only according to their ethnic roots, but also as Spaniards and members of a larger European community. Although in Catalonia, as in Croatia, factionalism threatened to tear apart the social fabric, an adoption of varying "selves" finally averted war.

3. Islands of Felicity:
Women Seeing Utopia in Seventeenth-Century France

1. Based on statistical analysis of the family background of salon members, Lougee argues that salons promoted an intermingling of nobility and the bourgeoisie, and that male mockery of preciosity arose from a fear of such a redistribution of power. *Le Paradis des Femmes: Women, Salons, and Social Stratification in Seventeenth Century France*) Stanton asserts that the "myth of preciosity" as a comical, exaggerated style of behavior was created to cover male fears of women's activities and influence. She speaks of the *précieuse* as representing "the castrating female who denies man's primacy" ("The Fiction of *Préciosité* and the Fear of Women", 126)

2. For further discussion of *préciosité*, see Backer, *Precious Women*; Lougee, *Le Paradis des Femmes: Women, Salons and Social Stratification in Seventeenth Century France*, and Pelous, *Amour précieux, amour galant.*

3. Conversations were extremely important in the long novels of the first half of the seventeenth century as a means of analyzing complex emotional and psychological questions. Mlle. de Scudéry repeatedly depicts her characters gathered in groups for conversation or the telling and discussion of tales. The conversations in her works were so highly valued that they were compiled and printed separately through the 1680s as *Conversations sur divers sujets*, *Conversations nouvelles sur divers sujets*, and so on.

The literary fairy tale owes even more to the discussions of the salons. As early as 1685, it was fashionable for ladies to tell fairy tales to one another in these gatherings. Mme. d'Aulnoy was the first to put such a tale into print, with her story, "L'Isle de la Félicité." In one of the volumes of her tales she even creates as a frame a group of women who tell the following tales to one another during a carriage ride. As Thelander writes in "Mother Goose and Her Goslings: The France of Louis XIV as Seen through the Fairy Tale," these tales "shared the ideals of the Paris salons, particularly those which cultivated the refinement of language and manners associated with the précieux" (469). For a more complete history of this phenomenon, see Robert's *Le conte de Fées littéraire en France de la fin du XVIIe à la fin du XVIIIe siècle* and Storer's *Un Episode littéraire de la fin du XVIIe siècle: La Mode des contes de fées (1685–1700)*.

The link between epistolary writing and conversation has long been established, as practitioners such as Mme. de Sévigné presented their letters as an attempt to sustain dialogue with the absent addressee. Because letters were then read aloud in social gatherings, the process of discussion and debate was further extended.

As these genres incorporated the salon's patterns of social interaction into their very structure, they facilitated "the transformation of narrator and audience into a private academy, an interpreting assembly joined together for the purpose of analyzing the significance of even the smallest element of the narrated stories" (De Jean 7). When the text presented an alternate society, this invitation to analysis may have also included reflection on the structures of society and its possible transformation.

4. Madeleine de Scudéry's novels include *Ibrahim ou L'illustre Bassa* (4 vols., 1641), *Artamène ou le Grand Cyrus* (10 vols., 1649–53), and *Clélie, Histoire romaine* (10 vols., 1654–60). She was also the author of novella: *Célinte, Nouvelle première* (1661), *Mathilde d'Aguilar* (1667), and *La Promenade de Versailles* (1669). Other works include poetry, essays on moral issues, and a set of discourses attributed to famous women of the past, *Les Femmes illustres ou Les Harangues héroïques* (1642–44). A helpful biography and brief discussion of her works may be found in Aronson.

5. For an analysis of Mlle. de Scudéry's ideal of conversation, see Goldsmith, *Exclusive Conversations: The Art of Interaction in Seventeenth-Century France.*

6. Her works met with success in Italy and England, and she has been called "a European novelist" (Aronson 153). For a study of the reception of her works, see Aronson, 137–70; and Alain Niderst, "Madeleine de Scudéry de 1660 à 1789."

7. The influence of *préciosité* on Mme. d'Aulnoy has been noted by numerous critics. Focusing principally on her language are Jacques Barchilon, "'Précieux' Elements in the Fairy Tale of the Seventeenth Century"; Teresa Di Scanno, *La Mode des contes de fées de 1690 à 1705*; and Marcelle Maistre Welch, "Les Jeux de l'Ecriture dans les Contes de Fées de Mme. d'Aulnoy." Welch also addresses *précieux* themes of love and sexuality in her article, "La Femme, le mariage et l'amour dans les contes de fées mondains du XVIIème siècle français."

8. According to Welch, "the typical heroine aspires as of right to earthly felicity and one not necessarily acquired through marriage. She claims free choice, she counts on immediate satisfaction of the senses" ("La Femme" 57). Unless otherwise indicated, all translations are my own.

Farrell qualifies this reading by stressing that, although the tales reflect "a feminine utopic vision" of power and pleasure (54), their presentation in the "frivolous" genre of the fairy tale provided only a vicarious fulfillment of needs, therefore neutralizing impulses toward real reform.

9. Most critics have focused on her biography or on the place of the tales in the development of the fairy tale as a genre. It is only recently that critics have begun to study the tales' style, symbolism, or ideological content. For a brief biography, see "Madame d'Aulnoy: Writer of Fantasy" in Wilson and Warnke, *Women Writers of the Seventeenth Century*. An interesting psychological interpretation of the tales has been offered by Amy DeGraff in *The Tower and the Well*.

10. She aided the nobles in revolt against the regent, Anne d'Autriche, and her minister, Mazarin during the Fronde (1648–53). She helped claim Orléans for the rebel cause and in Paris ordered the cannons of the Bastille to be turned on the royal troops.

11. Having refused or been denied numerous political matches, she fell in love at the age of forty-three with Lauzun, a man who could hardly be considered her social equal. The king initially gave permission for the marriage, then rescinded it a few days later and had Lauzun imprisoned.

12. In her study, "A House of Her Own: Marginality and Dissidence in the 'Memoires' of La Grande Mademoiselle (1627–1693)", Cholakian argues that, deprived of a significant role in the patriarchal society of the court, Mlle de Montpensier took pleasure in creating a home of her own, based on the maternal line. (The name Montpensier comes from property inherited from her mother.)

13. Leibacher-Ouvrard, 7.

14. For a discussion of utopias in the seventeenth century, see Manuel and Manuel, *French Utopias: An Anthology of Ideal Societies*; Leibacher-Ouvrard, *Libertinage et Utopies sous le règne de Louis XIV*, and Ronzeaud, "La femme dans le roman utopique de la fin du XVIIᵉ siècle".

15. Even the term "freedom" was defined less in political terms than in the language of personal need. Mlle de Gournay, one of the strongest voices in defense of women, spoke of freedom as "the phenomenon of being taken seriously, of having the opportunity for intellectual and artistic fulfillment and success" (Wilson and Warnke xxi).

16. From the viewpoints of history and contemporary politics, Mlle. de Scudéry had reasons to contrast violent Madrid and peaceful Avignon. In the fourteenth century, Pedro the Cruel (the Pedro whom Mathilde flees) was so infamous for his vicious behavior that he alienated not only the French but the English, his former allies. In the seventeenth century, Spain and France were constant rivals for policical supremacy, despite Louis XIV's marriage to Maria Teresa of Spain. In 1667, the year of publication of *Mathilde*, the War of Devolution between the two countries began. In contrast, Avignon was a papal state and neutral territory from 1309 to 1791, and the popes that ruled there during the time of Mathilde were French.

17. Beugnot sees this publication as a way of returning the debate to society, but suggests that such endorsement through an established medium limits the "corrosive" effect of the utopian ideal (31). This repeats Farrell's argument that a work legitimized by publication is thereby neutralized and deprived of its subversive potential. For a history of the circumstances surrounding the writing of the letters, their sources and what little critical attention they have received, see Bertaud, "En marge de leurs *Mémoires*, une correspondance entre Mlle de Montpensier et Mme de Motteville."

18. Bertaud cites *L'Astrée* as a source of Mlle. de Montpensier's vision, but she also acknowledges the importance of the novels of Mlle. de Scudéry, in particular a passage of *Clélie* that describes a tranquil society of "illustres Solitaires" (284–85).

19. Bertaud also underscores Mlle. de Montpensier's debt to *précieuse* society: "The polite society that she imagines is not so fantastical that it does not recall the world of the salons and the life of the *ruelle*, another source of her inspiration" (285). The *ruelle* refers to the space between a bed and the wall and is a reference to the bedchambers where much of *précieuse* social life was conducted.

20. For a discussion of how gender affected access rights and privacy in seventeenth-century France and how this could be conveyed in the novel, see Danahy, "Social, Sexual and Human Spaces in *La Princesse de Clèves*." Boundaries are less important for Mlle. de Scudéry, who, aside from her portrayal of the land of the new Sauromates, chose instead to illustrate the value of cosmopolitanism by describing countries where strangers were welcomed. Mlle de Montpensier also suggests a more relaxed attitude toward visitors, since she speaks of no barrier on the shady routes leading to her republic.

21. The island's allegorical meaning, as a figure for human happiness, is particularly clear at the beginning and end of the tale.

22. In an interesting detail, Zephire cannot carry the prince on his back, so carries him in his arms as he had borne Psyche. This reference to the ancient myth is highly significant; Psyche is taken against her will to the palace of Cupid, where she is kept in ignorance of his identity and restricted by his rules. Failure to obey the male results in punishment. Here Mme. d'Aulnoy revises the tale, reversing gender roles and transforming the tale of transgression and punishment to one of love and tragedy. Mme. d'Aulnoy was evidently fascinated with the story of Psyche, for she used it several times (for example, in "Le Serpent Vert" and "Gracieuse et Percinet") to explore the possibility of greater freedom and cooperation between the sexes.

23. It is important to note that Lutin does not fight as a conventional male, such as the Russian prince. Instead, he adopts the dress of one of the princess's Amazons and kills her enemy through trickery. This experimentation with gender roles is common in the tales of Mme. d'Aulnoy.

24. In her discussion of seventeenth-century fairy tales, Thelander writes that the blending of kingdoms through marriage is a common concept of the tales and indeed, to some extent, of the period overall. She cites Lucien Febvre: "Before the Revolution, people walked straight across the *limites:* aristocrats, scholars, traders crossed with no surprise. Frontiers existed only for the military and the prince—and only in times of war" (475). Thus the intermingling of two peaceable kingdoms is not astonishing, while the defenses of the "Isle de la Félicité" appear all the more significant as a sign of woman's fear and vulnerability.

25. According to Ronzeaud, men wished to eliminate or restrict the activities of women in their utopias through fear of their passions and sensuality (79). It is ironic that both sexes structured their ideal societies around fear of the other.

26. Jacques Du Bosc, *L'Honneste femme* (1632), quoted and translated by Lougee in *Paradis*, 21.

27. Beugnot also notes the limiting effect of the conditional mood: "these two reveries . . . establish a new abbey of Thélème, a true utopia, a place of 'nowhere' bounded by the recourse to the conditional." (29).

28. It seems clear from the context of the story that Parthénie is speaking of heterosexual love, yet she chooses the phrase "une personne," rather than a clearly

masculine form, such as "un amant," which in that time was an innocent term corresponding to "suitor." Her use of the feminine form may indicate that other relationships, such as friendship, could also be deeply satisfying or (and I feel this is more likely) it is a reflection of her unwillingness to state openly her desire for a man's love. The vague term "quelqu'un" may serve the same purpose.

4. Mothers and Monsters in
Sarah Robinson Scott's *Millenium Hall*

1. Biographical research on the life of Sarah Robinson Scott has been made difficult because at her request her personal papers were destroyed after her death. A short account of her life, including a list of her published books, written by Sir Egerton Brydges, the son-in-law of her younger brother, was published in 1805. The canon established by Brydges has not been challenged. One full-length study of Scott's life and work is available in book form, a 1932 doctoral dissertation by Walter M. Crittenden, which brought together nearly all of the biographical information that was available at that time. I have relied upon Crittenden's work extensively for the factual information given in this paper, although my interpretations of some of the facts differ from his.

2. According to Ferguson in *First Feminists* (128), their mother, Elizabeth Drake, had herself been educated at the academy of Bathsua Pell Makin, an early and influential proponent of advanced education for girls. The strong influence of their mother was probably enhanced even further by their grandmother's second husband, Dr. Conyers Middleton, who served as professor of Classical Literature at Cambridge. In addition to Ferguson (*First Feminists* 22–24, and 311–26), further biographical information can be found in Spencer's introduction to the 1986 Virago edition of *Millenium Hall*.

3. The practice of including a sister or a woman friend on the wedding trip and, eventually, in the household was common in the eighteenth century and does not, in itself, indicate anything unusual in the relationship between Sarah Scott and Lady Montagu or in Mr. Scott's response to it. However, a hint that Lady Montagu's presence might have created a difficulty in the marriage is found in the text of *Millenium Hall* in which Mr. Morgan, the husband of the character that comes nearest to being based on Scott's own life, refuses to allow his wife even to see her friend, Miss Mancel, thus forcing their separation until he becomes too ill to prevent their meeting.

4. A copy of the book in the library of Horace Walpole, who was a friend of her sister, comments on the flyleaf in pencil that the book "is the work of Lady Barbara Montagu and Mrs. Sarah Scott." Although the idea of a coauthored book about a female community is attractive, there is no corroborating evidence that Lady Montagu had any significant role in writing the book, and authorship has been attributed to Scott alone. All references to *Millenium Hall* will be to the 1955 edition edited by Crittenden.

5. Critical attention to Scott and *Millenium Hall* has been scarce. The novel itself was out of print from 1778 until 1955, when it was edited by Walter M. Crittenden. A facsimile of the 1762 edition followed in 1974, and a more accessible

paperback, edited and introduced by Jane Spencer, came out in 1986 but has since gone out of print. There have been two doctoral dissertations on the life and works of Scott, Crittenden's 1932 dissertation at the University of Pennsylvania, which is available in print through the University of Pennsylvania Press, and Gaby Esther Onderwyzer's 1957 unpublished dissertation at the University of California at Berkeley. *Millenium Hall* is listed with a brief plot outline in Lyman Tower Sargent's *British and American Utopian Literature, 1516–1985*. As a result of the renewed interest in women writers and the recent paperback edition, *Millenium Hall* is beginning to be mentioned, if only briefly, in books on the tradition of women's writing (Faderman 103–6; Grier 137; Mavor 83–86; Katherine M. Rogers 342–46; Spender 134–35; and Todd 342–46). In addition, the number of recently published sustained studies of the novel's meaning and significance is increasing. To date the most notable books with chapters on *Millenium Hall* include Boone's study of canonical and noncanonical novels, which groups it with Gaskell's *Cranford*, Jewett's *Country of the Pointed Firs*, and Gilman's *Herland* as works about female communities that run counter to the tradition of the marriage plot (288–95); and Lanser's excellent study of the uses of narrative voice by women writers, which reads *Millenium Hall* against Wollstonecraft's *The Wrongs of Women* as illustrative of the difficulties encountered by women writers in establishing a female communal voice (223–38). Among the increasing number of articles on Scott are Grow (9–15), Hill (107–30), Carretta (303–25), and Rabb (3–16).

6. The metaphoric uses of ruined health as a physical manifestation of a diseased soul as well as a synecdoche for the corruption of a male-dominated society are certainly not unique to *Millenium Hall*. I might cite, as particularly interesting and relevant examples, the use of deteriorated health in this way in the works of Mary Wollstonecraft, particularly the poor health of both male and female characters in her novels *Mary: A Fiction* and *Maria: or the Wrongs of Woman*, and in the works of Mary Shelley, her daughter, notably the poor health and ultimate death of Dr. Frankenstein in *Frankenstein* and the devastating plague of *The Last Man*.

7. This "Attick school," devoted to a study of the arts and the classics, falls into a tradition of writings about and experiments with advanced education for girls and women, including the works of Mary Astell and Bathsua Makin. I have already noted that Sarah Scott's mother is said to have attended Makin's school and it is likely that Scott and Lady Montagu were familiar with Astell's *A Serious Proposal to the Ladies*.

8. See note 3.

9. According to the *Oxford English Dictionary*, the word "monster," was used to describe human dwarfs and giants during the eighteenth century. The following is a broad definition for that period: "an animal or plant deviating in one or more of its parts from the normal type; specifically an animal afflicted with some congenital malformation."

10. I am using the term *heterosexual* here to denote sexual relations between men and women and the term *homosexual* to denote sexual relations between women, understanding that neither of these twentieth-century terms would have had meaning for Sarah Scott or her contemporaries. The question of whether we can accurately describe sexual or affectional relationships as homosexual or lesbian prior to the invention of these terms in the late nineteenth century is a controversial one that is

but merely to argue that the text of *Millenium Hall* does not support a reading of its characters' relationships as lesbian.

5. Gaskell's Feminist Utopia:
The Cranfordians and the Reign of Goodwill

1. For further discussion of Showalter and feminist literary utopias, see Pfaelzer, "The Changing"; and Kuryllo.

2. George Griffith's essay describes fully the long-lasting genre debate as to whether *Cranford* is in fact a novel, noting that critics have argued, variously, that it is or is not a novel, a collection of short stories, a "novella," a short fiction series, and a serial. For our purposes, since it is a long, prose narrative, we shall consider it a novel and refer the intersted reader to Griffith.

3. Although critics have often assumed that Gaskell's description of the Cranfordians as Amazons was intended to be ironic—see Keating and Dodsworth—Auerbach stresses the suitability of the term, noting that the text rejects the traditional military image of the Amazons, and that instead the "more womanly" Cranfordians are considered to be the "more Amazonian" (83). Fowler also makes a convincing argument for the appropriateness of the term: "*Cranford* begins with a joke about Amazons: 'Amazóns' possess the town, but ironically, are at once shown not to be Amazons at all but funny old ladies. In the end, though, the joke is on the reader, for these old ladies turn out to be the winners, the survivors, the heroines" (728).

4. The theoretical base for defining feminist literary utopias tends to differ from that of literary utopias in general. For example, Darko Suvin's widely accepted definition of a literary utopia is based on structure: "Utopia is the verbal construction of a particular quasi-human community where sociopolitical institutions, norms and individual relationships are organized according to a more perfect principle than in the author's community, this construction being based on estrangement arising out of an alternative historical hypothesis" ("Defining" 132). Similarly, Lyman Tower Sargent defines literary utopias through the establishment of three structural categories: "eutopia or positive Utopia, the dystopia or negative Utopia, and the satirical Utopia" ("Utopia" 143). Feminist utopias, on the other hand, are most often defined by content, and necessarily so; the extent to which a text is or is not feminist can only be determined through an examination of content. So while a text may be defined as a literary utopia according to its structure, it will be further defined as a feminist literary utopia, according to its content.

5. It must be noted, though, that while feminist utopias are, by definition, communal, communal utopias are not necessarily feminist.

6. Notably, *Cranford* differs from other feminist utopias in that it has a female narrator who initially enters the community as a visitor and then, after a conversion process, becomes a participating member.

7. Duthie notes that "It was certainly not unrealistic to show their [women's] numbers as considerable in any country town. The surplus of women over men was a large one in the first half of the nineteenth century, and middle-class widows and spin-

sters, who had no profession and could not seek employment in industry, naturally congregated there" (41). However, Cranford is exceptionally female, even considering the uneven demographics of the time.

8. Cranford is described as being without gentlemen, but the town does not lack men. In the course of the novel, we meet the surgeon, the shopkeeper, and several male domestics; however, these men obviously do not represent a threat to the authority of the genteel, middle-class Cranfordians.

9. Dodsworth's essay is worth reading for historical purposes. It offers an alternately shocking and amusing demonstration of what might once be acceptably said about women's literature. According to Dodsworth, Deborah's fundamental flaw is her "hidden desire to equal the male" (135). He sees the novel as having a steady progression from Deborah, who foolishly strives "to rival the male in his own world" (143) and who leads the other women to "pretend to be as good as, or even better than, men" (133), to the satisfactory conclusion where, under Peter Jenkyns's guidance, "the principle of male vitality returns to Cranford" (141) and "the women have been shown their own inadequacy" (143). For Dodsworth, Deborah ultimately demonstrates, as does the entire text, "the insufficiency of the female in a world of two sexes" (139).

10. There is, of course, the famous passage where Deborah scoffs at "the modern idea of women being equal to men. Equal, indeed! she knew they were superior" (51). Although Dodsworth takes this statement of Deborah's as further evidence of her feminist militancy, sentiments of this nature are standard tenets of Victorian patriarchy. In fact, John Ruskin, that most outspoken and prolific of Victorian misogynists, insisted, as does Deborah, upon women's inherent moral superiority: in "Of Queens's Gardens," Ruskin describes women as "enduringly, incorruptibly good" (119); he asserts further that "by her office, and place, she [woman] is protected from all danger and temptation" (117). Deborah's claim of female superiority, then, may more appropriately be seen as a statement of support for patriarchal values than as an endorsement of radical social reversals.

11. Charlotte Brontë kept her stock in an unstable company for the same reason; because her sister Emily had originally selected the company, Charlotte chose to maintain her investment regardless of financial losses.

12. Interestingly, the contemporary definition of feminism, as stated by the noted feminist historian Gerda Lerner, corresponds closely to that of Wollstonecraft: according to Lerner, feminism is a multifaceted theory involving, among other things, "(a) a doctrine advocating social and political rights for women equal to those of men; (b) an organized movement for the attainment of these rights; (c) the assertion of the claims of women as a group and the body of theory women have created; (d) belief in the necessity of large-scale social change in order to increase the power of women" (236).

13. In a letter to John Ruskin, Gaskell wrote of *Cranford*, "And it is true too, for I have seen the cow that wore the grey flannel jacket" (747).

14. Dodsworth makes the singular claim that Brown's "death is a terrible thing just because he is a representation of the Victorian male as a benign deity" (134); putting aside the question of why Brown might be considered a "deity," it is also questionable whether he is indeed "benign."

15. Hilary M. Schor, in "Affairs of the Alphabet: Reading, Writing and Narrating in *Cranford*," offers an interesting discussion of Mary and the "evolution of the narrator" (288). Schor argues, as do I, "that by telling the story of the Amazons, 'Mary Smith'—who had not looked at all like a character— has resolved her own choice of world and affiliations" (288). Schor's essay, however, focuses primarily on *Cranford* "as a woman writer's experiment with narrative, an extended commentary on the ways women are taught to read cultural signs, and a serious critique of the role of literature in shaping female readers" (288).

16. Mary's confession of her fear of eyes raises, yet again, a question that many feminist theorists have recently been asking: Is the gaze necessarily male? According to Kaplan, "The gaze is not necessarily male (literally), but to own and activate the gaze, given our language and the structure of the unconscious, is to be in the 'masculine' position" (30). In her recent discussion of the same issue, Newman explores the effects of both the male and female gaze in *Wuthering Heights*, and she suggests that a "gaze that escaped patriarchal specular relations would not simply reverse the positions of male and female, . . . but would eliminate the hierarchy altogether" (1032); she stresses, though, "the difficulty of doing that" (1032).

17. In the aftermath of the *Mary Barton* furor, Gaskell wrote a friend: "Some people here are very angry and say the book will do harm; and for a time I have been shaken and sorry" (*Letters* 70). Following the publication of *Ruth*, Gaskell wrote again: "I think I must be an improper woman without knowing it, I do so manage to shock people" (*Letters* 223).

6. Subjectivity as Feminist Utopia

1. See, for example, Ursula Le Guin, *The Dispossessed* (1974), Joanna Russ, *The Female Man* (1975), Marge Piercy, *Woman on the Edge of Time* (1976), and Judy Grahn, *Mundane's World* (1988).

2. See Carol Kolmerten's incisive study of women's experiences in nineteenth century intentional communities in *Women in Utopia: The Ideology of Gender in the American Owenite Communities*, in particular 90–100.

3. Benjamin develops the theory of intersubjectivity in three core texts, "The Bonds of Love: Rational Violence and Erotic Domination" (1980), "A Desire of One's Own: Psychoanalytic Feminism and Intersubjective Space" (1986) and *The Bonds of Love* (1988).

4. Marianne Hirsch argues that the repression of the fictional mother "stands at the very basis of the marriage plot." Hirsch suggests that we need to include maternal absence, silence, and negativity in this analysis. She also considers the impact of eliminating the mother on the heroine's development and allegiances. See in particular 46–50.

5. See Warshaw for a qualitative analysis of the mother-daughter separation process of young adult women.

6. Translated by Benjamin from *Phänomenologie des Geistes*; cited in Benjamin, *Bonds* 38.

7. See D. W. Winnicott, *The Child, the Family and the Outside World*, cited in Benjamin, *Bonds* 40–41.

8. See Pfaelzer, *Utopian Novel in America* 26–51, and "Immanence, Indeterminance, and the Utopian Pun in *Looking Backward*" in *Looking Backward 1988–1888*, ed. Patai, 51–67.

9. Some passages from this discussion of the texts of "The Harmonists" by Rebecca Harding Davis and of "Transcendental Wild Oats" appeared originally in "The Sentimental Promise and the Utopian Myth," in which I argue that these early critiques of utopia expose the fallacy of sentimentality, which promised security through male patronage. At the same time, they restore the promise of sentimentality, which provides for women's social, economic, and moral authority through the segregation of gender spheres.

10. Interesting discussions of celibacy in utopian communities can be found in Blair and Foster, *Religion and Sexuality*.

11. For histories of Fruitlands, see Bronson Alcott's *Letters* and *Journals*, and the historical material in Bazin, Cheyney, Elbert, Francis, Harrison, and Sears.

12. Habermas, in "A Theory of Communicative Competence," apparently first used the term in order to designate an individual capacity *and* a social domain. Benjamin appropriated the term, initially a human capacity, to designate a theoretical standpoint from which to criticize the exclusively intrapsychic conception of the individual in psychoanalysis. In *Bonds*, she traces the development of the term in psychological studies through Colin Trevarthen and Daniel Stein. See Benjamin, *Bonds* 19–20.

7. Texts and Contexts:
American Women Envision Utopia, 1890–1920

1. I have gathered my list of utopian novels from four main sources: Lyman Tower Sargent's classic bibliography, *British and American Utopian Literature, 1516–1985*; Kenneth Roemer's excellent annotated bibliography at the end of *The Obsolete Necessity: America in Utopian Writings, 1899–1990*; Carol Kessler's recently updated annotated bibliography in vol. 1 of *Utopian Studies*; and letters from utopian bookseller and scholar Stuart Teitler, of Kaleidoscope Books, who has delighted in telling me about utopian novels not listed in any of the standard bibliographies. All page numbers in the text refer to the first editions or the edition listed in the Works Cited.

2. Critics such as Jane Tompkins have shown us that, in Tompkins' words "out of the ideological materials they had at their disposal, the sentimental novelists elaborated a myth that gave women the central position of power and authority in the culture" ("Sentimental Power," 83). Barbara Welter, on the other hand, believes that women writing sentimental novels simply reflected stereotypes about women. See also Dee Garrison's "Immoral Fiction in the Late Victorian Library," where she argues that sentimental fiction subverts traditional male authority.

3. The only exception is Nettie Parrish Martin, *A Pilgrim's Progress* (1908). Martin writes that in her Martian utopia, women "have nothing to do but eat, sleep, and take their ease" (105).

4. We now know for certain that Lillian B. Jones was black. As I discovered in the Fort Worth city directories for 1916 through 1930, Jones was listed as a high school teacher at the "colored" school; Terrell High School; she then became a telephone operator in 1929. She owned her own home at 1109 East Humbolt Street in

Fort Worth. As was the practice for many southern city directories, the Fort Worth Directory placed a "(C)" after the names of black residents and such a designation was placed after Jones's name. The faculty pictures in the Terrell High School year-book for 1922 show "Mrs. L. B. Jones" to be a light-skinned black woman with an "A.B." who taught English.

5. DuPlessis (*Writing*) maintains that these tactics of writing beyond the ending might result in woman-to-woman bonds and forms of a communal protagonist. She finds the romance plot muffling the main female character by repressing quest, by valorizing heterosexual ties, and by offering coupling as a sign of personal and narrative success.

8. Consider Her Ways: The Cultural Work of Charlotte Perkins Gilman's Pragmatopian Stories, 1908–1913

1. I owe to Lee Cullen Khanna the insight to apply Jane Tompkins's concept of "cultural work" to feminist utopian fiction. Jane Donawerth and Carol Kolmerten provided invaluable encouragement and sound advice regarding revision, as have my Penn State colleagues Shirley Marchalonis and Ian Marshall. I thank them each.

2. Realize, however, that Bakhtin missed recognizing the applicability of his insight to boundaries marking gender, a locale of social change that was engaging ever more interest as he began his career. He lived from 1895 to 1975, overlapping the last forty years of Gilman's life. During the 1920s he was working on a treatise about the nature of moral responsibility and aesthetics, a relationship that had concerned Gilman during the previous two decades.

3. *The Forerunner* includes poems, short stories, fables, essays, editorials, plays, one serialized novel and one serialized work of nonfiction per volume. For each of the fourteen issues of volume 1, contents appear on the title page; indices for volumes 2–7 appear at the end of each volume.

4. See also Eisler, "Pragmatopia: Women's Utopias and Scenarios for a Possible Future," a paper delivered at the October 2–5, 1986 Conference of the Society of Utopian Studies at Asilomar, California. Eisler's study suggests an updated version of Gilman's 1898 *Women and Economics*, now including recent archeological discoveries and evolutionary theory. For further information on this recent research, see works cited by Elinor W. Gadon, Marija Gimbutas, and Lucy R. Lippard for archeology and Stephen Jay Gould for evolution.

5. The original Greek antecedents are *gy* from *gyne* for "woman"; "l" from English "linking," and Greek *lyein* or *lyo* having the double meaning: to solve or resolve (as in analysis) and to dissolve or set free (as in catalysis)"; *an* from *andros* for "man" (105).

6. Cranny-Francis, discussing Marge Piercy's *Woman on the Edge of Time* (1976), writes, "three intersecting narratives—realist, utopian, dystopian—construct a complex text in which Piercy deconstructs dominant ideological discourses, [and] examines the interpellation of the individual in ideology . . . [,] one of the principal means by which ideology is naturalized into the lives of individuals, the realist narrative" (137). See her chap. 4, "Feminist Utopias," 107–42.

7. In an earlier discussion of Gilman's story "Bee Wise," I discussed the relationship between utopian and realistic writing. I suggested that fictional solutions can

be called "utopian" to the extent that they do not anywhere exist; they can also be called "realistic" to the extent that they are possible. That "literary realism"—which I would here define as a rationally constructed vision of what could be possible in a currently existing society, hence "realistic"—was in fashion during Gilman's historical moment offered her a serendipitous coincidence, even though she wrote at the very end of that era. Perhaps one reason why all of her work was out of print by 1930 was that she had held to this literary fashion beyond its passing. The fact of a Great War did not dampen her expectation of human progress, nor did the furor over Freud temper her belief in human capacity to choose rationally.

8. *The Yellow Wallpaper*, written August 1890, was first published in the *New England Magazine* in January 1892.

9. Gilman explains in her autobiography, *The Living of Charlotte Perkins Gilman*, why this never reached completion: "One enthusiast, starting a new magazine, engaged me to write a serial novel for him, but was punished for his rashness by the prompt failure of his venture" (303). Only three installments appeared; a fourth exists as page proofs.

10. "Dr. Clair's Place" reverses "The Yellow Wallpaper" by demonstrating what *should be done* for exhausted women, instead of exposing gross error. Dr. Willy Clair, a southerner by birth and a specialist in psychopathy, established a sanatorium in southern California called The Hills. As her patient, Octavia Welch recovers genuine happiness. The story outlines Dr. Clair's procedure for accomplishing a "cure."

11. *The Reproduction of Mothering: Psychoanalysis and the Sociology of Gender* (1978); for a critical discussion of the theory, see also *Signs* 6, no. 3 (1981): 482–514 for critiques. A brief discussion appears in "Being and Doing: A Cross-Cultural Examination of the Socialization of Males and Females" (1978) in *Woman in Sexist Society*, edited by Vivian Gornick and Barbara K. Moran.

12. Benigna McAvelly (listen to the pun on Machiavelli!) also appears in the novel serialization *Benigna McAvelly* (1914).

13. Gilman's good friend, Martha S. Bensley Bruère, wrote for *The Survey* and in 1919 published in the *Ladies' Home Journal* a serialization of a utopian novel, *Mildred Carver, U.S.A.*—an updated, gender-revised version of the universal service to one's country imagined by Bellamy in *Looking Backward*.

14. Hayden argues that Gilman, though a self-proclaimed socialist, in fact supported highly individualistic social solutions based upon a "benevolent" capitalistic economy (107). If we are to classify her economic views according to her recommendations rather than her abstract preferences, then we must recognize that she advocated capitalism, albeit a grassroots version defiant of corporate hegemony. However, as Hayden notes, Gilman did not disturb the hierarchy of class structure.

15. From Proverbs 6:6–11 (King James version):

6 Go to the ant, thou sluggard; consider her ways, and be wise:

7 Which having no guide, overseer, or ruler,

8 Provideth her meat in the summer, *and* gathereth her food in the harvest.

9 How long wilt thou sleep, O sluggard? when wilt thou arise out of thy sleep?

10 Yet a little sleep, a little slumber, a little folding of the hands to sleep:
11 So shall thy poverty come as one that travelleth, and thy want as an armed man.

16. Gilman may have read the juvenile serialization "A Brave Girl" by Elizabeth Stuart Phelps, in Wide Awake, in which a former college woman becomes a business success.

9. Science Fiction by Women in the Early Pulps, 1926–1930

1. For help in locating these women writers, I wish to thank the librarians of the Rosenfeld Collection at the University of Maryland, Baltimore County, especially John Beck and Barry Wood; the librarians of the Library of Congress; and the librarians of McKeldin Library at the University of Maryland at College Park, especially Betty Day and Judith Cmero. Women writers are best represented in Tuck's Encyclopedia of Science Fiction and Fantasy through 1968, which includes four (Hansen, Harris, Lorraine, and Stone) of these eight writers. Tuck reports a story from F. J. Ackerman, that Hansen "appeared at a meeting of the Los Angeles Science Fiction Society in 1939" and said "she had placed these stories for her brother, a world traveller, who had written them" (1:205), but Tuck seems not to believe this denial of authorship. The story is hard to credit because, while it might be embarrassing for a woman to publish science fiction in the 1930s, it was not for most men; and because Hansen continued to publish, mainly nonfiction science works in Amazing Stories in the 1940s, and a long text in 1969 arguing a different configuration for a prehistoric Atlantic Ocean—The Ancient Atlantic. My analysis in this essay will not include women who published in the pulp magazines before the advent of science fiction specialty magazines; see Bleiler's bibliography, Science Fiction: The Early Years, for such writers. Most famous of these writers is Gertrude Barrows Bennett, who published under the pseudonym Francis Stevens, and whose stories anticipate many of the characteristics of the writers I discuss here (see Lloyd Arthur Eshback's introduction to Bennett's The Heads of Cerberus; Tuck 1:38; and Bleiler 703–5 and 40–41). Aladra Septama, who published "The Beast Men of Ceres" in Amazing Stories Quarterly in 1929, a detective story set in a utopian future where women retain their own names and residences even after marriage (and where women resolve the plot peacefully by arranging marriages with the aliens whom the men are trying to destroy), is written not by a woman but by Judson W. Reeves (see Day 97).

2. Mary Shelley's Frankenstein is alluded to in Clare Winger Harris, "Artificial Man," 79, 80, 82; Ellis, "Creatures of the Light," esp. 204; Ludwick, 536; and Hansen, "City on the Cloud," 427. Perhaps Hansen alludes to Mary Shelley's The Last Man in "Man from Space," esp. 1044. Besides Shelley as a model, many of the science fiction writers had published in other genres: see Irving, Songs; Rice, Dainty Dishes; and Harris, Persephone. References to science taught in college classrooms appear in Clare Winger Harris, "Evolutionary Monstrosity," "Fate of the Poseidonia," "Menace of Mars," and "Runaway World"; Hansen, "Man from Space," and "Undersea Tube";

Lorraine, "Into the 28th Century," and "Jovian Jest"; Stone, "Out of the Void"; and Ellis, "Slaves of Dust." The University of Illinois is mentioned in Clare Winger Harris, "Ape Cycle," 304; the University of Arizona in Lorraine, *Brain*, 7, and Hansen, "What the Sodium Lines Revealed," 130, 137; and the University of California in Hansen, "City on the Cloud," 426. On the history of science education for women in the United States, see Rossiter, esp. 1–50. Lilith Lorraine, the only writer on whom I have biographical information, was educated at the Universities of Arizona and California (see Donawerth, "Lilith Lorraine"). Hansen probably did graduate work in science at UCLA; see Hansen, *Ancient Atlantic*, 13.

3. For contemporary feminist science theorists who argue that women have a special empathy with other life forms, see Merchant, chapters 1 and 11; Rothschild; and Keller, esp. 101–3, 117–19, 145–51. Even in Rice and Tonjoroff-Roberts's "The Astounding Enemy," which treats insects as bug-eyed monsters, Mildred Sturtevant, the woman scientist captured by insects, has great empathy for them: "I have grown fond of these" giant lightning bugs (97); when the evil giant termite leader is killed, "to our amazement she ran to him and touched his face," mourning the death of this "great intelligence" (103).

4. In one case, I am almost convinced of direct influence: in both Charlotte Perkins Gilman's 1915 *Herland*, and in Lilith Lorraine's 1930 "Into the 28th Century," future utopians have developed cats who do not kill birds. See Gilman, *Herland*, 49–53, and Lorraine, "Into the 28th Century," 261.

5. In addition, the streets are safe for women even at night. In Hansen's "What the Sodium Lines Revealed," the streets are lighted from underneath in mosaic patterns (129). In Irving's "The Moon Woman," an alternate solution gives to every woman a "radiomatic" weapon so that she can protect herself (754).

6. The one story that pictures woman as a nurse presents her as a trained professional, idealizing nursing: "There is no finer or nobler [career] under heaven" (Ludwick 567).

7. Even in this early science fiction by women, there appear many versions of feminism, rather than a single coherent feminism. For reflections on the "feminisms" of later science fiction by women, I am indebted to Veronica Hollinger, "Feminisms, Criticisms, Science Fictions," revised as "Feminist Science Fiction: Breaking Up the Subject."

8. Harris's problem with a woman narrator and protagonist presages the problems that Judith Merril later faces, in the late 1940s and 1950s, when she experiments with female voice and housewife heroism in science fiction; Merril's problems are particularly noticeable in her novel *Shadow on the Hearth*.

10. Difference and Sexual Politics in Naomi Mitchison's *Solution Three*

1. Naomi Mitchison's books about Africa include some written specifically for the people of the tribe in Botswana that adopted her in the 1960s (i.e., *When We Become Men*), general history such as *The Africans*, and a biography of Bram Fischer (banned in South Africa) along with a collection of children's stories, *African Heroes, A Life for Africa*. For a full bibliography, see Benton.

2. I am offering only a sketch of Naomi Mitchison's life here. For a fuller picture of her life, writing, and politics, see Benton. Benton was given access to many private papers and letters.

3. Throughout her work, Naomi Mitchison has portrayed women who have eschewed conventional sexual and domestic roles. Her novel *We Have Been Warned* (1932), about the British Left, caused outrage across the political spectrum for its sympathy for women's aspirations toward sexual independence.

11. "There Goes the Neighborhood": Octavia Butler's Demand for Diversity in Utopias

1. Some of the recent texts that have particularly influenced my thinking about trends in women's utopian writing are Le Guin, *The Left Hand of Darkness*, *The Dispossessed*, and *Always Coming Home*; Russ, *The Female Man*; Wittig, *Les Guérillères*; Piercy, *Woman on the Edge of Time*; Gearhart, *The Wanderground*; Charnas, *Walk to the End of the World* and *Motherlines*; Tepper, *The Gate to Women's Country*; Elgin, *Native Tongue* and *The Judas Rose*; Slonczewski, *A Door Into Ocean*; Moffett, *Penterra*; Pamela Sargent, *The Shore of Women*; Felice, *Double Nocturne*; and Melissa Scott, *The Kindly Ones* and *Mighty Good Road*.

2. Zaki argues that "Butler believes that human nature is fundamentally violent and therefore flawed. The origin of violence, she suggests, lies in the human genetic structure, which is responsible for the contradictory impulses towards intelligence and hierarchy. These two conflicting impulses inevitably propel humans to wage war. . . . Connected to this trait is an inability to tolerate differences, usually physical differences of race and gender" (241), an argument Zaki takes nearly word for word from Butler's Oankali characters in *Xenogenesis*. I find it unconvincing in light of the adaptability of humans portrayed throughout Butler's work; but more important, the Oankali themselves prove to be wrong about many aspects of "human nature" through the course of the series. Dorothy Allison attempts to characterize Butler's views of men and women as essentialistic; again, I find the overall argument unconvincing, though she indicates points of contradiction in Butler's texts. Haraway's discussions of essentialism in Butler's work are much more complex. Haraway is troubled by what she perceives as the heterosexism of Butler's assumptions about human sexual behavior—a concern I share. But I would like to note that Butler's eradication of intercourse in *Xenogenesis* does not necessarily stem from her conservatism, as Zaki claims. Rather, Butler brings into question another "essential" component of humanity in bringing the "naturalness" of genital reproduction into question.

3. Sarah Lefanu, who notes that Butler is one of a number of women writing science fiction who uses "a traditional science fiction narrative framework . . . to undermine sexual and racial stereotypes," finds violence an essential component of Butler's feminist approach (88). "There is an element of violence . . . which is traditionally not a quality of 'feminine' writing," she writes. "[The violence] is transgressive; the construction of the inviolable body is a corollary of the construction of the coherent self" (99). Lefanu thus argues against the conception of Butler as having an essentialistic view of human nature.

4. Zaki's assertion that Butler's writing constitutes "dystopian pessimism, [which] assumes that dystopia is inevitable because its origins are ontological or otherwise metaphysical" and is therefore "anti-utopian and conservative," seems to me a misreading of Butler's project, particularly when Zaki states that "Butler's unmediated connections between biology and behavior have an implicit corollary: that abandoning the human body is a necessary prerequisite for real human alteration" (242). Butler's fiction insists on the possibilities for transforming a biological "human nature," which is fluid and unpredictable, responding to specific material forces as well as to biology. The characters in *Xenogenesis* who claim to have genetic "proof" of humanity's innate destructive tendencies are themselves perpetually surprised by human behavior, which a genetic map alone often does not help them to predict.

5. In regard to Butler's insistence on re-creating the human biological conditions of reproduction, it seems important to point out that many feminist critics target the social contract, which excludes women from participation in citizenship by positing them as objects rather than subjects of the political sphere, not the biological conditions of reproduction, as the juncture that renders patriarchy inevitable (and seemingly natural). See Pateman for a more thorough discussion of this argument. Three feminist utopias that follow a similar theme, removing women from the nuclear family structure and allowing them full interaction in the public sphere, are Shuler, *She Who Remembers*; Thomas, *Reindeer Moon*; and Holland, *Pillar of the Sky*. Since Zaki questions whether Butler's "conservative" family structures may arise from her sensitivity to "the increasing conservatism of the contemporary social and political order, which has made substantial inroads upon Afro-American communities" (245), it may be helpful to note three other recent novels by African-American women—Alice Walker, *The Temple of My Familiar* (1989); Toni Morrison, *Beloved* (1987); and Sherley Anne Williams, *Dessa Rose (1986)*; the first two of which fit into the fantasy genre—develop utopian themes based on radical restructurings of public and private spaces within the family and community.

6. Although the condition that afflicts the characters in *Clay's Ark* is described in earlier novels, I find it interesting that Butler chose to concentrate on the spread of the disease itself in the only Patternist novel published after the start of the AIDS epidemic. Like AIDS, the Clayark organism is spread through bodily fluids shared during physical contact, particularly during sex; when Keira chooses to lose her virginity with an infected man, she is fully aware that the consequence may be death. Yet rather than suggesting abstinence for affected individuals (as have some groups working to prevent the spread of AIDS), Butler insists that sexual activity is necessary for health: the disease exacerbates desire, and the individuals who shun physical contact die. She also insists that quarantine is an untenable solution, for a single individual who escapes can infect people "all over the world." Although the characters in *Clay's Ark* heroically attempt to isolate themselves, when the inevitable happens and the disease is spread beyond their community, they agree that "we knew it would happen sooner or later" (183).

7. "Mute" is a racial label as well as the name for a "handicap" in the Patternist books. In one of the contradictions of the dominant group, the mutes are alternately called "latents," implying the capacity to become telepathic, or treated as another

species entirely with nothing to offer the dominant group but their bodies. When one character in *Mind of My Mind* hears the term "mute," she exclaims, "I know what it means . . . it means nigger!"

8. Hortense Spillers's "Mama's Baby, Papa's Maybe" discusses the physical inscription of the body by torture as a discursive signifier. The black body is "interpreted" by the white master discourse to mean "slave"; it is then reinscribed, by whippings or brandings, as the property of a particular owner, available alone for his interpretation. The relationship between this bodily "text" and the written text of slave narratives is extremely complicated, but Spillers links the two as spaces of resistance to a hegemonic interpretation. As such, the slave narrative text may be seen as utopian because it necessarily posits a place outside the site of the master discourse that made its writing necessary.

9. I want to thank Jane Donawerth for helping to shape my ideas about Butler's writing and for editing this essay through several different drafts. I also want to thank my husband, Paul Anderson, for proofreading and fact-checking.

12. The Frozen Landscape in Women's Utopian and Science Fiction

1. See Freibert, 67–84.

2. In her play "The Convent of Pleasure" (1668), Cavendish further explores this conflict between a woman's utopia and the biological/reproductive roles that are metaphorically eliminated or deferred in the frozen world. A young heiress determines not to marry and forms an all-female community, devoted to sensual and intellectual indulgence. Counterpointed to the contentment of Lady Happy and her friends is a theatrical performance representing the ills they have escaped by retiring from the world of men: two "mean Women" lament their husbands' profligacy and abuse, stories repeated by women of higher status in later scenes; a lady "breeding a Child" complains that she has "not one minutes time of health" (in Ferguson, *First Feminists* 93); another Lady runs mad with grief at the loss of a child; a woman in labor crosses the stage groaning and praying for ease; a pair of "Ancient Ladies" recount the worthlessness of their grown children; two lady's-maids recount the sufferings of a woman in labor as they seek a midwife to help her; another woman, in labor for three days, is "delivered" only of life. Cavendish's heroine rejects these miseries by establishing the "convent," hoping to evade the dangers and responsibilities of reproduction by evading men. Though a luxurious and blooming place, this convent of pleasure is metaphorically a frozen landscape, for its inhabitants are frozen in a sort of eternal girlhood, a zone of safety from the distresses of marriage, childbirth, and childrearing. Lady Happy's utopia ends when she marries a prince who, disguised as a woman, has shared its pleasures. The tone of the ending is not ironic, but it is difficult to avoid the ironic implication that the heroine has been tricked into marriage by a man pretending to share her goals, and that when she marries and gives up the name of Lady Happy, she will also give up her happiness. For more on Cavendish's critique of the consequences of childbearing for women, see Hilda L. Smith, 75–95.

3. Much excellent recent criticism has taken up the questions of gender and the motif of parenthood in Shelley. See, for example, Moers, 140–51; Rubenstein; Levine and Knoepflmacher, eds.; Mary Poovey; and William Veeder.

4. Little is known of the author. According to the editor of the 1889 edition, Bradley Lane was a proper lady, "indifferent" to fame, who "kept herself in concealment so closely that even her husband did not know that she was the writer who was making this stir"(5).

5. Pfaelzer (*Utopian Novel*, 141–58) discusses the congruence of Lane's depiction of the essence of femininity with the pure, passive True Woman of the nineteenth century.

6. See, for example, Moore, *Al-Modad*; Adolph, *Arqtiq: A Study of Marvels at the North Pole*; or Sutton, *White City, A Novel*. The "white, dead wilderness" (205) of the Antarctic is the setting for a brilliant scientist's attempt to control reproduction and speed the process of human evolution in Ellis's "Creatures of the Light," 197–220. His physically perfect Adam and Eve need no sleep or food, and are distinguished by their "icy" blue eyes. The arctic motif is wittily treated, if less central, in Carrington's surrealist comedy *The Hearing Trumpet*, where a new ice age allows a group of old women to escape a dystopian nursing home and establish a utopia of their own.

7. For more on this novel, see Byrd, 234–44.

8. See Khouri, 49–61; and Moylan, 91–120.

9. Thanks are due to Carol Kolmerten, Jane Donawerth, and Nancy Foss for their comments and suggestions on earlier versions of this article.

Works Cited

Adolph, Mrs. Anna. *Arqtiq: A Study of Marvels at the North Pole*. Hanford, Calif.: author, 1899.

Albinski, Nan Bowman. *Women's Utopias in British and American Fiction*. London: Routledge, 1988.

Alcott, Bronson. *Journals of A. Bronson Alcott*. Edited by O. Shepard. Boston: Little, Brown, 1938.

———. *The Letters of A. Bronson Alcott*. Edited by Richard Herrnstadt. Ames: Iowa State Univ. Press, 1969.

Alcott, Louisa May. "Transcendental Wild Oats." In *Alternative Alcott*, edited by Elaine Showalter, 364–79. New Brunswick: Rutgers Univ. Press, 1988.

———. *Transcendental Wild Oats and Excerpts from the Fruitlands Diary*. Edited by William Henry Harrison. Cambridge, Mass.: Harvard Common, 1984.

Allison, Dorothy. "The Future of Female: Octavia Butler's Mother Lode." In *Reading Black, Reading Feminist: A Critical Anthology*, edited by Henry Louis Gates, Jr., 471–78. New York: Meridian, 1990.

Almond, Gabriel, and Sidney Verba. *The Civic Culture: Political Attitudes and Democracy in Five Nations*. Newbury Park, Calif.: Sage, 1989.

Annas, Pamela. "New Worlds, New Words: Androgyny in Feminist Science Fiction." *Science Fiction Studies* 5 (July 1978): 143–56.

Aptheker, Bettina. *Tapestries of Life: Woman's Work, Woman's Consciousness, and the Meaning of Daily Experience*. Amherst: Univ. of Massachusetts Press, 1989.

Arnold, Birch [Bartlett, Alice Elinor Bowen]. *A New Aristocracy*. New York: Bartlett, 1891.

Aronson, Nicole. *Mademoiselle de Scudéry*. Translated by Stuart R. Aronson. Boston: Twayne, 1978.

Astell, Mary. *A Serious Proposal to the Ladies. Parts I & II.* 4th ed. London, 1701. Reprint. New York: Source Book, 1970.

Auerbach, Nina. *Communities of Women: An Idea in Fiction.* Cambridge, Mass.: Harvard Univ. Press, 1978.

Aulnoy, Marie-Catherine de. "L'Isle de la Félicité." In volume 2 of *Histoire d'Hypolite, Comte de Duglas,* 99–125. Paris: Louis Sevestre, 1690.

———. "Le Prince Lutin." In Volume I of *Les 'Contes des Fées,* 133–99. Paris: La Compagnie des Librairies, 1774.

Backer, Dorothy. *Precious Women.* New York: Basic Books, 1974.

Bakhtin, M[ikhail]. M[ikhailovich]. "Response to a Question from *Novy Mir*" [1970]. In *Speech Genres and Other Late Essays,* edited by Caryl Emerson and Michael Holquist, and translated by Vern W. McGee,1–7. Austin: University of Texas Press, 1986.

Bammer, Angelika. *Partial Visions: Feminism and Utopianism in the 1970s.* New York: Routledge, 1991.

Barchilon, Jacques, " 'Précieux' Elements in the Fairy Tale of the Seventeenth Century." *L'Esprit Créateur* 3, no. 3 (1963): 99–107.

Barr, Marleen. *Alien to Femininity: Speculative Fiction and Feminist Theory.* New York: Greenwood, 1987.

———. *Feminist Fabulation: Space/Postmodern Fiction.* Iowa City: Univ. of Iowa Press, 1992.

———. "Food for Postmodern Thought." In *Feminism, Utopia, and Narrative,* edited by Sarah Webster Goodwin and Libby Falk Jones, 21–33. Knoxville: Univ. of Tennessee Press, 1990.

———, ed. *Feminist Science Fiction.* Special issue of *Women's Studies International Forum* 7, no. 2 (1984).

———, ed. *Future Females: A Critical Anthology.* Bowling Green: Bowling Green State Univ. Popular Press, 1981.

———, and Patrick D. Murphy, eds. *Feminism Faces the Fantastic.* Special issue of *Women's Studies* 14, no. 2 (1987).

———, and Nicholas D. Smith, eds. *Women and Utopia: Critical Interpretations.* Lanham, Md: Univ. Press of America, 1983.

Bartkowski, Frances. *Feminist Utopias.* Lincoln: Univ. of Nebraska Press, 1989.

Baruch, Elaine, and Ruby Rohrlich, eds. *Women in Search of Utopia.* New York: Schocken, 1984.

Baym, Nina. "Melodramas of Beset Manhood: How Theories of American Fiction Exclude Women Writers." *American Quarterly* 33 (1981): 123–39.

Bazin, Edith. *Alcott Memoires.* Boston: Richard Badger, 1915.

Beal, Frances M. "Black Women and the Science Fiction Genre." *Black Scholar* 17 (Mar.–Apr., 1986): 14–18.

Bellamy, Edward. *Looking Backward, 2000–1881.* Edited by John L. Thomas. 1888. Reprint. Cambridge, Mass.: Belknap Press/Harvard Univ. Press, 1967.

Belsey, Catherine. "Constructing the Subject: Deconstructing the Text." In *Feminist Criticism and Social Change: Sex, Class, and Race in Literature and Culture*, edited by Judith Newton and Deborah Rosenfelt, 45–64. New York: Methuen, 1985.

Benjamin, Jessica. *The Bonds of Love: Psychoanalysis, Feminism, and the Problem of Domination*. New York: Pantheon, 1988.

———. "The Bonds of Love: Rational Violence and Erotic Domination." In *The Future of Difference*, edited by Hester Eisenstein and Alice Jardine, 41–70. Boston: G. K. Hall, 1980.

———. "A Desire of One's Own: Psychoanalytic Feminism and Intersubjective Space." In *Feminist Studies/Critical Studies*, edited by Teresa de Lauretis, 78–101. Bloomington: Indiana Univ. Press, 1986.

Bennett, Gertrude Barrows [Francis Stevens]. *The Cerberus Heads*. 1919; Reprint. Reading, Pa.: Polaris, 1952.

———. "Friend Island." Reprinted in *Under the Moons of Mars*. Edited by Sam Moskowitz. New York: Holt, Reinhart, and Winston, 1970. (Originally published in *All Story Weekly*, 7 September 1918).

Benton, Jill. *Naomi Mitchison: A Century of Experiment in Life and Letters*. London: Pandora, 1990.

Bertaud, Madeleine. "En marge de leurs Mémoires, une correspondance entre Mlle de Montpensier et Mme de Motteville." *Travaux de Littérature* 3 (1990): 277–95.

Beugnot, Bernard. "Y a-t-il une problématique féminine de la Retraite?" In *Onze études sur l'image de la femme dans la littérature française du dix-septième siècle*, edited by Wolfgang Leiner, 29–49. Paris: Jean-Michel Place, 1978.

Blair, Don. *The New Harmony Story*. New Harmony, Ind.:n.p., n.d.

Bleiler, Everett F., with Richard K. Bleiler. *Science Fiction: The Early Years*. Kent: Kent State Univ. Press, 1990.

Boone, Joseph Allen. *Tradition Counter Tradition: Love and the Form of Fiction*. Chicago: Univ. of Chicago Press, 1987.

Bowerbank, Sylvia. "The Spider's Delight: Margaret Cavendish and the 'Female' Imagination." *English Literary Renaissance* 14 (1984): 392–408.

Brantenberg, Gerd. *The Daughters of Egalia*. Translated by Louis MacKay. London: Journeyman, 1978.

Brontë, Charlotte. *Villette*. 1853. Reprint. Oxford: Oxford Univ. Press, 1990.

Bruère, Martha Bensley. *Mildred Carver, U.S.A.* New York: Macmillan, 1919.

Bryant, Dorothy. *The Kin of Ata Are Waiting for You*. New York: Random House, 1976.

Butler, Octavia E. "Bloodchild." In *The 1985 Annual World's Best SF*, edited by Donald A. Wollheim, 193–212. New York: DAW, 1985. (Originally published in *Isaac Asimov's Science Fiction Magazine* [June 1984]).

————. *Clay's Ark*. New York: St. Martin's, 1984.

————. "The Evening and the Morning and the Night." In *The Year's Best Science Fiction Fifth Annual Collection*, edited by Gardner Dozois, 280–302. New York: St. Martin's, 1988.

————. *Kindred*. Boston: Beacon, 1988.

————. *Mind of My Mind*. New York: Doubleday, 1977.

————. *Patternmaster*. New York: Doubleday, 1976.

————. "Speech Sounds." In *The New Hugo Winners*, edited by Isaac Asimov, 199–216. New York: Wynwood, 1989. (Originally published in *Isaac Asimov's Science Fiction Magazine* [Dec. 1983]).

————. *Survivor*. New York: Doubleday, 1978.

————. *Wild Seed*. New York: Doubleday, 1980.

————. *Xenogenesis: Dawn, Adulthood Rites, Imago*. New York: Warner, 1987, 1988, 1989. Reprint. New York: Guild America, 1989.

Byrd, Deborah. "Gynocentric Mythmaking in Joan Vinge's *The Snow Queen*." *Extrapolation* (Fall 1986): 234–44.

Caldecott, Leonie. "Naomi Mitchison." In her *Women of Our Century*, 11–34. London: Arile Books, 1984.

Carretta, Vincent. "Utopian Limited: Sarah Scott's *Millenium Hall* and *The History of Sir George Ellison*." *The Age of Johnson: A Scholarly Annual* 5 (1992): 303–25.

Carrington, Leonora. *The Hearing Trumpet*. New York: St. Martin's, 1976.

Cavendish, Margaret. *The Description of a New World, Called the Blazing-World*. London: A. Maxwell, 1668.

————. *Grounds of Natural Philosophy*. London: A. Maxwell, 1668.

————. *Nature's Pictures Drawn by Fancies Pencil to the Life*. 1656. Reprint. London: A. Maxwell, 1671.

————. *Observations upon Experimental Philosophy, To which is added, the Description of a New Blazing-World*. 1666. Reprint. London: A. Maxwell, 1668.

————. *Playes*. London: A. Warren, for John Martin, James Allestrye, and Tho. Dicas, at the Bell in Saint Paul's Churchyard, 1662.

————. *Plays, Never before Printed*. London: A. Maxwell, 1668.

————. *The Worlds Olio*. London: J. Martin and J. Allestrye at the Bell in St. Paul's Churchyard, 1655.

Charnas, Suzy McKee. *Motherlines*. New York: Berkley, 1978.

————. *Walk to the End of the World*. New York: Ballantine, 1974.

Cheyney, Edna. *Louisa May Alcott: Her Life, Letters, and Journals*. Boston: Little, Brown, 1928.

Chodorow, Nancy. "Being and Doing: A Cross-Cultural Examination of the Socialization of Males and Females." In *Woman in Sexist Society: Studies in Power and Powerlessness*, edited by Vivian Gornick and Barbara K.

Moran, 173–97. New York: Basic Books, 1978.

———. "Gender, Relation and Difference in Psychoanalytic Perspective." In *The Future of Difference*, edited by Alice Jardine and Hester Eisenstein, 3–19. Boston: G. K. Hall, 1980.

———. *The Reproduction of Mothering: Psychoanalysis and the Sociology of Gender*. Berkeley: Univ. of California Press, 1978.

Cholakian, Patricia Francis. "A House of Her Own: Marginality and Dissidence in the 'Mémoires' of La Grande Mademoiselle (1627–1693)." *Prose Studies* 9, no. 3 (1986): 3–20.

Cornell, Drucilla, and Adam Thurschwell. "Feminism, Negativity, Intersubjectivity." In *Feminism as Critique: On the Politics of Gender*, edited by Seyla Benhabib and Drucilla Cornell, 143–89. Minneapolis: Univ. of Minnesota Press, 1987.

Cranny-Francis, Anne. *Feminist Fiction: Feminist Uses of Generic Fiction*. Cambridge: Polity, 1990.

Crittenden, Walter Marion. "The Life and Writings of Mrs. Sarah Scott—Novelist (1723–1795)." Ph.D. diss. Univ. of Pennsylvania, 1932.

Danahy, Michael. "Social, Sexual and Human Spaces in *La Princesse de Clèves*." *French Forum* 6, no. 3 (1981): 212–24.

Davis, Rebecca Harding. "The Harmonists." *Atlantic Monthly* 17 (May 1866): 529–38.

Davison, Jane. *The Fall of a Doll's House: Three Generations of American Women and the Houses They Lived In*. New York: Holt, Rinehart and Winston, 1980.

Day, Donald B. *Index to the Science Fiction Magazines, 1926–1950*. Boston: G. K. Hall, 1952.

DeGraff, Amy Vanderlyn. *The Tower and the Well: A Psychological Interpretation of the Fairy Tales of Madame d'Aulnoy*. Birmingham, Ala.: Summa Publications, 1984.

De Jean, Joan. "The Female Tradition." *L'Esprit Créateur* 23, no. 2 (1983): 3–8.

de Lauretis, Teresa. *Technologies of Gender: Essays on Theory, Film, and Fiction*. Bloomington: Indiana Univ. Press, 1987.

Di Scanno, Teresa. *La Mode des Contes de Fées de 1690 à 1705*. Genova: Università di Genova, 1968.

Dodderidge, Esmé. *The New Gulliver, or The Adventures of Lemuel Gulliver Jr. in Capovolta*. New York: Taplinger, 1979.

Dodsworth, Martin. "Women Without Men at Cranford." *Essays in Criticism* 13 (1963): 132–45.

Donawerth, Jane. "Lilith Lorraine: Feminist Socialist Writer in the Pulps." *Science Fiction Studies* 17 (1990): 252–58.

———. "Teaching Science Fiction by Women." *English Journal* 79 (March 1990): 39–46.

———. "Utopian Science: Contemporary Feminist Science Theory and Science Fiction by Women." *NWSA Journal* 2, no. 4 (Autumn 1990): 535–57.

Douglas, Ann. *The Feminization of American Culture.* New York: Knopf, 1977.

DuPlessis, Rachel Blau. "The Feminist Apologues of Lessing, Piercy, and Russ." *Frontiers* 4 (Spring 1979): 1–8.

———. *Writing Beyond the Ending.* Bloomington: Indiana Univ. Press, 1985.

Duthie, Enid L. *The Themes of Elizabeth Gaskell.* Totowa, N.J.: Rowman and Littlefield, 1980.

Eisler, Riane. *The Chalice and the Blade: Our History, Our Future.* San Francisco: Harper and Row, 1988.

———. "Pragmatopia: Women's Utopias and Scenarios for a Possible Future." Paper delivered at the 1986 Conference of the Society of Utopian Studies, Asilomar, Calif., Oct., 1986.

Elbert, Sarah. *A Hunger for Home: Louisa May Alcott and Little Women.* Philadelphia: Temple Univ. Press, 1984.

Elgin, Suzette Haden. *The Judas Rose.* New York: DAW, 1986.

———. *Native Tongue.* New York: DAW, 1984.

Ellis, Sophie Wenzel. "Creatures of the Light." *Astounding* 1, no. 2 (Feb. 1930): 197–220.

———. "Slaves of the Dust." *Astounding* 4, no. 3 (Dec. 1930): 295–309.

Faderman, Lillian. *Surpassing the Love of Men: Romantic Friendship and Love Between Women from the Renaissance to the Present.* New York: William Morrow, 1981.

Farrell, Michèle L. "Celebration and Repression of Feminine Desire in Mme d'Aulnoy's Fairy Tale: *La Chatte blanche.*" *L'Esprit Créateur* 29, no. 3 (1989): 52–64.

Felice, Cynthia. *Double Nocturne.* New York: DAW, 1987.

Ferguson, Moira, ed. *First Feminists: British Women Writers, 1578–1799.* Bloomington: Indiana Univ. Press, 1985.

———. "A Wise, Wittie, and Learned Lady: Margaret Lucas Cavendish." In *Women Writers of the Seventeenth Century*, edited by Katharina M. Wilson and Frank J. Warnke, 305–18. Athens: Univ. of Georgia Press, 1989.

Fetterley, Judith. *The Resisting Reader: A Feminist Approach to American Fiction.* Bloomington: Indiana Univ. Press, 1981.

Firestone, Shulamith. *The Dialectic of Sex: The Case for Feminist Revolution.* 1970. Reprint. New York: Bantam, 1972.

Fisher, Mary A. *Among the Immortals.* New York: Shakespeare Press, 1916.

Fitzmaurice, James. "Fancy and the Family: Self Characterizations of Margaret Cavendish." *Huntington Library Quarterly* 53 (Summer 1990): 199–209.

Flax, Jane. "The Family in Contemporary Feminist Thought." In *The Family in Political Thought*, edited by Jean Bethke Elshtain, 223–53. Amherst: Univ. of Massachusetts Press, 1982.

Foster, Frances S. "Octavia Butler's Black Female Future Vision." *Extrapolation* 23 (1982): 37–49.

Foster, Lawrence. *Religion and Sexuality: The Shakers, the Mormons, and the Oneida Community*. Urbana: Univ. of Illinois Press, 1984.

———. *Women, Family, and Utopia: Communal Experiments of the Shakers, the Oneida Community, and the Mormons*. Syracuse: Syracuse Univ. Press, 1991.

Fowler, Rowena. "*Cranford*: Cow in Grey Flannel or Lion *Couchant?*" *Studies in English Literature 1500–1900* 24 (1984): 717–29.

Francis, Richard. "Circumstances and Salvation: The Ideology of the Fruitlands Utopia." *American Quarterly* 25 (1973): 202–34.

Freibert, Lucy. "World Views in Utopian Novels by Women." In *Women and Utopia: Critical Interpretations*, edited by Marleen Barr and Nicholas D. Smith, 67–84. Lanham, Md.: Univ. Press of America, 1983.

Friend, Beverly. "Virgin Territory: Women and Sex in Science Fiction." *Extrapolation* 14 (Dec. 1972): 49–58.

Fry, Lena Jane. *Other Worlds*. Chicago: author, 1905.

Frye, Northrop. "Varieties of Literary Utopias." In *Utopias and Utopian Thought*, edited by Frank E. Manuel, 25–49. Boston: Beacon, 1965.

Gadon, Elinor W. *The Once and Future Goddess: A Symbol for Our Time*. San Francisco: Harper and Row, 1989.

Gale, Zona. *Romance Island*. Indianapolis: Bobbs-Merrill, 1906.

Gallagher, Catherine. "Embracing the Absolute: The Politics of the Female Subject in Seventeenth-Century England." *Genders* 1 (Spring 1988): 24–39.

Gamble, Sarah. " 'Shambleau . . . and Others': The Role of the Female in the Fiction of C. L. Moore." In *Where No Man Has Gone Before*, edited by Lucie Armitt, 29–49. London: Routledge, 1991.

Garrison, Dee. "Immoral Fiction in the Late Victorian Library." *American Quarterly* 28 (1976): 71–80.

Gaskell, Elizabeth. *Cranford/Cousin Phillis*. 1851–53, 1863–64. With an introduction by Peter Keating. Harmondsworth, England: Penguin, 1976.

———. *The Letters of Mrs. Gaskell*. Edited by J. A. V. Chappel and Arthur Pollard. Cambridge, Mass.: Harvard Univ. Press, 1967.

Gearhart, Sally Miller. *The Wanderground: Stories of the Hill Women*. Watertown, Mass.: Persephone, 1979.

Gilbert, Sandra, and Susan Gubar. *The Madwoman in the Attic: The Woman Writer and the Nineteenth-Century Literary Imagination*. New Haven: Yale Univ. Press, 1979.

———. *No Man's Land*. 2 vols. New Haven: Yale Univ. Press, 1989.

Gilligan, Carol. *In a Different Voice: Psychological Theory and Women's Development*. Cambridge, Mass.: Harvard Univ. Press, 1982.

Gillmore, Inez Haynes. *Angel Island*. New York: Henry Holt, 1914.

Gilman, Charlotte Perkins. "Aunt Mary's Pie Plant." *Woman's Home Companion* 6 (June 1908): 14, 57, 58.

———. "Bee Wise." *The Forerunner* 4, no. 7 (July 1913): 169–73.

———. *Benigna McAvelly*. *The Forerunner* 5, nos. 1–12 (1914).

———. "A Council of War." *The Forerunner* 4, no. 8 (Aug. 1913): 197–201.

———. "Dr. Clair's Place." *The Forerunner* 6, no. 6 (June 1915): 141–45.

———. "Forsythe & Forsythe." *The Forerunner* 4, no. 1 (Jan. 1913): 1–5.

———. "A Garden of Babies." *Success* 12 (June 1909): 370–71, 410–11.

———. "Her Housekeeper." *The Forerunner* 1, no. 4 (Jan. 1910): 2–8.

———. "Her Memories." *The Forerunner* 3, no. 8 (Aug. 1912): 197–201.

———. *Herland. 1915*. Reprint. With an Introduction by Ann J. Lane, New York: Pantheon, 1979.

———. *The Living of Charlotte Perkins Gilman: An Autobiography*. With a Foreword by Zona Gale. New York: Appleton-Century, 1935. Reprint. Edited by Ann J. Lane. Madison: Univ. of Wisconsin Press, 1990.

———. "Maidstone Comfort." *The Forerunner* 3, no. 9 (Sept. 1912): 225–29.

———. "Masculine Literature." Chapter 5 of *Our Androcentric Culture; or, The Man-Made Culture*. *The Forerunner* 1, no. 5 (Feb. 1910): 18–22.

———. *Moving the Mountain*. *The Forerunner* 2 (1911). Reprint. New York: Charlton, 1911.

———. "Mrs. Hines' Money." *The Forerunner* 4, no. 4 (Apr. 1913): 85–89.

———. *What Diantha Did*. *The Forerunner*. 1, no. 11 to 2, no. 10 (Nov. 1909–Oct. 1910).

———. *With Her in Ourland*. *The Forerunner* 7 (1916).

———. "A Woman's Utopia." Box 21, Folder 260. Arthur and Elizabeth Schlesinger Library, Radcliffe College.

———. *Women and Economics: A Study of the Economic Relation Between Men and Women as a Factor in Social Evolution*. 1898. Edited and with an Introduction by Carl N. Degler. New York: Harper Torchbooks, 1966.

———. *The Yellow Wallpaper*. 1891. Reprint. With an Afterword by Elaine R. Hedges. Old Westbury, N.Y.: Feminist Press, 1973.

Gimbutas, Marija. *The Civilization of the Goddess*. New York: Harper Collins, 1991.

———. *The Gods and Goddesses of Old Europe: Myths and Cult Images*. Berkeley: Univ. of California Press, 1982.

Goffman, Erving. *The Presentation of Self in Everyday Life*. Garden City, N.Y.: Doubleday, 1959.

Goldsmith, Elizabeth C. *Exclusive Conversations: The Art of Interaction in Seventeenth-Century France*. Philadelphia: Univ. of Pennsylvania Press, 1988.

Goodwin, Sarah Webster, and Libby Falk Jones, eds. *Feminism, Utopia, and Narrative*. Knoxville: Univ. of Tennessee Press, 1990.

Gotlieb, Phyllis. *Son of the Morning and Other Stories*. New York: Ace Science Fiction Books of Berkley Publishing, 1983.

Gould, Stephen Jay. *The Mismeasure of Man*. New York: Norton, 1981.

Graffigny, Françoise de. *Lettres d'une Peruvienne*. 1747. Translated as *Letters Written by a Peruvian Princess*. London, 1748.

Grahn, Judy. *Mundane's World*. Freedom, Calif.: Crossing, 1988.

Grant, Douglas. *Margaret the First: A Biography of Margaret Cavendish,Duchess of Newcastle, 1623–1673*. Toronto: Univ. of Toronto Press, 1957.

Greer, Germaine, and Susan Hastings, Jeslyn Medoff, Melinda Sansone. *Kissing the Rod: An Anthology of 17th-Century Women's Verse*. New York: Farrar, Straus and Giroux, 1988.

Grier, Barbara. *The Lesbian in Literature*. Revised 3d ed. Tallahassee, Fl.: Naiad, 1981.

Griffith, George V. "What Kind of Book is 'Cranford'?" *Review of International English Literature* 14, no. 2 (1983): 53–65.

Griffith, Mary. *Three Hundred Years Hence*. 1836. Reprint. Boston: G. K. Hall, 1975.

Gross, John. "Mrs. Gaskell." In *The Victorian Novel: Modern Essays in Criticism*, edited by Ian Watt, 217–28. Oxford: Oxford Univ. Press, 1971.

Grow, L. M. "Sarah Scott: A Reconsideration." *Coranto, Journal of the Friends of the Libraries, University of Southern California* 9, no. 1 (1973): 9–15.

Gubar, Susan. "C. L. Moore and the Conventions of Women's Science Fiction." *Science Fiction Studies* 7 (1980): 16–27.

Habermas, Jürgen. "A Theory of Communicative Competence." *Recent Sociology No. 2* (1970):115–48.

Hansen, L[ouise]. Taylor. *The Ancient Atlantic*. Amherst, Wis.: Amherst Press, 1969.

———. "The City on the Cloud." *Wonder Stories* 2, no. 5 (Oct. 1930): 426–31.

———. "The Man from Space." *Amazing Stories* 4 (Feb. 1930): 1034–44.

———. "The Prince of Liars." *Amazing Stories* 5 (Oct. 1930): 582–99.

———. "The Undersea Tube." *Amazing Stories* 4 (Nov. 1929): 720–25.

———. "What the Sodium Lines Revealed." *Amazing Stories Quarterly* 21 (Winter 1929): 120–38.

Haraway, Donna Jeanne. *Primate Visions: Gender, Race, and Nature in the World of Modern Science*. New York: Routledge, 1989.

Harris, Clare Winger. "The Ape Cycle." Reprinted in *Away From the Here and Now: Stories in Pseudo-Science*, 296–365. Philadelphia: Dorrance, 1947.

———. "The Artificial Man." *Science Wonder Quarterly* 1 (Fall 1929): 79–83.

———. "A Certain Soldier." Reprinted in *Away From the Here and Now: Stories in Pseudo-Science*, 71–95. Philadelphia: Dorrance, 1947.

———. "The Diabolical Drug." *Amazing Stories* 4 (May 1929): 156–61, 180.

———. "The Evolutionary Monstrosity." *Amazing Stories Quarterly* 2 (Winter 1929): 70–77.

———. "The Fate of the Poseidonia." *Amazing Stories* 2 (June 1927): 245–52, 267.

———. "The Fifth Dimension." *Amazing Stories* 3 (Dec. 1928): 823–25, 850.

———. "The Menace of Mars." *Amazing Stories* 3 (Oct. 1928): 582–97.

———. "The Miracle of the Lily." *Amazing Stories* 3 (Apr. 1928): 48–55.

———. *Persephone of Eleusis: A Romance of Ancient Greece.* Boston: Stratford, 1923.

———. "A Runaway World." *Weird Tales* (July 1926). Reprinted in *Away From the Here and Now: Stories in Pseudo-Science*, 7–36. Philadelphia: Dorrance, 1947.

———, and Miles J. Breuer. "A Baby on Neptune." *Amazing Stories* 4 (Dec. 1929): 790–99.

Harris, William H., and Judith S. Levey, eds. *The New Columbia Encyclopedia.* New York: Columbia Univ. Press, 1975.

Harrison, William Henry. *Transcendental Wild Oats and Excerpts from the Fruitlands Diary.* Cambridge, Mass.: Harvard Common, 1984.

Hayden, Delores. *The Grand Domestic Revolution: A History of Feminist Designs for American Homes, Neighborhoods, and Cities.* Cambridge, Mass: MIT Press, 1981.

Henley, Carra Dupuy. *A Man From Mars.* Los Angeles: Baumgardt, 1901.

Hill, Bridget. "A Refuge from Men: The Idea of a Protestant Nunnery." *Past and Present* 117 (1987): 107–30.

Hirsch, Marianne. *The Mother/Daughter Plot: Narrative, Psychoanalysis, Feminism.* Bloomington: Indiana Univ. Press, 1989.

Holland, Cecelia. *Pillar of the Sky.* New York: Knopf, 1985.

Hollinger, Veronica. "Feminisms, Criticisms, Science Fictions." Science Fiction Research Association Conference. Miami University, Oxford, Ohio. 25 June, 1989.

———. "Feminist Science Fiction: Breaking Up the Subject." *Extrapolation* 31 (Fall 1990): 229–39.

Hopkins, Annette B. *Elizabeth Gaskell: Her Life and Work.* 1952. Reprint. New York: Octagon, 1971.

Irving, Minna [Minnie Odell]. "The Moon Woman." *Amazing Stories* 4 (Nov. 1929): 746–54.

———. *Songs of a Haunted Heart.* Chicago: Belford, Clarke, 1888.

Jameson, Frederic. *The Political Unconscious: Narrative as a Socially Symbolic Act.* Ithaca: Cornell Univ. Press, 1981.

Jones, Alice Ilgenfritz. *Beatrice.* Chicago: McClurg, 1895.

————, and Ella Merchant. *Unveiling a Parallel: A Romance*. 1893. Reprint. Edited and with an Introduction by Carol A. Kolmerten. Syracuse: Syracuse Univ. Press, 1991.

Jones, Kathleen. *A Glorious Fame: The Life of Margaret Cavendish*. London: Bloomsbury, 1988.

Jones, Lillian B. *Five Generations Hence*. Fort Worth, Tex.: Dotson Jones, 1916.

Jordan, Judith V., and Janet L. Surrey. "The Self-in-Relation: Empathy and the Mother-Daughter Relationship." In *The Psychology of Today's Woman*, edited by Toni Bernay and Dorothy W. Cantor, 81–104. Hillsdale, N.J.: Analytic Press, 1986.

Kaplan, E. Ann. *Women and Film: Both Sides of the Camera*. New York: Routledge, 1983.

Keating, Peter. Introduction to *Cranford*, by Elizabeth Gaskell, 7–26. Middlesex, Harmondsworth, England: Penguin, 1976.

Keller, Evelyn Fox. *A Feeling for the Organism: The Life and Works of Barbara McClintock*. New York: Freeman, 1983.

Kellogg, Davida. Interview, by Naomi Jacobs. Winter 1986. Univ. of Maine, Orono, Maine.

Kessler, Carol Farley. "Bibliography of Utopian Fiction by United States Women 1836–1988." *Utopian Studies* 1, no. 1 (1990): 1–58.

————, ed. *Daring to Dream: Utopian Stories by United States Women, 1836–1919*. Boston: Pandora, 1984.

Khanna, Lee Cullen. "Frontiers of Imagination: Feminist Worlds." *Women's Studies International Forum* 7, no. 2 (1984): 97–102.

Khouri, Nadia. "The Dialectics of Power: Utopia in the Science Fiction of Le Guin, Jeury and Piercy." *Science Fiction Studies* 7 (Mar. 1980): 49–61.

Kinkaid, Mary. *Walda*. New York: Harper, 1903.

Kitch, Sally. *Chaste Liberation, Celibacy, and Female Cultural Status*. Urbana: Univ. of Illinois Press, 1989.

Klein, George. *Psychoanalytic Theory: An Explanation of Essentials*. New York: International Universities Press, 1976.

Kolmerten, Carol. *Women in Utopia: The Ideology of Gender in the American Owenite Communities*. Bloomington: Indiana Univ. Press, 1990.

Kuryllo, Helen. "'A Woman's Text in the Wild Zone': The Subversiveness of Elizabeth Gaskell's *Cranford*." In *Utopian Studies II*, edited by Michael Cummings and Nicholas Smith, 102–8. Lanham, Md.: Univ. Press of America, 1989.

Lane, Charles. "Social Tendencies." *The Dial* 4 (Oct. 1843): 188–204.

Lane, Mary E. Bradley. *Mizora: A Phophecy*. *The Cincinnati Commercial* (Nov. 1880–Feb. 1881). Reprint. With Introductions by Stuart A. Teitler and Kristine Anderson. Boston: Gregg, 1975.

Lansbury, Coral. *Elizabeth Gaskell: The Novel of Social Crisis*. London: Paul Elek, 1975.

Lanser, Susan Sniader. *Fictions of Authority: Women Writers and Narrative Voice*. Ithaca, N.Y.: Cornell Univ. Press, 1992.

Le Guin, Ursula K. *Always Coming Home*. New York: Harper and Row, 1985.

———. *Dancing at the Edge of the World: Thoughts on Words, Women, Places*. New York: Harper and Row, 1989.

———. *The Dispossessed*. New York: Harper and Row, 1974.

———. "Is Gender Necessary?" In *The Language of the Night: Essays on Fantasy and Science Fiction*, edited by Susan Wood, 161–69. New York: Putnam, 1979.

———. *The Language of the Night: Essays on Fantasy and Science Fiction*, edited by Susan Wood. New York: Putnam, 1979.

———. *The Left Hand of Darkness*. 1969. New York: Ace, 1976.

———. "Sur: A Summary Report of the Yelcho Expedition to the Antarctic, 1909–10." *New Yorker* 1 (Feb. 1982): 38–46.

Lefanu, Sarah. *In the Chinks of the World Machine*. London: Women's Press, 1988. Reprinted as *Feminism and Science Fiction*. Bloomington: Indiana Univ. Press, 1989.

Leibacher-Ouvrard, Lise. *Libertinage et Utopies sous le règne de Louis XIV*. Geneva: Librairie Droz, 1989.

Lerner, Gerda. *The Creation of Patriarchy*. New York: Oxford Univ. Press, 1986.

Lessing, Doris. *The Marriages Between Zones Three, Four, and Five*. New York: Knopf, 1980.

Levine, George, and U. C. Knoepflmacher, eds. *The Endurance of Frankenstein*. Berkeley: Univ. of California Press, 1979.

Levitas, Ruth. *The Concept of Utopia*. Syracuse: Syracuse Univ. Press, 1990.

Lippard, Lucy R. *Overlay: Contemporary Art and the Art of Prehistory*. New York: Pantheon, 1983.

Lorde, Audre. *Sister Outsider*. Trumansburg: Crossing, 1984.

Lorraine, Lilith [Mary Maude Dunne Wright]. *Banners of Victory*. Atlanta, Ga.: Banner Press of Emory University, 1937.

———. *The Brain of the Planet*. Science Fiction Series No. 5. New York: Stellar, 1929.

———. "Into the 28th Century." *Science Wonder Quarterly* 1 (Winter 1930): 250–67, 276.

———. "The Jovian Jest." *Astounding* 2, no. 2 (May 1930): 228–33.

Lougee, Carolyn C. *Le Paradis des Femmes: Women, Salons, and Social Stratification in Seventeenth-Century France*. Princeton: Princeton Univ. Press, 1976.

Ludwick, Kathleen. "Dr. Immortelle." *Amazing Stories Quarterly* 3, no. 4 (Fall 1930): 560–69, 574.

Makin, Bathsua. *An Essay to Revive the Antient Education of Gentlewomen*. London, 1673. Reprinted as Augustan Reprint Society Publication No. 202. Los Angeles: William Andrews Clark Memorial Library, 1980.

Manuel, Frank E., and Fritzie P. Manuel. *French Utopias: An Anthology of Ideal Societies*. New York: Free Press, 1966.

Martin, Nettie Parrish. *A Pilgrim's Progress in Other Worlds*. Boston: Mayhew, 1908.

Mason, Caroline. *A Woman of Yesterday*. New York: Doubleday, 1900.

Mavor, Elizabeth. *The Ladies of Llangollen: A Study of Romantic Friendship*. 1971. New York: Penguin, 1973.

McDowell, Deborah E. "Witnessing Slavery After Freedom—*Dessa Rose*." In *Slavery and the Literary Imagination*, edited by Deborah E. McDowell and Arnold Rampersad, 144–63. Baltimore: Johns Hopkins Univ. Press, 1989.

McLeod, Glenda K. "Madame d'Aulnoy: Writer of Fantasy." In *Women Writers of the Seventeenth Century*. edited by Katharina M. Wilson and Frank J. Warnke, 91–118. Athens: Univ. of Georgia Press, 1989.

Mellor, Anne K. "On Feminist Utopias." *Women's Studies* 9 (1982): 241–62.

Mendelson, Sara Heller. *The Mental World of Stuart Women: Three Studies*. Amherst: Univ. of Massachusetts Press, 1987.

Merchant, Carolyn. *The Death of Nature: Women, Ecology, and the Scientific Revolution*. San Francisco: Harper and Row, 1980.

Merril, Judith. *Shadow on the Hearth*. Garden City, NY.: Doubleday, 1950.

Mews, Hazel. *Mrs. Gaskell: Novelist and Biographer*. Cambridge, Mass.: Harvard Univ. Press, 1966.

Mitchison, Naomi. *African Heroes*. London: Bodley Head, 1968.

———. *The Africans*. London: Anthony Blond, 1970.

———. *All Change Here: Girlhood and Marriage*. London: Bodley Head, 1975.

———. *Among You Taking Notes — The Wartime Diary of Naomi Mitchison 1930–1945*. Edited by Dorothy Sheridan. London: Gollancz, 1985.

———. *As It Was: An Autobiography 1897–1918*. Glasgow: Richard Drew, 1988.

———. *The Corn King and the Spring Queen*. London: Jonathan Cape, 1931.

———. *Early in Orcadia*. Glasgow: Richard Drew, 1987.

———. *Memoirs of a Spacewoman*. New York: Berkley, 1962.

———. *Not by Bread Alone*. London: Marion Boyars, 1983.

———. *Solution Three*. London: Dobson, 1975.

———. *Travel Light*. London: Faber and Faber, 1952.

———. *We Have Been Warned*. London: Constable, 1935.

———. *When We Become Men*. London: Collins, 1965.

———. "Words." In *Despatches from the Frontiers of the Female Mind*, edited by Jen Green and Sarah Lefanu, 164–74. London: Women's Press, 1985.

———. *You May Well Ask: A Memoir*. London: Gollancz, 1979.

Moers, Ellen. *Literary Women*. 1976. Reprint. New York: Oxford Univ. Press, 1985.

Moffett, Judith. *Penterra*. New York: Worldwide, 1988.

Montpensier, Anne Marie Louise d'Orléans. *Lettres de Mademoiselle de Montpensier, de Mesdames de Motteville et de Montmorenci, de Mademoiselle du Pré, et de Madame la marquise de Lambert*. Paris: L. Collin, 1806.

Moore, C[atherine]. L. "No Woman Born." 1944. Reprinted in *The Best of C. L. Moore*, edited by Lester Del Rey, 200–42. Garden City, N.Y.: Doubleday, 1975.

Moore, M. Louise. *Al-Modad; or Life Scenes Beyond the Polar Circumflex, A Religio-Scientific Solution of the Problems of Present and Future Life*. Shell Bank, Cameron Parish, La.: Moore and Beauchamp, 1892.

Morrison, Toni. *Beloved*. New York: Knopf, 1987.

Moylan, Tom. *Demand the Impossible: Science Fiction and the Utopian Imagination*. New York: Methuen, 1986.

Newman, Beth. " 'The Situation of the Looker-On': Gender, Narration, and Gaze in *Wuthering Heights*." *PMLA* 105 (1990): 1029–41.

Niderst, Alain. "Madeleine de Scudéry de 1660 à 1789." *Oeuvres et critiques* 12, no. 1 (1986–87): 31–41.

Onderwyzer, Gaby Fisher. "Sarah Scott: Her Life and Works." Ph.D. diss., Univ. of California, Berkeley, 1957.

Osborne, Dorothy. *Letters from Dorothy Osborne to Sir William Temple*. Edited by G. C. Moore Smith. Oxford: Clarendon, 1928.

Paloma, Dolores. "Margaret Cavendish: Defining the Female Self." *Women's Studies* 7 (1980): 55–66.

Patai, Daphne. "Beyond Defensiveness: Feminist Research Strategies." In *Women and Utopia: Critical Interpretations*, edited by Marleen Barr and Nicholas D. Smith, 148–69. Lanham, Md.: Univ. Press of America, 1983.

———. "Utopia for Whom?" *Aphra* 5 (Summer, 1974): 2-16.

———, ed. *Looking Backward, 1988–1888*. Amherst: Univ. of Massachusetts Press, 1988.

Pateman, Carole. *The Sexual Contract*. Stanford: Stanford Univ. Press, 1988.

Pearson, Carol. "Women's Fantasies and Feminist Utopias." *Frontiers: A Journal of Women's Studies* 2, no. 3 (1977): 50-61.

Pelous, J. M. *Amour précieux, Amour galant (1654-1675)*. Paris: Klincksieck, 1980.

Perry, Ten Eyck Henry. *The First Duchess of Newcastle and Her Husband as Figures in Literary History*. London: Ginn, 1918.

Pfaelzer, Jean. "The Changing of the Avant-Garde: The Feminist Utopia." *Science Fiction Studies* 15 (Nov. 1988): 282–94.

———. "Immanence, Indeterminance, and the Utopian Pun in *Looking Backward*." In *Looking Backward, 1988–1888*, edited by Daphne Patai, 51–67. Amherst: Univ. of Massachusetts Press, 1988.

———. "The Sentimental Promise and the Utopian Myth: Rebecca Harding Davis's 'The Harmonists' and Louisa May Alcott's 'Transcendental Oats.'" *American Transcendental Quarterly*, n.s. 3, no. 1 (Mar. 1989): 85–100.

———. *The Utopian Novel in America, 1886–1896: The Politics of Form*. Pittsburgh: Univ. of Pittsburgh Press, 1984.

Phelps, Elizabeth Stuart. *A Brave Girl*. Serialized in *Wide Awake* 18–19 (Dec. 1883–Aug. 1884).

Piercy, Marge. *Woman on the Edge of Time*. New York: Knopf: Reprint. New York: Fawcett, 1976.

Pohl, Frederick. Panel discussion. Science Fiction Research Association Meeting, Oxford, Ohio. 24 June 1989.

Poovey, Mary. *The Proper Lady and the Woman Writer*. Chicago: Univ. of Chicago Press, 1984.

Rabb, Melinda Alliker. "Making and Rethinking the Canon: General Introduction and the Case of *Millenium Hall*." *Modern Language Studies* 18, no. 1 (1988): 3–16.

Rice, Louise. *Dainty Dishes from Foreign Lands*. Chicago: Library Shelf, 1909.

Rice, Louise, and Tonjoroff-Roberts. "The Astounding Enemy." *Amazing Stories Quarterly* 3, no. 1 (Winter 1930): 78–103.

Rich, Adrienne. *On Lies, Secrets and Silence: Selected Prose, 1966–1978*. New York: Norton, 1979.

Richberg, Eloise O. *Reinstern*. Cincinnati, Ohio: Editor Publishing, 1900.

Robert, Raymonde. *Le Conte de fées littéraire en France de la fin du XVIIᵉ à la fin du XVIIIᵉ siècle*. Nancy: Presses Universitaires de Nancy, 1981.

Roemer, Kenneth. "The Literary Domestication of Utopia: There's No *Looking Backward* Without Uncle Tom and Uncle True." *American Transcendental Quarterly* 3, no. 1 (Mar. 1989): 101–22.

———. *The Obsolete Necessity: America in Utopian Writings*. Kent State: Kent State Univ. Press, 1976.

Rogers, Bessie Story. *As it May Be*. Boston: Gorham, 1905.

Rogers, Katherine M. *Feminism in Eighteenth-Century England*. Urbana: Univ. of Illinois Press, 1982.

Rohrlich, Ruby, and Elaine Hoffman Baruch, eds. *Women in Search of Utopia: Mavericks and Mythmakers*. New York: Schocken Books, 1984.

Ronzeaud, Pierre. "La femme dans le roman utopique de la fin du XVIIᵉ siècle." In *Onze études sur l'image de la femme dans la littérature française du dix-*

septième siècle, edited by Wolfgang Leiner, 103–30. Paris: Jean-Michel Place, 1978.

Rose, Mary Beth. "Gender, Genre, History: Seventeenth-Century English Women and the Art of Autobiography." In *Women in the Middle Ages and the Renaissance: Literary and Historical Perspectives*, edited by Mary Beth Rose, 245–78. Syracuse: Syracuse Univ. Press, 1986.

Rosenfelt, Deborah. "Feminism, 'Postfeminism,' and Contemporary Women's Fiction." In *Tradition and the Talents of Women*, edited by Florence Howe, 268–91. Urbana: Univ. of Illinois Press, 1991.

Rosinsky, Natalie M. *Feminist Futures: Contemporary Women's Speculative Fiction*. Ann Arbor, Mich.: UMI Research, 1984.

Rossiter, Margaret W. *Women Scientists in America, Struggles and Strategies to 1940*. Baltimore: Johns Hopkins Univ. Press, 1982.

Rothschild, Joan. "A Feminist Perspective on Technology and the Future." *Women's Studies International Quarterly* 4 (1981): 65–74.

Rubenstein, Marc A. " 'My Accursed Origin': The Search for the Mother in *Frankenstein*." *Studies in Romanticism* 15, no. 2 (Spring 1976): 165-94.

Ruskin, John. "Of Queens' Gardens." In *Sesame and Lilies and the Political Economy of Art*. 1865. Reprint. London: n.p., n.d.

Russ, Joanna. *The Female Man*. New York: Bantam, 1975.

———. "The Image of Women in Science Fiction." In *Images of Women in Fiction*, edited by Susan Koppelman Cornillon, 79–94. Bowling Green: Bowling Green Univ. Popular Press, 1972.

———. *Magic Mommas, Trembling Sisters, Puritans & Perverts: Feminist Essays*. Trumansburg, N.Y.: Crossing, 1985.

Salvaggio, Ruth. *Suzy McKee Charnas: Octavia Butler: Joan D. Vinge*. Mercer Island, Wash.: Starmont, 1986.

Sarasohn, Lisa T. "A Science Turned Upside Down: Feminism and the Natural Philosophy of Margaret Cavendish." *Huntington Library Quarterly* 47 (1984): 289–307.

Sargent, Lyman Tower. Address. Society for Utopian Studies Annual Meeting, Lexington, KY. Nov., 1990.

———. *British and American Utopian Literature 1516–1985: An Annotated Chronological Bibliography*. New York: Garland, 1988.

———. "The Political Dimensions of Utopianism." In *Per una definizione dell'utopia: Metodologie e discipline a confronto. Atti del convegno internazionale di Bagni di Lucca, 12–14 Settembre 1990*, edited by Vita Fortunati and Nadia Minerva, 185–210. Ravenna, Italy: Longo Editrice, 1992.

———"Utopia—The Problem of Definition." *Extrapolation* 16, no. 2 (1975): 137–47.

———. "Women in Utopia." *Comparative Literature Studies* 10 (Dec. 1973): 302–16.

Sargent, Pamela. *The Shore of Women.* New York: Crown, 1986.

———, ed. *Women of Wonder: Science Fiction Stories by Women about Women.* New York: Random House, 1974.

Schor, Hilary M. "Affairs of the Alphabet: Reading, Writing and Narrating in *Cranford.*" *Novel: A Forum on Fiction* 22, no. 3 (1989): 288–304.

Schweikart, Patrocinio. "What If . . . Science and Technology in Feminist Utopias." In *Machina Ex Dea: Feminist Perspectives on Technology*, edited by Joan A. Rothschild, 198–211. New York: Pergamon, 1983.

Scott, Melissa. *The Kindly Ones.* New York: Baen, 1987.

———. *Mighty Good Road.* New York: Baen, 1990.

Scott, Sarah. *Agreeable Ugliness or the Triumph of the Graces.* London, 1754.

———. *A Description of Millenium Hall.* 1762. Reprint. Edited by Walter M. Crittenden. New York: Bookman Associates, 1955.

———. *A Description of Millenium Hall.* With an Introduction by Jane Spencer. London: Virago, 1986.

Scudéry, Madeleine de. *Artamène ou le Grand Cyrus.* 1649–53. Reprint. Geneva: Slatkine, 1972.

———. *Mathilde (d'Aguilar).* 1667. Reprint. Geneva: Slatkine, 1979.

Sears, Clara Endicott. *Bronson Alcott's Fruitlands.* Boston: Houghton Mifflin, 1915.

Septama, Aladra [Judson W. Reeves]. "The Beast-Men of Ceres." *Amazing Stories Quarterly* 2 (Winter 1929): 90–110.

Shelley, Mary Godwin. *Frankenstein; or, The Modern Prometheus.* Edited by James Rieger. 1818. Reprint. Chicago: Univ. of Chicago Press, 1982.

———. *The Last Man.* Edited by Hugh J. Luke, Jr., 1826. Reprint. Lincoln: Univ. of Nebraska Press, 1965.

Shelley, Percy, Bysshe. "Mont Blanc." In *English Romantic Writers*, edited by David Perkins, 968–970. New York: Harcourt, Brace, and World, 1967.

Showalter, Elaine, ed. *Alternative Alcott.* New Brunswick, N.J.: Rutgers University Press, 1988.

———. "Feminist Criticism in the Wilderness." In *The New Feminist Criticism: Essays on Women, Literature, and Theory*, edited by Elaine Showalter, 243-70. New York: Pantheon, 1985.

———. *A Literature of Their Own.* Princeton: Princeton Univ. Press, 1977.

———, ed. *The New Feminist Criticism: Essays on Women, Literature, and Theory.* New York: Pantheon, 1985.

Shuler, Linda Lay. *She Who Remembers.* New York: Arbor House, 1988.

Slonczewski, Joan. *A Door Into Ocean.* New York: Arbor House, 1986.

Smith, Curtis C., ed. *Twentieth-Century Science-Fiction Writers.* 2d ed. Chicago: St. James, 1986.

Smith, Hilda L. *Reason's Disciples: Seventeenth-Century English Feminists.* Urbana: Univ. of Illinois Press, 1982.

Spencer, Jane. Introduction to *A Description of Millenium Hall*, by Sarah Scott, v–xv. London: Virago, 1986.

Spender, Dale. *Mothers of the Novel*. London: Pandora, 1986.

Spillers, Hortense J. "Mama's Baby, Papa's Maybe: An American Grammar Book." *Diacritics* (Summer 1987): 64–81.

Spivack, Gayatri Chakravorty. *In Other Worlds: Essays in Cultural Politics*. New York: Routledge, 1987.

Staicar, Tom, ed. *The Feminine Eye: Science Fiction and the Women Who Write It*. New York: Ungar, 1982.

Stanton, Domna C. "The Fiction of *Préciosité* and the Fear of Women." *Yale French Studies* 62 (1981): 107–34.

Stepan, Alfred. "What is Democracy." Radio program 3, No. 91R50F043,BB3. Moderated by Barbara Goodwin. 28 April 1991.

Stone, Leslie F. "Letter of the Twenty-Fourth Century." *Amazing Stories* 4 (Dec. 1929): 860–61.

———. "Men With Wings." *Air Wonder Stories* 1 (July 1929): 58–87.

———. "Out of the Void, Part I." *Amazing Stories* 4 (Aug. 1929): 440–55.

———. "Out of the Void, Part II." *Amazing Stories* 4 (Sept. 1929): 544–65.

———. "Through the Veil." *Amazing Stories* 5 (May 1930): 174–80.

———. *When the Sun Went Out*. Science Fiction Series No. 4. New York: Stellar, 1929.

———. "Women With Wings." *Air Wonder Stories* 1 (May 1930): 984–1003.

Storer, Mary Elizabeth. *Un Episode Littéraire de la fin XVIIe siècle: La Mode des contes de fées (1685–1700)*. 1928. Reprint. Geneva: Slatkine, 1972.

Strauss, Sylvia. "Women in 'Utopia.'" *South Atlantic Quarterly* 75 (Winter 1976): 115–31.

Sutton, Paralee Sweeten. *White City, A Novel*. Palo Alto, Calif.: Palopress, 1949.

Suvin, Darko. "Defining the Literary Genre of Utopia: Some Historical Semantics, Some Geneology, a Proposal and a Plea." *Studies in the Literature of the Imagination* 6, no. 2 (Fall 1973): 121–45.

———. *Metamorphoses of Science Fiction: On the Poetics and History of a Literary Genre*. New Haven: Yale Univ. Press, 1979.

Tepper, Sheri S. *The Gate to Women's Country*. New York: Doubleday, 1988.

Thelander, Dorothy R. "Mother Goose and Her Goslings: The France of Louis XIV as Seen Through the Fairy Tale." *Journal of Modern History* 54 (1982): 467–96.

Thomas, Elizabeth Marshall. *Reindeer Moon*. Boston: Houghton Mifflin, 1987.

Tinckner, Mary Agnes. *San Salvador*. Boston: Houghton Mifflin, 1892.

Todd, Janet. *Women's Friendship in Literature.* New York: Columbia Univ. Press, 1980.

Tompkins, Jane. *Sensational Designs: The Cultural Work of American Fiction 1790–1860.* New York: Oxford Univ. Press, 1985.

———. "Sentimental Power: *Uncle Tom's Cabin* and the Politics of Literary History." In *The New Feminist Criticism: Essays on Women, Literature, and Theory,* edited by Elaine Showalter, 81–104. New York: Pantheon, 1985.

Travitsky, Betty. "His wife's prayers and meditations MS Egerton 607." In *The Renaissance Englishwoman in Print: Counterbalancing the Canon,* edited by Anne M. Haselkorn and Betty Travitsky, 241–60. Amherst: Univ. of Massachusetts Press, 1990.

Tuck, Donald H. *The Encyclopedia of Science Fiction and Fantasy Through 1968.* 3 vols. Chicago: Advent, 1974.

Turberville, A. S. *History of Welbeck Abbey and Its Owners.* London: n.p., 1938.

Ulrich, Laurel Thatcher. *Good Wives: Image and Reality in the Lives of Women in Northern New England.* New York: Oxford Univ. Press, 1980.

Veeder, William. *Mary Shelley and Frankenstein: The Fate of Androgyny.* Chicago: Univ. of Chicago Press, 1986.

Vinge, Joan. *The Snow Queen.* New York: Dial Press, 1980.

Von Frank, Albert J. "Sarah Pierce and the Poetic Origins of Utopian Feminism in America." *Prospects* 14 (1991): 45–63.

Washington, Mary Helen. *Black-Eyed Susans: Classic Stories By and About Black Women.* Garden City, N.Y.: Anchor Books, 1975.

Waisbrooker, Lois Nichols. *A Sex Revolution.* Topeka, Kans.: author, 1894.

Walker, Alice. *The Temple of My Familiar.* New York: Harcourt Brace Jovanovich, 1989.

Walpole, Horace. *The Castle of Otranto.* London: n.p., 1765.

Warshaw, Susan. "College Women's Psychological Separation From Their Mothers: A Psycholanalytic Perspective." Ph.D. diss., California School of Professional Psychology, 1991.

Waugh, Patricia. *Feminine Fictions: Revisiting the Postmodern.* London: Routledge, 1989.

Weinkauf, Mary. "So Much For the Gentle Sex." *Extrapolation* 26 (1985): 231–39.

Welch, Marcelle Maistre. "La Femme, le mariage et l'amour dans les contes de fées mondains du XVIIème siècle francais." *Papers on French Seventeenth Century Literature* 10, no. 18 (1983): 47–58.

———. "Les Jeux de l'Ecriture dans les Contes de Fées de Mme D'Aulnoy." *Romanische Forschungen* 101, no. 1 (1989): 75–80.

Welter, Barbara. "The Cult of True Womanhood." *American Quarterly* 18 (1966): 151–74.

Williams, Sherley Anne. *Dessa Rose*. New York: William Morrow, 1986.

Wilson, Katharina M., and Frank J. Warnke. *Women Writers of the Seventeenth Century*. Athens: Univ. of Georgia Press, 1989.

Winnicott, D. W. *The Child, The Family, and the Outside World*. Harmondsworth, Middlesex, England: Penguin Books, 1964.

Winslow, Helen. *Salome Shepard, Reformer*. Boston: Arena, 1893.

———. *A Woman for Mayor*. Boston: Arena, 1909.

Wittig, Monique. *Les Guérillères*. Boston: Beacon, 1985.

Wolfe, Patricia A. "Structure and Movement in *Cranford*." *Nineteenth-Century Fiction* 23, no. 2 (1968): 161–76.

Wollstonecraft, Mary. *Mary, A Fiction*. 1788. Reprint. London: Oxford Univ. Press, 1976.

———. *Vindication of the Rights of Woman*. Harmondsworth, England: Penguin, 1982.

———. *The Wrongs of Woman*. 1798. Reprint. London: Oxford Univ. Press, 1976.

Woolf, Virginia. *A Room of One's Own*. New York: Harcourt and Brace, 1929. Revised ed. 1957.

Yates, Francis A. *Giordano Bruno and the Hermetic Tradition*. Chicago: Univ. of Chicago Press, 1964.

———. *The Occult Philosophy in the Elizabethan Age*. London: Routledge, 1979.

Yourell, Agnes Bond. *A Manless World*. New York: Dillingham, 1891.

Zaki, Hoda. "Utopia, Dystopia, and Ideology in the Science Fiction of Octavia Butler." *Science Fiction Studies* 17 (1990): 239–51.

Index